Penguin Education

Children and Race

D0666316

CHILDREN AND RACE

David Milner

Penguin Books

Penguin Books Ltd,
Harmondsworth, Middlesex, England
Penguin Books Inc.,
7110 Ambassador Road, Baltimore, Maryland 21207, U.S.A.
Penguin Books Australia Ltd,
Ringwood, Victoria, Australia
Penguin Books Canada Ltd,
41 Steelcase Road West, Markham, Ontario, Canada
Penguin Books (N.Z.) Ltd,
182–190 Wairau Road, Auckland 10, New Zealand

First published 1975
Copyright © David Milner, 1975

Made and printed in Great Britain by
Cox & Wyman Ltd, London, Reading and Fakenham
Set in Monotype Plantin

Contents

Introduction   7

1   Prejudice and Psychology   9
2   The Socialization of Attitudes and Identity   35
3   Children's Racial Attitudes   61
4   Racism and Black British Children   101
5   Black Identity and Mental Health   140
6   Education and Black Children   168
7   Education against Prejudice   211

Appendix 1: Sources of books, material and
information concerning the lives and backgrounds of black
people in Britain   253
Appendix 2: A select list of multi-racial books for
the primary school   255
References   259

Introduction

This book is principally concerned with children's racial attitudes.
Two aspects of these attitudes will be central to the discussion:
the process by which children develop racial attitudes in societies
where prejudice is widespread, and secondly, the psychological
effects of this climate of prejudice on black children. Particular
emphasis is given to the situation of black 'immigrant' children
in Britain. Until four or five years ago there had been very little
research concerning this or indeed any other aspect of immigrant
experience. More recently, race-relations research became a
growth industry, such that the last published register of research
listed some 131 projects concerned with 'Commonwealth immigrants',[1] but this boom may be short-lived.[2] The previous dearth
of British research has required that we lean heavily on studies
conducted in the United States; by far the greatest volume of
relevant research emanates from there, both as a result of that
country's pre-eminence in social scientific research, and of the
central importance of race relations in its social and political
life.

The perspective from which these issues will be discussed is a
socio–psychological one. That is, we are here concerned with the
nexus of a number of social forces within the individual child and
the racial attitudes they foster; and we are concerned with the
reactions to the conflicts engendered by these forces, in black
children. Prejudice and discrimination do violence to the individual in many ways, over and above the poor material environment
in which they confine him. Racist attitudes characterize his group
in a derogatory way, and by implication, himself. This devalued
identity is one which may be difficult to accept for it negates his
normal sentiments towards his own group, and in some cases, even
his self-esteem. After an historical prologue, these issues are

discussed at length in Chapters 2 to 5; Chapters 6 and 7 are devoted to their educational implications.

This book has been difficult to write through attempting to satisfy at least two different audiences; on the one hand, social psychologists and educationalists, and on the other, teachers, local education authorities, community workers and others, who have rather different interests and needs, through dealing with these issues at a practical rather than theoretical level. Academic readers, therefore, should try to forgive the occasional intrusion of the real world, while other readers must try to bear with the anaesthetic prose style of the research reports from which so much of the material is drawn.

Unwillingly, I must acknowledge my debt to those politicians without whose activities this book might not have been necessary. Others to whom unequivocal thanks are due include Rosalind Street-Porter, whose studies of children's literature contributed to Chapter 7, Professor Henri Tajfel for his intellectual and personal support, Amblavaner Sivanandan for his inspiration, Annabel Alcock and Lesley Stelling for typing the manuscript, Valerie Walkerdine and Graham Vaughan for their critical reading of particular chapters of the work and their suggestions, and the past and present students of the MSc Race Relations course at the University of Bristol for their tolerance of it all. Finally, to include under one rubric the many people who have contributed in other ways, I would like to thank my 'significant others'.

Bristol   D.M.
December 1973

1 Prejudice and Psychology

Prejudiced attitudes about human groups have almost certainly existed since numbers of people first distinguished themselves from one another. In essence, they are irrational, unjust or intolerant dispositions towards other groups. They are often accompanied by stereotyping. This is the attribution of supposed characteristics of the *whole* group to all its *individual* members. Stereotyping has the effect of exaggerating the uniformity within a group, *and* its distinction from others. The entire group is tarred with the same brush, obscuring individual differences. The process is made easier where there are visible physical differences between groups; these can be convincingly depicted as signifying other, more profound differences, and hence a 'reason' for differential treatment. In this way, prejudiced attitudes have expedited the oppression of groups of people throughout history, and where there have been differences in skin-colour, the most obvious and intractable of physical differences, the process has been facilitated.

This 'racial' prejudice is not essentially different from religious, political or other prejudices, as we shall show later; similar derogatory ideologies may develop between peoples who are visually indistinguishable but who differ according to other, quite abstract, criteria. Indeed, prejudiced attitudes need bear so little relation to real distinctions between groups that they may be fostered where no such distinctions exist. Walter Lippmann[1] has described how Aristotle understood that 'to justify slavery he must teach the Greeks a way of *seeing* their slaves that comported with the continuance of slavery', for no obvious differences distinguished slaves and masters. Aristotle decreed that 'He is by nature formed a slave who is fitted to become the chattel of another person, and on that account is so.'[2] In this way he imputed constitutional characteristics to the slaves which predetermined their social role so justifying their exploitation as a part of the natural order of things. As Lippmann remarks, 'Our slave must be a slave by nature, if we are Athenians who wish to have no qualms.'

The essence of this is the recourse to quasi-scientific explanation of imaginary group differences to rationalize an exploitative social arrangement. It is a common feature of such social relationships, regularly repeated over the course of the following millennia and no doubt pre-dating this era also. The superstructure of group prejudice has invariably been supported by formal or informal theories of group differences, supposedly 'justifying' these attitudes.

It was not until the eighteenth and nineteenth centuries that 'scientific' theories of race became widespread, and only comparatively recently that race attitudes themselves came to be studied. This introduction will convey something of the climate of racial thought in the period leading up to the time when social psychology came to focus on these issues; we will show how the study of race and racial attitudes has been influenced by both academic and lay conceptions of racial groups and the context of social relations surrounding them.

Hostile attitudes towards black people in Britain are not a new phenomenon. Queen Elizabeth I, for example, declared herself 'discontented at the great numbers of Negroes and blackamoors who had crept in since the troubles between Her Majesty and the King of Spain', a theme with which politicians have been happy to associate themselves in the 1960s, despite the intervening centuries of civilization.

The voyages of 'discovery' to the African continent and its subsequent colonization had marked the first sustained contact between the 'white' peoples of Western Europe and the 'black' peoples of Africa, and provided a great stimulus to the development of attitudes towards these 'races'. Long before this, however, notions of dark and mystical beings were common in Western cultures and may have influenced the ways in which black people were later to be regarded. One of the earliest instances of this is found in the writings of John Cassian, a monk of Bethlehem around A.D. 400. He tells of his conversations ('Conferences') with the Egyptian hermits who directed their lives towards the attainment of a vision of God. The experience of one such ascetic after two days of fasting is described in the following way:

And when at last he sat down to eat, the devil came to him in the shape of a hideous negro, and fell at his feet saying: 'Forgive me for making you undertake this labour.'[3]

Another pilgrim to the desert, having had only palm leaves and dry bread to eat for twenty days,

... saw the demon coming against him. There stood before him a person like a Negro woman, ill-smelling and ugly. He could not bear her smell and thrust her from him.

The hallucinogenic circumstances of these visions are not important; what is relevant is that here is evidence of a very early association of the Negro with the Devil, with filth and with ugliness.

The association of blackness with evil is a common theme both historically and cross-culturally. 'Black' had a highly pejorative connotation in this country in and before the sixteenth century. Its meanings included 'deeply stained with dirt, soiled, dirty, foul . . . having dark or deadly purposes, malignant; deadly, disastrous, sinister',[4] and so on. White had a correspondingly pure connotation. The two colours 'being coloures utterlye contrary',[3] denoted the polarity of good and evil, virtue and baseness, God and the Devil. The associations of these colours can be seen in literature, folk-lore and mythology for centuries before this time, and indeed till the present day. James I wrote a book on witchcraft called *The Demonologie* in which many of the stories related to the 'master of the coven' who was not only the personification of the Devil but was also always portrayed as black. Nor is this usage restricted to the literature of the occult. Gergen[6] points out that in the mainstream of English literature, 'a tendency to use white in expressing forms of goodness and black in connoting evil' is discernible in the works of Chaucer, Milton, Shakespeare Hawthorne, Poe and Melville; and Bastide[7] detects the same tendency in religious art and literature.

The same colour usage has been demonstrated to exist in a variety of different cultures. Gergen cites anthropological evidence from Tibet, Siberia, Mongolia, West Africa, Rhodesia, Nigeria, and from the North American Creek Indians, all of which provide parallel instances of these same colour-values. This rather suggests that there may be some almost universal cultural experiences which have evolved these colour-meanings; the association of night and darkness with fear and isolation, and day with brightness and life is a possible candidate, as is the instruction of children in cleanliness.

This is not to argue for an explanation of racial prejudice in terms of universal cultural experiences with the colours black and white. Rather, it conveys something of the cultural context within which the newly discovered dark people were evaluated, in this period.

It was not until the mid-sixteenth century that English travellers landed in Africa although the Portuguese had already been involved in exploration and trading within the continent for 100 years. Shortly, the first accounts of these 'Black soules' reached London, as did a sprinkling of the black people themselves. This was, then, a very sudden introduction to a people whose existence had been virtually unacknowledged, save for mention of Ethiopia in the Bible, and reference to the 'sub-Sahara' in the literature of antiquity. Moreover, the colour of these persons was the antithesis of the contemporary ideal – of alabaster skin and cheeks like roses. Extending the highly negative connotations of blackness and black objects to black *people* was therefore a logical step. The equation of whiteness with goodness and humanity defined these totally 'opposite' beings as somehow un-human. In Hakluyt's *Principall Navigations, Voiages and Discoveries of the English Nation* Robert Baker described the beings he encountered in Guinea in 1562, 'whose likelinesse *seem'd* men to be, but all as blacke as coles'.[8] From the unwittingly ethnocentric perspective of the Europeans, this sub-human character was thoroughly confirmed by the black man's 'heathen' religions, 'savage' behaviour, his geographical proximity to the most human-like animals, the apes, and his libido. Bastide[7] detects, as a result, the progressive Aryanization of Christ in religious painting from this time onwards in an effort to avoid the stigma attaching to 'darker' physical characteristics.

Curtin[9] argues that the travellers themselves were not unduly antagonistic towards black men and that the savage image of Africans was fostered less by them than by writers in England. The public's taste for the curious and the exotic and the 'libidinous fascination for descriptions of other people who break with impunity the taboos of one's own society' ensured that these aspects of African life were related in the greatest detail. These writings inevitably affected popular conceptions of the black man although these conceptions were not markedly hostile.

Jordan[4] suggests that 'It was not until the slave trade came to require justification, in the eighteenth century that some Englishmen found special reason to lay emphasis on the Negro's savagery'. Certainly the exotic accounts of the Africans from the preceding centuries coloured later public attitudes and assisted this process. The colonization of the New World demanded an unlimited supply of cheap labour in order for its enterprises to survive. Native crops required 'labour intensive' cultivation, and Africa contained unlimited amounts of the human commodity. From the fifteenth century onwards the Portuguese had captured Africans, 'put yrons upon their legges',[8] and carried them into slavery. Early in the sixteenth century black slaves were supplied to their settlements in America; later, a few Englishmen supplied the Spanish with slaves, but the English did not significantly enter into the slave trade until the seventeenth century.

Some fifteen million slaves were landed in the Americas from the sixteenth to the nineteenth centuries. As Segal[10] writes:

The slave trade was more than the hinge of colonial exploitation ... it was the basis of British – as well as French and American – mercantile prosperity ... and the source of industrial expansion ... It was the huge profits from the slave and sugar trades which produced much of the capital for Britain's industrial revolution ... The technological achievements which were to give the West political and economic dominance over so wide an area of the world were made possible by the miseries of the middle passage.

The brutalities of slavery are amply documented elsewhere; they will not be reiterated here. Accompanying and 'justifying' the systems were certain racial ideologies quite as brutalizing as the material conditions of plantation life. These were in large part a reflection of the conflict between the whites' treatment of slaves and the puritan ethics they espoused. Explanations of the discrepancy were generated, couched in terms of the inferiority of the slaves, and the social arrangements embodied in slavery were legitimized in law. The code of South Carolina portrayed Negroes as 'of barbarous, wild, savage natures',[10] and many states passed laws which confined the slaves (and their offspring) to bondage for life, forbade inter-marriage, education, religious practice and even social life for slaves.

Racial thought in the eighteenth and nineteenth centuries

Coincident with the period of slavery was the infancy of scientific thought about human types. This was not fortuitous, but a result of intellectual curiosity aroused by white Europeans' first prolonged contact with the apparently different variety of human beings they had found in Africa. Developments in biology, and later in anthropology, stimulated interest further. The earliest racial theorizing in Europe sought to explain the political ascendancy of particular European races by their superiority according to certain mental and physical criteria. Boulainvilliers[11] was a proponent of this type of view as early as the seventeenth century, eulogizing the Germanic race; though this was not a new notion, it helped to re-furbish the myth of Nordic superiority which in turn undoubtedly influenced the evaluation of the starkly contrasting dark peoples of the world.

As well as being politically expedient, theories which sought to classify human types reflected similar developments in biology. In 1735, Karl Linnaeus published his *Systema Naturae*[12], classificatory scheme for all plant and animal life, including man. This made some sense of the wealth of information about living things emerging from the scientific discoveries of the period. Later Linnaeus distinguished four varieties of man, black, yellow, red and white, but he did not order them in any way.

At about the same time, an ancient equivalent, 'The Great Chain of Being', was resurrected. This was a conception of all living things as an ordered hierarchy, headed by man (who had close ties with Heaven by way of the next link upwards, the angels).

This notion reassured men that they were both superior to animals and nearly divine, and, as Jordan[4] notes, served 'to satisfy the eighteenth century's ravenous appetite for hierarchical principles in the face of social upheaval'. Fairly soon a synthesis of various systems emerged, and although few explicit references were made to the hierarchical ordering of the races, it was an automatic assumption that the white European race was the primary stock, which was obvious from its civilization and cultural ascendancy. And, as Curtin[9] points out, 'If whiteness of skin was the mark of the highest race, then darker races would be inferior in increasing order of their darkness', assigning the Africans to the lowest human station, the nearest link with the apes.

The following 150 years, until the start of the twentieth century, was the most fertile period for the development of racial thought. Barzun,[13] Curtin,[9] Gossett,[14] and Stanton,[15] amongst others, provide admirable histories of this scientific era. Two themes of this period are particularly relevant for our purposes: the implicit racism of so much racial theory, and the relation between that theory and wider social and political developments.

To take the second of these first, it is possible to relate particular currents of racial thought to their authors' declared positions on wider racial issues. This is not to posit a simple cause–effect relationship between the two in either direction. But it is equally wrong to deny the intercourse, conscious or otherwise, between these two kinds of 'beliefs'. The teachings of science *are* enlisted, now as then, to justify social and political policy; similarly, actual social arrangements are adduced as the living proof of scientific theory. Thus in the debate over slavery some of the 'polygenist' theorists, who believed in the separate (or implicitly unequal) creation of the races of man, were themselves pro-slavery in their writings, while the teachings of the 'monogenists' who adhered to the 'official' account of Adam and Eve's procreation of the human race spoke for (or were recruited by) the other side. When we set aside individual examples and look at the whole period of history, it is impossible to ignore the correlation between scientific thought and actual social arrangements. It is clear that scientists are influenced by the social arrangements and climate of values around them, and their own ideologies, *and* that scientific theory consequently plays a role in sustaining those arrangements. It is, as they say, 'no coincidence' that the period during which white people – through the slave trade, slavery itself, colonialism and imperialism – was the period which saw the zenith of racist scientific thinking. There *is* a sense in which it was 'necessary' for certain ideologies concerning black people to develop among the public at large, in order to reconcile humanitarian religious beliefs with the actual treatment black people were receiving; and the scientific community was not immune from this. This is the other theme which emerges clearly from this era: that whatever the individual persuasion of racial theorists on the origins of races, or the significance of racial differences, the common thread that runs through nearly all racial theory of this time is the fundamental assumption of the current inferiority of black people.

A representative sample of the principal racial theorists illustrates these theories. Of British racial theorists, Edward Long, a biologist resident in Jamaica, exemplified both currents. He maintained that Africans were 'brutish, ignorant, idle, crafty, treacherous, bloody, thievish, mistrustful, and superstitious people'.[16] An avid pro-slavery campaigner, it seems he was not above fabricating evidence from his Jamaican experiences to support his arguments. At a more scientific level, Banton[17] suggests that Robert Knox's *The Races of Men*[18] was the first systematic racist treatise, 'one of the most articulate and lucid statements of racism ever to appear'. His writings were enormously influential and his ideas found their way into the speeches of politicians, Emerson and Disraeli among them. His predecessor in Edinburgh, James Prichard, was far more enlightened, and in fact anticipated much of Darwin's evolutionary theory. But although, as Curtin points out, he attempted 'to defend the racial equality of mankind through the theory of monogenesis',[9] he shared the assumption that Africans were *presently* an inferior race.

In Europe, the French Count Arthur de Gobineau was the most prominent of racist thinkers and was internationally influential. Barzun[13] discusses the complex relationship between his thought and the social and cultural climate of his time. Nietzsche and W. S. Chamberlain, for example, were to take up his theories, and if they 'were the visible agents of dissemination for the Count's ideas of race, it is also true that they were helped by others, anonymous and unconscious propagandists about whom we can talk only as the "forces" or the "movements" of the century'.[13] The political influence of Gobineau's writings survived him by many years; his belief in the supremacy of the Nordic-Aryan race, and in the degeneracy of 'semitized' and 'nigridized' races was resurrected to bolster the doctrines of National Socialism in pre-war Germany.

In the New World racial theory had a more vital aspect: it spoke to the immediate domestic situation of the relations between races. The polygenist teachings of Morton and the 'American School' (primarily Nott and Gliddon) underwrote Southern slavery in justifying Negro subordination through 'scientific' evidence of innate inferiority. In an obituary of Morton, it was said:

> We can only say that we of the South should consider him as one benefactor, for aiding most materially in giving to the Negro his true position as an inferior race.[19]

In retrospect it can be seen that the opposing monogenists, though more humanitarian in motive, abetted this process by conceding the central tenet of Negro inferiority. Some, like Bachman, were prevented from admitting the possibility of racial equality by their own ownership of slaves. To assert that racial theory in this period was itself implicitly racist is not to make a value judgement from a superior contemporary perspective; perhaps with the exception of the out-and-out propagandists, 'these were the teachings of science at its best for its own time'[9] and we would do well to evaluate current theory in the same light.

The advent of Darwinism might have diverted racial thought into more enlightened directions having established the fundamental kinship of the human races. But it is a measure of the grip that racist thinking held on the scientific community and the public at large that Darwin's theories, and their derivatives, were interpreted to provide a framework which could encompass racial strife and the subjugation of one race by another. As Gosset shows,

> ... Darwin provided a new rationale within which nearly all the old convictions about race superiority and inferiority could find a place

. . . The idea of natural selection was translated into a struggle between individual members of a society, between members of classes of a society, between different nations and between different races. This conflict, far from being an evil thing, was nature's indispensable method for producing superior men, superior nations and superior races.[14]

These interpretations were given added weight by Spencer's beliefs – 'the survival of the fittest' was his concept. Spencer and his contemporaries helped to lay the foundations of sociology in America, and their influence extended to neighbouring disciplines like psychology. Similar racial thinking prevailed here too. Francis Galton's 'Eugenics' movements provided further allies, for it was concerned to demonstrate the transmission of human abilities, through heredity, and the resulting hierarchy of abilities extended to races as well as individuals. Galton considered that 'the average intellectual standard of the Negro race is some two grades below our own', and, as if to clinch the argument, reminds us that 'it is seldom that we hear of a white traveller meeting with a black chief whom he feels to be a better man . . .'[20] It must be remembered that this was very much the alchemical period of the social sciences. Nevertheless, the net result was little respite from racist thinking throughout the scientific community. Around the turn of the century new attitudes began to permeate racial thought, the result of anthropological data, and the dawning realization that there are no pure races. As we shall see, these developments were slow to influence psychology.

Social psychology and racial attitudes

Although the nineteenth century produced a surfeit of theory about race, racial *attitudes* were not studied at all. There are several reasons for this. The most obvious is that the social sciences were still very young, even in the last decades of the century. And if sociology and psychology were in their infancy, social psychology was still a twinkle in the Founding Fathers' eyes.

Very few social phenomena had been scientifically studied at all, and social attitudes fell somewhere between the interests of sociologists and the concern of psychologists with the individual.

Social scientists had not yet fostered the degree of objectivity necessary to consider attitudes *per se*, apart from their referents. There were two other, related reasons, namely current racial attitudes among the public at large, and the state of scientific knowledge about race. Simply prejudiced racial attitudes did not present themselves as an obvious candidate for study because they appeared to be legitimate. The lingering belief in the innate inferiority of the Negro, supported by scientific findings, was reason enough for the feeling of prejudice against him. What could be less remarkable?

Social psychology, in many respects linking psychology and sociology, did not emerge until the first two decades of this century. It was slow to turn its attention to racial attitudes and not until the mid twenties did it seriously do so. We can trace the development of thought about race and racial attitudes through the very early textbooks of social psychology; like their predecessors in other disciplines, they seem to mirror current scientific and public opinion.

One exception to this rule was a paper by a sociologist of the Chicago School, W. I. Thomas, who attempted to explain the psychology of race prejudice. Thomas pointed to the mechanisms of discrimination in the smallest micro-organism which make sense of the environment, serving 'to choose between the beneficial and the prejudicial'. Emotional states become associated with these distinctions which then may be aroused in other circumstances by suggestion and association. The vicissitudes of food-gathering and reproduction insist that individuals 'single out characteristic signs of personality in others and attach an emotional value to them'. Associations are formed with fellows of common interest and feuds struck against enemies. Distinctive characteristics are fostered for solidarity within the group, in contrast to others. Design, and later habit ensure that 'the usual is felt as comfortable and safe, and a sinister view is taken of the unknown'. A group, like an individual, 'has a feeling of intimacy with itself' and 'signs of unlikeness in another group are regarded with prejudice'.

Race prejudice is in one sense a superficial matter. It is called out primarily by the physical habits of an unfamiliar people – their colour, form and feature, and dress – and by their activities and habits in only a secondary way ... [But] ... this prejudice is intense and immediate, sharing in this respect the character of the instinctive reactions in general.

However, when race-prejudice is complicated by caste-feeling,

the antipathy of a group for an alien group is reinforced by the contempt of the higher caste for the lower ... Under these conditions it is psychologically important to the higher caste to maintain the feeling and show of superiority ... *signs* of superiority and inferiority (like racial characteristics) being thus aids to the manipulation of one class by another, acquire a new significance and become more ineradicable.[21]

This was written in 1904, and is a strange mixture of the naïve and the sophisticated. However, it appears not to have been acknowledged in the early textbooks of social psychology, which are much less enlightened about these issues, where they mention them at all. Another sociologist, Edward Ross, actually produced the first book entitled 'Social Psychology',[22] in which prejudice is only briefly discussed. His own racial stereotypes, however, suggest a less informed and objective stance than Thomas's. He cites 'negro volubility, Singhalese treachery, Magyar passion for music' as 'arising directly or indirectly out of race endowment'. Although he cautions that 'probably they are much less congenital than we love to imagine', he goes on to claim that *social attitudes* towards these groups have an innate aspect also: both 'class antipathy and race prejudice (are) inherited venoms [which] no force of logic can kill'. His own social attitudes were far from progressive and frequently intruded into his writing.

William MacDougall, remembered benignly as the first real social psychologist, was similarly uncritical of popular ideas. The Negro merits only one mention in his textbook, *Social Psychology*,[23] which first appeared in 1908. In discussing man's sex instinct, he stressed the deleterious consequences of 'unrestrained and excessive indulgence of the sexual appetite', and adds this footnote:

It has often been maintained, and not improbably with justice, that the backward condition of so many branches of the negro race is in the main determined by the prevalence of this state of affairs.

The book contains no reference to either attitudes or behaviour towards Negroes; race relations, it seems, were not yet legitimate objects of research for social psychology.

Floyd Allport,[24] another of the 'fathers' of the discipline, at first appeared to be not very much more enlightened, some sixteen years later. He also emphasized the Negro's backwardness and cited evidence which quantified this in a quasi-scientific fashion. He said:

Various investigators rate the intelligence of the full-blooded Negro as roughly between two-thirds and three-fourths of that of the white race . . . it is fairly well established, however, that the intelligence of the white race is of a more versatile and complex order than that of the black race. It is probably superior also to that of the red or yellow races.

However, he later referred to white people's *behaviour* to black people, apparently the first social psychologist to do so; he also indicated that such behaviour might not be entirely justified. He said:

This discrepancy in mental ability is not great enough to account for the problem which centers around the American Negro or to explain fully *the ostracism to which he is subjected*.

This seems to contain the rudiments of a value-judgement – the slightest implication that this state of affairs is to be regretted. This is some advance over previous views which accepted the situation as entirely natural. Although Allport cites evidence for physical differences between Negroes and whites – differences in blood pressure, emotionality and inhibition – he attributes differences in behaviour primarily to *social* causes. He maintains that 'The reason why the Negro tends to be asocial is that, growing up in an environment of poverty and ignorance, where stealth and depredation are often the accepted means of livelihood, he has had no opportunity for developing socialized traits.' He goes on to argue for 'organized supervision of the moral influences brought to bear on Negro children'.

However moralistic this position now appears, it did at least acknowledge the importance of *social* and *cultural* influences on the Negro's character and abilities. This was not solely Allport's responsibility, but it reflected a very important development, for in relinquishing the doctrine of innate inferiority, it introduced the idea of potential equality. It took the Negro's 'inferiority' out of the realm of pre-determined racial characteristics, and, *ipso facto*, introduced the possibility of change. If 'the Negro' was more a product of his environment than his race, and his environment was a product of the white man, then it was quite clear where the responsibility for the Negro's degraded position lay. Not only was the white man vulnerable to this moral censure, but, in the context of the idea of potential equality, his *prejudice* against the Negro could now be seen as totally unfair. With their 'scientific' support removed, prejudiced attitudes appeared to be irrational and unjust; from the mid-twenties onwards racial attitudes *per se* became an urgent object of study by social scientists.

Clearly, this was a highly significant change of attitude on the part of the scientific community. An entirely new perspective on an old and troubling problem had been attained, which had revolutionary implications for social science and, more importantly, for the society itself. If we look at the first twenty years of the century during which time this change came about, or at least crystallized, we can see a number of contributory causes.

In social science itself, the development of anthropology was breaking down the old ethnocentric ideas of foreign peoples. The wealth of information from studies of primitive societies all over the world, showed that there could be infinite varieties of civilization, all equally satisfying to their peoples, so questioning the monolithic superiority of Western culture. Alien peoples could no longer be caricatured and dismissed as inferior, nor could the 'alien' peoples at home, the Negroes. Also during this period the elements of a sociology of Negro life came to be written. Du Bois and Booker T. Washington wrote powerfully of the black man's predicament, from within the black community; but perhaps the single most influential 'white' contribution was made by Ray Stannard Baker, a journalist who travelled in both the North and the South, 'following the colour line'. His writings[25] were serialized in the press and caused a tremendous stir in the white community; without sociological tools of inquiry, he provided a systematic and disciplined account of the Negro's disadvantagement, and the discrimination he suffered in all areas of life. His assessment of the total situation was particularly acute: 'It keeps coming to me that this is more a white man's problem than it is a Negro problem.' This detachment is more remarkable when considered against the hysterical anti-Negro attitudes current in the South at that time (1908), where some of his researches were carried out. This climate is very powerfully conveyed, unwittingly in the title of one section of his writing, which is called 'Difficulty of breaking the lynching habit'.

Studies of Negro life in several major cities were also conducted, among them Ohio, Boston, New York and Chicago. In some cases these were the result of the issues forcing themselves to the attention of social scientists and politicians, through race riots. These were local symptoms of a general movement, the emergence of the Negro from slavery and its aftermath to demand full citizenship.

The movement was led by the Negro intellectuals aided by Northern Liberals; the moderate wing was represented by Booker T. Washington, who argued for Negro education, industrial training and business institutions. He sought to advance the Negro without offending white society, which led to him being described as an 'Uncle Tom'. He wrote:

... the Negro is fast learning the lesson that he cannot afford to act in a manner that will alienate his Southern white neighbours from him ... The wisest among my race understand that the agitation of questions of social equality is the extremest folly.[26]

W. E. B. du Bois was identified with a much more militant position, arguing that Negroes must stand up against segregation and discrimination, and emphasizing the need to discover talent and leadership within the race. During this time Negro organizations proliferated; the first decade of the century saw the founding of the National Negro Business League, the Niagara Movement, and the National Association for the Advancement of Coloured People, followed by the National Urban League. With them flourished campaigning periodicals, like the NAACP's *Crisis*, and Negro politics and literature gained prominence.

Two events, more than anything else, accelerated the Negro's emergence. The First World War saw discrimination in the armed services replaced by greater equality than some Negroes had ever enjoyed before; it also gave thousands of whites their first experience of black men with equal or occasionally even superior military status. Many Negroes distinguished themselves in war service, and the contribution of the race as a whole underlined their right to citizenship in peacetime. The other factor was the exodus from the South. From wartime onwards a massive migration to the industrial cities of the North took place, encouraged by the prospects of high wages and less segregation.

Increasing numbers in the North meant more coloured voters, more coloured factory-workers, and potentially, better-educated Negroes ready to assume leadership in every area of American life, racial and non-racial.[27]

And whereas the 'colour problem' had been previously restricted to the South, the migration ensured that prejudice and discrimination against black people became a nation-wide issue. Over and above this, the massive immigration of Europeans during these years made the issues of nationality, race and citizenship very controversial.

In the twenties, social psychology's enduring concern with racial attitudes began. While the 'founding fathers' of the discipline had speculated about the problem this had been haphazard and unproductive, for in the absence of reliable evidence they had leant too heavily on 'common knowledge' with all the biases that entails. The mid-twenties saw the first *empirical* studies of racial attitudes, an attempt to ground explanations on a firm foundation of scientific evidence. Emory Borgardus was a pioneer in this early work. Initially[28] he asked large numbers of people to simply assign a variety of race, nationality and language groups to particular categories, according to whether the individual had a 'friendly feeling' towards each, a 'feeling of neutrality' or 'feelings of antipathy'. Rather surprisingly, Turks had the most antipathy directed against them by the student subjects involved; the categories 'Negro' and 'Mulatto' came close behind them, and their combined scores exceeded that of the Turks. Bogardus then went on to ask each subject to 'select the race for which he felt the greatest antipathy and describe in detail the circumstances as nearly as he could recall them under which his dislike originated and developed'. He found that an important source of attitudes was 'traditions and accepted opinions' – hearsay evidence picked up from adults, literature and news items, and this accounted for nearly all the antipathy felt against the Turks, for few students had ever met one. Another source was direct experience of particular groups in childhood, usually involving fear or disgust; finally, experiences in adulthood with individuals were also generalized to the whole group, and fear and disgust figured in these, too. In another study[29] Bogardus encouraged his subjects to make their antipathies more specific and at the same time bring them into the realm of everyday experience. He asked them to indicate to which of a number of social groupings and relationships each would admit various nationalities, from 'to close kinship by marriage' at one extreme, through 'to employment in my occupation', to 'Would exclude from my country'. Averaged over one hundred and ten raters, the English were admitted to the most social categories, the Turks to the fewest, with Negroes and mulattoes close to the latter.

The subject matter of these studies reflected the public concern with immigration from Europe and the rights of aliens, quite as much as any concern with racial prejudice towards the indigenous minority, the Negroes. Bogardus wrote a book in 1928 called *Immigration and Race Attitudes* in which this emphasis continued. In the book he reported the results of a great number of social-distance tests like those described, and further accounts of racial experiences. He re-asserted that the origins of racial prejudice lay in 'direct' and 'derivative' personal experiences; direct experiences involved either physical repulsion due to appearance, smell, habits, living environment or social behaviour, while derivative experiences were the second-hand experiences and attitudes culled from friends, relations, public speakers, newspapers and the like. Thus,

antipathy against the Negro is due to differences in biological appearances and forms, variations in cultural levels, and to widespread propaganda ... [it] often begins with prejudice *caught by* children from their parents.

This was perhaps the first acknowledgement of childhood prejudices, and an early conception of prejudice as a social 'disease'.

During this period, then, the study of racial attitudes developed a methodology. The idea of *measurement* of attitudes, of locating a person's sympathies and antipathies on a numerical scale of intensity, brought an atmosphere of objectivity to a very personal and subjective issue. The new attitude scaling techniques of Thurstone[30] and others encouraged these developments. But not all research relied on these methods, for they were not suited to all aspects of the problem. And for the first time, children were studied in the search for the roots of prejudice, for whom sophisticated attitude scales were clearly inappropriate.

The strength and pervasiveness of prejudice suggested that it might be innate and some people argued that racial antagonism was instinctive (an argument which had the additional advantage of making prejudice somehow legitimate). Others held that this could not be so, for children, bless them, were entirely free of prejudice; but it was clear that prejudice could not appear suddenly in adulthood. Bruno Lasker[31] directed the first study of the development of racial attitudes through childhood. He collected adult opinions on these issues by circulating questionnaires to discussion groups, social and religious organizations and the like rather than eliciting attitudes directly from children. In the light of what we now know about coercive pressures in group discussions, and 'second-hand' accounts of childhood behaviour, this circuitous method seems rather questionable. Nevertheless, Lasker made a very acute distillation of hundreds of adult opinions which anticipates the findings of many of the later studies of children themselves. He described how the child is

certain to have his mind canalized, even before he starts going to school, into habitual acceptance of the prevailing [racial] attitudes of the group within which he lives ... the average child is made to notice outer differences and to accept them as signs of inner differences in value.

Lasker correctly identified the role of the parents in transmitting attitudes, by accident or design, and the importance of the school, church, and other social institutions in reinforcing them.

As important as the findings of this study are the assumptions which lay behind it. It portrayed racial prejudice, unequivocally, as a social evil. And so, in thirty years, the tacit acceptance of white attitudes towards blacks was replaced by a quite opposite perspective. The emergence of the Negro to demand equality with the white man pinpointed the injustice of racial prejudice, and this notion itself became one of the assumptions of many social scientists working on prejudice. This was to be called the 'social problems' approach to the study of prejudice; it was a remarkable development, for it entailed a value-judgement – that prejudice was bad – and thus an element of subjectivity. It was the more remarkable for coming at a time when American psychology was in the grip of the hyper-objective Behaviourist school.

It would be wrong to give the impression that all research was conducted from this perspective; other investigators adopted a stance of 'ethical neutrality' which avoided value-judgement about prejudice. And through the thirties a variety of different methodologies were brought to bear on the problems, from anthropological studies of communities to laboratory studies of individual, cognitive aspects of prejudice, like racial stereotyping. Nevertheless, 'prejudice' retained its pejorative connotation, reinforced by liberal public opinion, and this perspective increasingly held sway.

*

During and after the Second World War there was a great upsurge of interest in racial, religious and minority-group prejudice. It had become imperative to understand this phenomenon which had persuaded large numbers of people to cooperate in the systematic extermination of others. This was a world-wide concern, but one which particularly engaged a generation of psychologists whose discipline, they felt, should explain such things, and in some cases whose background or sympathies personally involved them. Bruno Bettelheim, who co-authored *The Dynamics of Prejudice*,[32] was himself a survivor of the concentration camps; other psychologists in America were European Jewish refugees and played a prominent role in these studies.

The War more than anything else insisted that prejudice be viewed from the 'social problems' perspective. In the climate of opinion during the following years an entirely neutral stance about prejudiced attitudes was inappropriate; and the effect of recent events in Europe was to define prejudice as unmistakably bad, a social cancer to be excised. Whereas prejudice had earlier been ignored or justified in terms of the inadequacies (innate or cultural) of the groups against whom it was directed, these positions were no longer tenable, if only because of the cultural, intellectual and commercial eminence of the persecuted minority.

This 'social problems' approach, then, was characterized by the importation of the social scientists' *values* into the study of prejudice. The War produced another emphasis; this might be called the 'abnormal' notion of prejudice. Precisely because of the excesses of race hatred perpetrated in Germany, prejudice was necessarily seen as an *abnormal* phenomenon, in some way the product of disturbed minds. It was difficult to accept that normal people were capable of actions, or even acquiescence to actions, like genocide. Therefore the emphasis was on finding the determinants of the 'prejudiced personality', the factors which were responsible for producing people who would be the most susceptible to these disturbed attitudes.

This was the intention of the Authoritarian Personality studies of Adorno and his associates in 1950.[33] They set out to investigate the co-variation in individuals of racial or religious attitudes (like anti-Semitism), ethnocentrism (or attitudes towards the racially or culturally different), political and economic conservatism, and 'potentiality for fascism' (usually referred to as authoritarianism). In addition the authors tried to identify the antecedents of these attitudes in childhood experience, through investigation of parents' attitudes, and their beliefs and practices concerning child-rearing.

The studies showed that anti-Semitism, ethnocentrism and authoritarianism were stongly correlated in certain people, but that while these things were associated with political and economic conservatism, this association was not so great as their inter-relation with one another. This inter-related system of attitudes and personality characteristics was highly functional for the individual in interpreting and coping with the social world; it was also shown to be related to certain modes of parental attitudes and behaviour.

In other words, the authors argued that authoritarian methods of child-rearing and accompanying attitudes tend to develop in the child a personality which is disposed towards certain types of ideology – (like anti-Semitism or for that matter colour-prejudice) and towards ethnocentrism and authoritarianism, all of which fulfil a need for that personality. Prejudice, then, was seen as a dynamic part of the functioning of this kind of personality.

Subsequently, volumes of research were conducted in the same area, purporting to reinforce or contradict these findings, and many methodological objections to the original studies were raised and sustained. What most concerns us are the implications these studies held for the view of prejudice current in social science at that time. While it has been established beyond doubt that prejudiced attitudes are often found in persons with this sort of 'abnormal' personality, this explanation cannot account for the currency of these attitudes among large populations of apparently 'normal' people.

This restriction of prejudice to a small population of disturbed people distracted attention from the much wider problem – the incidence of racial and religious prejudice throughout whole societies, of whom the majority were not of this personality type. Explanation of the larger problem would require that prejudice be seen as a *normal* social attitude. Although this admission was a thoroughly realistic appraisal of current racial attitudes, it ran counter to the ideal values of the academic community, and indeed of the Constitution itself. This was the discrepancy, between ideal values and actual attitudes and practices, which Myrdal had described as 'The American Dilemma'.[34]

The perspective of the Authoritarian Personality study had its roots in psychoanalytic theory. During the same period other views of the aetiology of prejudice were debated, which had a similar ancestry. One such view was an unlikely marriage of Freudian theory and learning theory, giving issue to the Frustration–Aggression Hypothesis and the scapegoat theory of prejudice. Simply it was argued that the accumulation of frustration in individuals generates aggression. These aggressive impulses may be directed against the causes of the frustration but as often as not, this is impossible or dangerous. Then it is suppressed but may find expression against other targets, for example, minority-groups like Jews or Negroes who are not in a position to retaliate. Thus the hostility is displaced on to a scapegoat and the individual rationalizes this hostility by finding fault with the group as a whole. This takes the form of ascribing undesirable characteristics to them, and projecting on to them undesirable qualities of one's own. Now this got away from the idea of prejudice being restricted to an abnormal minority, for everyone endures frustrations and was assumed to respond aggressively. But it was still basically an 'individual' notion of prejudice, explaining it in terms of individual motivation and experience. Like the Authoritarian Personality theory, it was an *externalization* theory, that is, it viewed prejudice as an external expression of the inner needs, motivations and conflicts of the *individual*. Seldom in psychological literature is there any acknowledgement of specifically *social* processes; only the implicit assumption that social phenomena are some kind of aggregate of individual phenomena. And like the Authoritarian Personality theory, it was content to look after the individuals and let the groups look after themselves.

Until the late 1950s there was an almost complete divide between psychological and sociological explanations of prejudice. As Pettigrew wrote:

Along the continuum of prejudice theories, two extreme positions have been popular. One strongly emphasizes the personality of the bigot and neglects his cultural milieu; the other views intolerance as a mere reflection of cultural norms and neglects individual differences. Recent evidence lends little support to either pole.[35]

His own studies in South Africa showed that while 'externalizing personality factors like authoritarianism contributed to prejudice, these factors were no more prevalent than in more tolerant areas. He concluded that:

... In areas with historically imbedded traditions of racial intolerance, externalizing personality factors underlying prejudice remain important, but socio-cultural factors are unusually crucial and account for the heightened racial hostility.

Since this time, socio-psychological research has concentrated less on wide-ranging explanations of prejudice than on the more specific factors involved: the various socio-cultural influences which encourage or ameliorate prejudice, like socio-economic status, education, contact between the races; its developmental course in children and adolescents and the cognitive aspects of prejudice. This work will be discussed in some detail later on. For the last ten or fifteen years the majority of studies have embodied a perspective which is an amalgam of the various approaches described so far. The 'social problems' approach is still the dominant perspective, but conceiving of prejudice as a *widespread* social problem not one of individual deviancy. This replaces the emphasis on the disturbed individual with a notion of prejudice as a normal consequence of socialization within a culture or sub-culture in which prejudiced attitudes are widely held and approved. (In many cases the terms of the discussion – 'positive and negative inter-group attitudes' rather than the more pejorative 'prejudice' – derive from the 'ethical neutrality' approach, perhaps to enhance the flavour of scientific objectivity.) This is the perspective from which this book is written. *Prejudice is seen, unequivocally, as a harmful and divisive social phenomenon, but one which is the almost inevitable result of the socialization of the child within an environment in which prejudiced attitudes are commonly held, rather than solely a consequence of individual personality dispositions.* Implicit in this is the main emphasis of the book, the developmental aspect. Since Lasker's work the child's innocence of prejudice has been seen to be a myth. However, most studies of childhood attitudes have been conducted piecemeal, without an overall theoretical perspective. We shall try as far as possible to integrate this wealth of information within a framework which assumes the central role of *social influence* in the development of prejudice.

*

In the history of racial thought, then, we see a gradual change of emphasis. Initially only the objects of racial attitudes were considered – the 'dark peoples'. The 'causes' of relations between races, and accompanying attitudes, were seen to be located firmly in the people themselves – in their innate character and abilities. As ideas of human equality came to be reinforced by scientific evidence, emphasis shifted to the cultural factors that might determine racial differences. This was a very crucial step, for it admitted that black people's deprivations and 'inadequacies' stemmed not from immutable genetic characteristics, but from the environment in which they found themselves – which *could*, in theory, be changed. That this environment was largely a creation of white people placed the moral responsibility for its history and its future, with them. The notion of potential equality carried with it the implication that white attitudes towards blacks were unjust, and insisted that they be examined. In this way, racial attitudes *per se* became the object of study. Attention was directed away from black people, to white people, as perpetrators of these attitudes. The nature of prejudice, its determinants even potential 'cures', were all studied in an attempt to understand and perhaps solve this 'social problem'.

This has been a continuing emphasis ever since this time; it is appropriate, for it is concerned with the causes of prejudice in white people. However, the switch away from the original concern with black people as the *reasons* for prejudice involved a neglect of them as *recipients* of these attitudes. Only comparatively recently has very much attention been paid to the psychology of experiencing prejudice – living, as it were, at the 'receiving end' of hostile and rejecting attitudes.

This is not to say that there has been no attempt to articulate the Negro's predicament and that of other oppressed racial minorities. There is a rich literature of black protest from the days of slavery onwards, some of which speaks to the psychological problems of Negro life. But social science itself, within whose domain these issues fall, has not attempted to formulate a comprehensive psychology of the black American until the last two decades.

Du Bois, one of the earliest and most prolific contributors to Negro literature, had an acute and intuitive understanding of Negro psychology. He described how black men had become ashamed of their colour because white society had forced them to accept its own appraisal of them. In 1903 he wrote:

... [the] American world ... yields him no self-consciousness, but only lets him see himself through the revelation of the other world. It is a peculiar sensation, this double consciousness, this sense of always looking at oneself through the eyes of others, of measuring one's soul by the tape of a world that looks on in amused contempt and pity.[36]

He saw the antidote in the attainment of an independent sense of self, a process of 'dawning self-consciousness, self-realization, self-respect'. James Baldwin took up the same theme some sixty years later: 'there was not, no matter where one turned, any acceptable image of oneself, no proof of one's existence';[37] and elsewhere,[38] of his brother: '. . . he was defeated long before he died because, at the bottom of his heart, he really believed what white people said about him'. Baldwin realized that acceptance by white society entailed acceptance of that society's portrayal of him; and 'one of the prices an American Negro pays – or can pay – for what is called his 'acceptance' is a profound, almost ineradicable self-hatred'.[37]

Until quite recently the solitary attempt at a Negro psychology by psychologists was Kardiner and Ovesey's *Mark of Oppression*.[39] Published in 1951, its authors used a psychodynamic approach, gathering material from life histories, accounts of daily life, and so on 'through the agency of free associations, dreams and reactions to the interviewer'. Twenty-five Negroes were studied, twelve of whom were patients in psychotherapy, weighting the account towards the extreme or abnormal modes of adjustment. But they concluded that for all Negroes,

. . . The central problem of . . . adaptation . . . is the discrimination he suffers and the consequences of this discrimination for the self-referential aspects of his social orientation. In simple words it means that his self-esteem suffers . . . because he is constantly receiving an unpleasant image of himself from the behaviour of others to him.'

Kardiner and Ovesey felt confident that their study had revealed the 'basic personality' of the Negro. This personality is essentially an unhappy, stressful one, suffering more and enjoying less than white men. The need for vigilance and personal control is ever present, which is 'distractive and destructive of spontaneity and ease . . . it diminishes the total social effectiveness of the personality'. The remedies seemed clear:

Obviously Negro self-esteem cannot be retrieved, nor Negro self-hatred destroyed, as long as the status is quo. What is needed by the Negro is not education but reintegration. It is the white man who required the education. There is only one way that the products of oppression can be dissolved and that is to stop the oppression.

Since this time there has been an accelerating interest in Negro life and behaviour, which correlates with the emergence of black movements in America, first as vehicles of protest and later as a political force. But once again, psychological studies have tended to be disparate and narrowly focused; taken together, however, they cover a lot of ground.

Naturally, a black psychology must start with the child, for like the white man, none of the black man's attitudes, nor his personality, nor his own way of being-in-the-world appear miraculously in adulthood. The black child, of course, is father to the black man. His grasp of the more complex issues of race may be weak, but the emotional conflicts which inhere in 'being black' are a reality to him. They may structure his childhood and adolescence more powerfully than any other influence on him.

This, then, is the other principal concern of this book: to describe aspects of a black developmental psychology, and in particular the intrusion of white attitudes into his identity. Simply we shall attempt to define some of the consequences for black children of living at the 'wrong end' of prejudice, and draw out the implications of this situation for mental health and education.

2 The Socialization of
   Attitudes and Identity

Attitudes, unlike the stars of the stage and screen, are made rather than born. Social attitudes do not unfold from germ plasm or inhere in particular genetic configurations; they are not innate, nor do they enter human tissue for transmission to future generations (for which we should be eternally grateful). They arise, are communicated and are sustained in the social life of man.

Recently there has been a vogue for quasi-scientific writing which has tried to establish the essentially animal-like nature of man. Konrad Lorenz, Robert Ardrey and Desmond Morris in particular, have enjoyed enormous popularity through assuring vast numbers of people of their *instinctive*, and therefore inevitable, bestiality. This has been dubbed 'the litany of innate depravity',[1] and it rests on analogies drawn between aggressive behaviour in man and instinctive aggression in various lower animals. We will not dwell on it here, for to attempt to find its value is to look for a needle in a straw man, and it has been effectively demolished elsewhere. These views are only important for the currency they have gained among the general public. This has happened because people need to understand their aggressive feelings and behaviour and:

if no other rational explanation appeals, or even when it does, instinct is likely to trump every other card in the pack because it appears to be so fundamental, so recondite, so all-embracing and so simple.[1]

Now while these notions have been principally applied to man's aggressive *behaviour*, there is a danger that they may be seen to embrace his aggressive (or prejudiced) attitudes also. If the former is mischievous, the latter is positively dangerous for people are virulent enough in their prejudices against one another without 'scientific' reinforcement.

As Berger and Luckmann[2] have written, '*Homo sapiens* is *homo socius.*' And in the last analysis, whatever analogies and equations between man and animals may be employed, supported by science, anecdote or dogma, we are left with the monolithic fact of man as a *thinking, communicating* organism, which separates him from all others. Social attitudes are communicational phenomena above all else. As such, they simply belong to a different realm of discourse to that which is concerned with the vicissitudes of animal life.

Socialization

We are primarily interested in the *child's* social attitudes. If these are not God-given then we have to consider the other sources of information and emotion in a relatively restricted social world. It is bounded by the home, the street, the school and to some extent the mass media, yet within these limits the child will learn most of what he needs to know about the world. This knowledge is the child's cultural inheritance; its transmission to the child is called the socialization process. All the ways of doing things practised in his group and in his culture are conveyed to him, intentionally and by accident, with or without his realization. The notion that the child begins to absorb the culture with his mother's milk is no exaggeration.

We are not here concerned with weaning and toilet-training, nor the inculcation of table manners; however, while racial attitudes could hardly seem further removed from these domestic imperatives, we may say categorically that they have their beginnings in the same milieu at the same time. For in the socialization process the child learns not only 'what to do' but also 'how things are' and 'why they are like that'. He begins to absorb and, to some extent, to construct for himself a *description* of the world as it is; and not just the physical world of objects but all the events which impinge on his consciousness, from the passage of time to the love of his parents. In other words he begins to *order* these disparate objects and events, and to make sense of them so that he may cope with them adequately. Otherwise he would be bombarded by a maelstrom of experiences which he could not understand nor respond to appropriately.

For the child, the foundations of this ordering are laid by the parents, for their own construction of the world, of reality, is contained more or less explicitly in the way they explain things to him. Older siblings, friends, and later teachers will complement the parents' 'structuring' of the child's experience. These principal figures who, more than anyone else, retail reality to the child have been called the 'significant others'.[3] Of these significant others, the parents are the most important and they are almost the sole performers of this role in the first few years of life.

Because of his lack of ready access to nonsocial sources of information, the child is peculiarly vulnerable to those social sources appearing and reappearing in the immediate environment. Parents and older siblings find themselves in positions of great power, the power that comes with having answers (right or wrong) to resolve the child's uncertainties. In the early years of socialization this power is almost monopolistic. Alternative answers or explanations are absent, and the child's earliest contacts with the broader universe are filtered through all the biases and distortions in his parents' conception of reality.[4]

In the beginning, then, the parents *define* the child's world: they explain that world and themselves define its limits. That other realms exist beyond them need not concern him; he

does not internalize the world of his significant others as one of many possible worlds. He internalizes it as *the* world, the only existent and only conceivable world, the world *tout court*.[2]

What is this reality, this constructuion of the world which is absorbed by the child ? It is the aggregate of *experience*, the experience of perceiving people, objects, and events, discriminating between them, understanding them, evaluating them and reacting to them. *And this aggregate of experience coheres in a symbolic representation of the world coloured by attitudes, values and beliefs about the world*. Through the socialization of experience the adult world passes on 'all the news that's fit to imprint'.

It would be quite wrong to portray this as a kind of indoctrination, to depict the child as a passive *tabula rasa*, on which parents scratch, indelibly, at will. A very great deal of this teaching is unconscious and occurs through example or implicitly. And the child is a very active participant, at first eager for information from the available sources, and later seeking out his own sources, which may retail quite different versions of reality. Nevertheless, children do become aware of their parents' attitudes and values and frequently absorb and reproduce them as their own. How does this happen, in concrete everyday behaviour ? Three overlapping processes are primarily responsible: direct tuition, indirect tuition and role-learning.

Direct tuition

Clearly, direct teaching of explicit attitudes is the simplest and most obvious vehicle. 'Your father and I think that . . . is wrong' is its simplest form. It can be applied to individual acts (read 'hitting little girls' in the previous sentence), through more generalized patterns of behaviour (read 'playing with coloured children') all the way up to complex social attitudes (read 'voting Labour'). For many years the parents are almost the sole arbiters of concepts of 'right' and 'wrong', while their children are unaware that these are less matters of fact than opinion. The parents' exclusive satisfaction of the child's biological, material and emotional needs ensures that they acquire a very high value to him. This is both a primary value – through the provision of tangible rewards – and a secondary value, shown in the child's desire to please and receive approval – as a reward. At the very least, the parents' sheer power over him underwrites their influence.

It seems intuitively likely that parents provide a great deal of direct instruction about values and attitudes. Most people, particularly those from middle-class families, can recall occasions from their own childhood when their parents declared their own beliefs about a particular issue, and encouraged them to feel likewise. Although recollections like these are notoriously unreliable, there is a good deal of research evidence which bears them out.

One of the more revealing studies of this kind of influence was conducted in the 1930s in a rural community in Tennessee. The authors[5] of the study found that

the [child's] attitude towards Negroes seems to have its origin with the child's parents. Apparently parents give *direct instruction* in these attitudes and *cannot recall having done so*: (Italics added.)

The Socialization of Attitudes and Identity 39

Some short quotations from interviews with the parents and the children illustrate this:

MOTHER: . . . He never played with any Negro children. I have to chase them out of the back yard, they keep coming around, but I never had to tell C— not to play with the niggers . . .

CHILD: Mamma tells me not to play with black children, keep away from them.

CHILD: One time I slipped off and played with some coloured people, back of our house when she told me not to, and I got a whipping.

Clearly these examples involve tuition in attitudes which are central to the social life of a particular community. However, there is evidence from much nearer home that attitudes towards less crucial issues are also communicated directly. Johnson[6] has studied the development of children's attitudes towards foreign nations; their parents

claim to speak to their children quite a lot about foreign countries in general, about contemporary and past wars, and about specific nations . . . the parents preferences for nations appear similar to those of their children.

This by no means proves that they teach attitudes to the children directly or intentionally, for their discussions might be of a purely factual nature. However, it is a plausible hypothesis that their attitudes and evaluations of countries are made known to the child in the process. In fact it is precisely this element of the discussions which seems to be most readily absorbed by the child, as we shall see later.

Related to the direct prescriptions and proscriptions that parents make are others which are more subtle, for particular attitudes are implicit within them, not explicitly stated. Parents' attitudes towards different social classes, for example, emerge from a variety of ways in which they guide their children's experience: the comics they are allowed to read, the clothes and hair-styles they may affect, and the ways in which they are encouraged to spend their money and their time. Here we are talking about the encouragement of paricular *styles* of behaviour, of whole social atmospheres created by parents rather than their discrete acts. They are rather less tangible than direct instruction but probably even more effective in conveying how 'we' think about things, how 'we' do things, and ultimately, who 'we' are.

We shall have more to say about this later on, for it overlaps with one of the other important ways in which attitudes are transmitted, which we have called indirect tuition. Before that, let us briefly look at an instance of this tuition in action. Sometimes behaviour may be directly taught, involving implicit attitudes which seem to have little relation to the behaviour itself. Examples are hard to give without a detailed scenario but a typical one might imply or directly state, that 'Good Jewish boys *don't* . . .!' At a stroke, the child is made aware of proscribed behaviour, his identity and a norm of 'goodness', all of which need have precious little relation to one another, but which in combination carry an unmistakable message. The machiavellian parent could more or less ensure obedience with this tripartite bind on the child, especially if delivered in a suitably coercive tone.*

Indirect tuition

This category includes the processes by which children reproduce aspects of adult behaviour, in this case their attitudes, without conscious or intentional teaching on the part of the parents. We shall concentrate on two of these processes, identification and modelling.

Identification

Children of two years and older have a tendency to act in a number of ways like their parents. They adopt parental mannerisms, play parental roles, and in the later pre-school years *seem to incorporate in their value-systems many of the values, restrictions and ideals of the parents.*[8] (Italics added.)

---

*Note: We should not underestimate the potency of these communications; 'extra' meaning is often imparted to apparently ordinary statements and demands, by words, emphasis or gesture. Laing[7] and others have shown how such 'paralinguistics' can contribute to schizophrenic conditions when a person is made aware of conflicting demands in the same communication, or 'double-binds'. 'Don't be so dependent on me!', for example, demands independence and obedience/dependence simultaneously.

In the absence of reward or punishment, or indeed any kind of guidance, the child's behaviour becomes a microcosm of the parents':

> It is as if the child had learned a principle 'to be like my father and mother'. He then incorporates many of their psychological properties into his own repertoire of properties . . . [this] . . . leads to the hypothesis of identification which short cuts the direct training process.[8]

The term 'identification' has been used in a variety of different senses, so that a good deal of confusion surrounds the concept.[9] Different views of the aetiology of identification account for some of the confusion. The range of behaviour to which the term has been applied has been very wide, so that Mussen has proposed we restrict the scope of what we refer to as 'identification behaviour'.

> Identification, then, may be described as an hypothesized process, accounting for the child's imitation of a model's complex, integrated patterns of behaviour, rather than discrete reactions or simple responses – emitted spontaneously without specific training or direct reward for emulation.[10]

Freudian theorists have attributed a great deal of significance to identification. In fact it was Freud himself who originated the concept, first to account for the pathology of melancholia,[11] and later,[12,13] to describe the development of the super-ego, ego-ideal and sex-typing. He suggested that the boy's identification with his father developed out of the resolution of the Oedipus complex, initiating the process of super-ego development. This he termed 'defensive' identification, in contrast with the 'anaclitic' identification of the girl with her mother, based on attachment, love and fear of the loss of her love. Most of the different types of identification described by other Freudian theorists corresponds with one or other of these. 'Defensive' identification (Freud and Mowrer[14]), 'aggressive' identification (Bronfenbrenner[15]) and Anna Freud's[16] 'identification' with the aggressor relate to essentially the same process; they arise from envy of the model's control over 'resources', whether these be the love of the mother, or as Whiting[17] suggests also 'food, privilege, information, freedom, love and praise'.

The child identifies with the model, then, to allay fears of aggression from him, and to enjoy the rewards accruing to his position:

> The child believes that if he is similar to the model . . . he would command the desired goals that the model can command. For a child, perception of similarity between himself and the model is rewarding and strengthens the identification response.[10]

Freud[18] rightly stressed that the model which the child imitates is not only the immediate image which the parents present, but also the 'ideal standard reflecting the parent's aspirations rather then his actual behaviour'.

The other variety of identification has variously been called 'primary' or 'anaclitic' (Freud) and 'developmental' (Mowrer). It is rooted in positive feelings of love for the model, the parent, who provides love, nurturance, comfort, etc., and it is these primary rewards which ensure that the model acquires a secondary reward value for the child. The prerequisite of this identification is the dependency of the child on the mother (Sears, Rau and Alpert[19]). Sears[8] describes how

> . . . Among the acquired forms of self-reward [are] the whole class of imitated maternal behaviour, such as gestures, postures, task performances, and expressions of feeling; and ultimately, as the child's cognitive capacities develop, and *he begins to perceive and absorb belief-systems, values and ideological positions, he imitates these aspects of his available models also.*

Clearly, identification is an important vehicle through which the parents unwittingly transmit not only particular ways of behaving, but their whole world-view; and these items of 'knowledge' are the more potent for emanating from very influential models.

Modelling

Whether these phenomena are explained in terms of psychoanalytic theory or learning theory[20] or indeed any other theory, it is clear that the child purposefully models his behaviour on that of his parents to a considerable extent. Learning-theory explanations have the advantage of also accounting for modelling behaviour where the model is not one of the parents, for example when an older brother or sister serves as the model.

Various writers, in particular Bandura and his associates have put forward 'modelling' theories of aggressive behaviour;[21,22] the underlying principles of the theory are equally applicable to other sorts of behaviour also. They simply propose that:

observation of aggressive models, either in real-life or in fantasy production, increases the probability that the observers will behave in an aggressive manner if the model is rewarded, or at least does not receive punishment for aggressive behaviour.

Empirical tests of the hypothesis have been largely confirmatory.[21-4]

There is every reason to believe that verbal behaviour is also accessible to imitation in the same way. Children are sensitive to the social connotations of some adult speech very early on, long before they fully understand the meaning; hence young children often swear to each other or to their parents knowing the effect the words will have, while knowing nothing of the anatomy, bodily functions or sexual acts that the words denote! In the same way, more complex speech involving factual statements, or attitudes and values, is often imitated far in advance of any comprehension of the concepts involved, but with their evaluative or affective sense faithfully reproduced.

Pushkin[25] reports a vivid example of this; he administered a 'tea-party' test to a six-year-old white boy in which the child was required to 'invite' a number of dolls (representing real people) home for a tea-party. When asked why he had always rejected the dolls representing coloured children, the boy replied, 'If I have to sit next to one of those I'll have a nervous breakdown.' There can be few more graphic examples of (one hopes) unintentional parental influence.

There have been very few systematic studies of the precise ways in which parents directly or indirectly teach children attitudes; those that exist are reviewed in some detail in the next chapter. For the moment, the results of one study (which looked at children's attitudes in relation to their mother's attitudes and behaviour) serve to summarize the general findings in the area:

The results unequivocally support the conclusion that ethnic attitudes of children are related to the ethnic attitudes of their

mothers ... the transmission of ethnic prejudice from mother to
child is certainly not surprising since children easily adopt prejudiced
attitudes if these are displayed by parents who typically have great
reinforcement value.[26]

Role-learning

Role-learning, the third aspect of socialization we shall deal with
overlaps with both direct and indirect tuition. It is an important
part of the socialization process, integrating the child into the
different facets of the social matrix, through his acquisition of the
behaviour appropriate to each. From birth, the individual finds
himself inexorably entangled in a web of relationships with others.
The first roles he plays are 'infant' and 'child'; the supporting
cast are the parents, brothers and sisters, and various 'extras' with
little part in the action. All these people, however have a clear idea
of 'what' the child is, that is, his role, and demand appropriate
behaviour from him in accordance with that role. As Laing[27] has
written: 'One is in the first instance the person that other people
say one is ... we discover who we already are.'

In other words, a role carries rather precise prescriptions for
the occupant's behaviour. These prescriptions reflect the social
reality of which the role is an integral part, and so similar roles will
carry quite different prescriptions in different social classes, cultures, or periods of history. In learning roles, the individual must
learn 'to behave, feel and see the world in a manner similar to
other persons occupying the same position'.[28] So it also involves
attaining a particular view-of-the-world and subscribing to certain norms and values. The perspective is strengthened when the
person comes to make emotional responses to conformity or deviation from these norms and values.

In the early years most role-learning takes place in relation to
the parents; role behaviour is essentially reciprocal behaviour, and
the parents are the 'others' who recur most frequently in the
child's world. Here again the parents directly influence the behaviour, shaping it to conform to their conception of appropriate
role behaviour, and implanting within it an appropriate conception of the world. And once again, it is not a calculated process of
indoctrination, in fact it may be largely unconscious. But as the

child learns the role, and enacts it, he becomes aware of the rather precise way in which it relates him to others; further he becomes aware of himself *as* performer of that role. The process continues into adulthood, in exactly the same way. In each new role,

... Both self and other can be apprehended as performers of objective, generally known actions, which are recurrent and repeatable by any actor of the appropriate type ... it is not difficult to see that, as these objectifications accumulate ('nephew-thrasher', 'sister-supporter', 'initiate warrior', 'rain-dance virtuoso' and so forth) an entire section of self-consciousness is structured in terms of these objectifications.[2]

Clearly, the parents' attitudes and values enter into the process of teaching the child his early roles; how they conceive of the role in turn determines how he behaves in that role, and ultimately, how he understands the reality surrounding him.

Identity and social reality

Role-learning illustrates the two aspects of the socialization process that concern us most: the child's acquisition of an understanding of the world about him, and his acquisition of an identity. For as he attains a perspective on the social world viewed from a particular role within it, so does he attain a notion of himself *as* enacting that role. It becomes a part of his identity. Thus, the person's view of the world and view of himself are indissolubly linked, through the roles he plays. They are opposite sides of the same coin, the currency being social roles.

Identity is a concept which has been much used and abused in psychological theory. The term 'identity' has been a repository for a variety of imprecise ideas about what people are and how they see themselves. It has been all things to all theorists, and it is not our intention to redefine it here in yet another way. It seems more useful to integrate the concept into a wider schema which does not exclude its previous usage, but operates at a different level of explanation. Peter Berger and Thomas Luckmann[2] have developed such a schema, aspects of which have already been introduced in this chapter.

Their thesis proceeds from the central tenet that reality is socially constructed; the 'knowledge that guides conduct in everyday life' is taken for granted as reality. It originates in the thoughts and actions of individuals and is communicated socially. This 'knowledge' is not the body of ideas we refer to as intellectual knowledge; rather it is the ordinary common-sense knowledge of our environment, way of living and so on.

However, we do not always view the world in exactly the same way. How we do so depends on who we are, where we are, what we are doing, why, when, how, and so on. In any one day, a man may see the world from the very different perspectives of early riser, father, *Times*-reader, commuter, bank employee, saloon-bar raconteur, bedtime story-teller, and perhaps even Great Lover. In other words, we pass through different realities as a matter of course; and we can recall them to consciousness at will Now it would be totally disorientating if all these realities involved *completely* different views of the world. In fact there is a strong common thread which runs through them all, the paramount reality which orders our behaviour in a consistent way, despite these variations. This is the reality of everyday life; it is shared by other people and it appears to exist independently of us all:

> The reality of everyday life is taken for granted *as* reality. It does not require additional verification over and beyond its simple presence. It is simply *there*, as self-evident and compelling facticity. I *know* that it is real.[2]

It is this everyday reality which smoothes the transition between the different realities that our lives involve, so that we hardly notice our passage from one to another. But each way of being-in-the-world has its own perspective on the world, its own universe of meaning. This applies not only to the major roles of 'parent' and 'child' but also to the fleeting 'walk-on' roles already mentioned. And we get momentary glimpses of yet other perspectives as, for example, when we show unusual courage or fall unexpectedly or pass before some fortuitous social mirror.

Each of these different spheres of experience involve different ways of construing the world and hence different ways of construing ourselves. Each requires different qualities and behaviours from us; each emphasizes some of our attributes and ignores or actually suppresses others, and we construe ourselves accordingly. Different realities require different identities. At the rally I am a Fascist but I return home to become a loving husband and father.

The recognition that, theoretically, a person possesses as many identities as he has attributes, distinguishes this approach from the many previous conceptions of identity as a stationary, unitary entity. However, it is no more true that 'identity' is the *sum total* of attributes an individual possesses, of demographic categories to which he belongs, and of roles which he plays. But these are the raw materials of identity. At a given time, his identity is an abstraction from this mass of characteristics he possesses – a sample of them, on which a particular reality focuses. Any situation in which he finds himself has its own reality. This acts like a filter; it filters out his less relevant attributes (our Fascist's passion for dogs, for example) and amplifies the salient ones (his anti-Semitism). These are the elements of the identity the person sees himself as having in this social reality and which he acts out. And the 'filter' is simply the 'knowledge' of that reality, and the attributes appropriate to it.

What we customarily understand by 'identity' in this system becomes simply the identity construed by the individual in his *everyday* reality – that is, the identity construed from the small number of attributes which recur again and again in the different realities he inhabits. These form the central core of his identity; they provide an ongoing sense of himself which gives him a foundation of consistency throughout his activities.

None of this implies that each inhabitant of a particular social reality has exactly the same identity. Any one individual will arrive at a notion of his identity partly as a result of the pressure a particular reality exerts on him – in the ghetto, for example, 'race' will be a crucial aspect of identity for many people, figuring importantly and frequently in their experience with highly emotional overtones. Yet for some long-standing residents, the importance of race may have receded, so that other attributes like 'King's Head dominoes champion' or 'friendly neighbourhood postman' are more central to their notions of themselves. Other differences in the identities which individuals deem important arise from the different attributes they possess and develop, their different experiences, and of course, differences in personality which produce different emphases on each of these. Nevertheless, to the extent to which people occupy similar realities in any given social situation, so will there be some consensus as to the importance of particular attributes, and some correspondence of identities.

Childhood identity

For the child this system is very much simpler. His social experience is far more restricted, as is his cognitive development, so that he does not alternate between different perspectives on his own and other people's behaviour with the dexterity with which adults do. That is, he inhabits only a few social realities – the home, the school, the street and the recreation ground – with correspondingly fewer 'identities'. Yet essentially the same system operates: social reality is made evident to him in an unsophisticated form mediated by the 'significant others' in his world. They monitor his behaviour according to the rules of that reality, and convey to him the qualities in himself which are appropriate to it. Through their appraisals he absorbs an idea of his standing in terms of those qualities, that is, a rudimentary sense of identity. He is aware that his mother believes the sun to shine out of his very mouth, his teacher perpetually reprimands him for talking in class, and his gang listen to his words with rapt attention. In each of these situations he perceives himself to be a slightly different person, but with some qualities common to each.

The central qualities which recur in many different realities, and so contribute most to his enduring sense of identity, will be different from one social milieu to another. Some, however, are likely to be crucial in most contexts. The child's sex, for example, determines his behaviour, dress and treatment in every situation in which he finds himself. It not only figures frequently, but also the context – that is, surrounded by emphatic taboos – impresses it firmly in his mind; consider the reaction from both teachers and friends if a boy goes into the girls' cloakroom at school, or wants to play with dolls in the gang. Age, too, is a very important attribute. It sets limits on permissible behaviour and it locates the child in the hierarchies of the family and the school. We would thus expect it to be an important aspect of the child's identity.

Age and sex are relatively simple categories that the child fully understands. However, there are categories which are conceptually complex, and not fully understood by the child, but which nevertheless crucially contribute to his identity. Certainly 'religion' is just such a category for Ulster children. As this is written, young children daily demonstrate this aspect of their identity in the streets, even without profound knowledge of the historical, ecclesiastic, or dogmatic issues between Protestantism and Catholicism. It is sufficient that from the earliest age the children associate the religious category-names with their adult evaluative connotations, and from that basis evolve an intense identification with their own group, and rejection of the other group. We shall have more to say about this process shortly.

Where the relations between groups are the subject of strong feelings, or where they are regulated by widely-held values and norms, or where they are institutionalized in compulsory segregation, there would we expect the relevant attribute (like 'race' or 'religion') to enter most strongly into people's identities. Further, the more explicitly the category figures in the social reality, the more pronounced this is likely to be. In racially segregated areas, then, race may be more crucial to the inhabitants than in unsegregated areas, even though the opportunities for inter-racial contact are reduced. Thus the *de jure* segregation of the American South may have enhanced the salience of the race category in comparison with the *de facto* segregation of the North. Morland[29] has provided some evidence which points in this direction; he found that Southern white children had a significantly greater ability to make racial distinctions than did Northern whites or Negroes. Moreover, Horowitz and Horowitz,[5] in the study cited earlier, showed that this pronounced intrusion of the 'race' category into the social reality can enhance the importance of the racial aspects of the child's identity over and above all others – even fundamental ones like 'sex'. They compared the importance of sex, age, race and socio-economic status identifications in their young Southern subjects; using three separate tests, they found consistent, clear evidence that with the children in these communities race is a more fundamental distinction than sex . . . The general order of importance of these attributes appears to be race first, then sex, age and socio-economic status.[5]

We have shown then, how social attitudes and identity are closely linked; both emanate from the reality that surrounds the child. A multi-racial society creates realities which demand a heightened awareness of particular attitudes and identities. Here the child comes to view his world and himself through race-tinted spectacles, whether he be black or white.

*

We can summarize the argument so far in the following way: in the course of socialization, society teaches children not only ways-of-doing things but also its *values*. Parents are central to this process; they are the interpreters and instructors. They encapsulate and inculcate society's message, by accident and design. Children come to hold many of these values as their own. Among them are values concerning other groups in the society – social classes, religious denominations and racial groups are the most obvious of these. Not all parents share the majority's attitudes and values so that their children may develop dissenting views. But that young children will absorb many of their parents' views is automatic and inevitable. And to the extent to which a view of the world prevails among a majority of adults, so will that perspective influence the next generation. As far as those children's attitudes and values are concerned, this is the beginning rather than the end of the story. All kinds of influences intervene before adulthood to affect these attitudes, most significantly the educational process. But we should be clear about the enormity of social pressures towards conformity to the majority view, exerted by the socialization process at home and at school.

Our central concern, racial attitudes, is not a special case, but one part of this larger view. In the remainder of this chapter and the following ones, we single out this aspect of the socialization process and its consequences. We first consider whether society teaches us ways of seeing *all* groups who are 'different' from ourselves, irrespective of how profound or superficial these differences may be.

The development of intergroup attitudes

Some recent work by Tajfel[30] and his associates has looked at the very minimum conditions necessary for numbers of individuals to perceive themselves as groups and behave discriminatorily against other groups. In this study, a number of children were divided into two groups – according to their preference for paintings by Klee or by Kandinsky, reproductions of which were shown to them with a slide projector. This was deliberately selected as a superficial and unimportant criterion for dividing up a group of children who knew each other well. The children were then individually given a series of tasks which required them to assign monetary rewards to *other* members of their own group (the ingroup) and the other group (the outgroup). It turned out that there was consistent discrimination in favour of their own group and against the other group, even though there was no 'reason' for enmity. Nor did the individual stand to gain personally by this discrimination. Further, the children seemed to try and maximize the difference between rewards accruing to ingroup and outgroup members, even if this involved sacrificing certain other advantages. One explanation of this behaviour is the following:

It is, however, possible that certain societies create, or contribute to what might be called a 'generic' outgroup attitude (Tajfel[31]); in other words, that norms, values and expectations present in their modes of socialization and education foster or reinforce a tendency to behave differentially towards outgroups and ingroups even when such behaviour has no 'utilitarian' value to the individual or to his group, and even when a particular categorization has very little meaning in terms of the emotional investment that it represents and in terms of differences between groups on which it is based.

The child strives to understand his environment, to recognize regularities in it, and to order it. He categorizes objects and events in order to respond to them appropriately. This includes the categorization of people and their behaviour. From these experiments it seems that our society encourages children to develop a notion of 'own-groupness', that is, a solidarity with 'similar' people and a tendency to discriminate against 'different' people, no matter how superficial is the basis for categorizing them in that way. So as the child is learning about real social groups, those about whom unmistakable adult values exist, like black people, are very easily assimilated into this 'us' and 'them' scheme of things. In other words, if children develop a slightly negative disposition towards 'other groups' when there is no important reason for discriminating against them, how much more easily must categorization and discrimination takes place when there are real differences between groups and powerful values surrounding them.

Racial attitudes, in the examples cited earlier, are generated where there is some degree of contact between the groups involved, where the groups are physically distinguishable, and often written or unwritten rules exist governing their conduct towards each other. None of these 'cues', however, are strictly necessary for prejudice to develop between racial groups; although given a climate of hostility, they certainly make discrimination and bigotry more easy.

If we consider the converse of this, namely situations where there is little or no contact between the groups concerned, and no obvious physical differences, it becomes clear that these cues are like the icing on the cake. The development of attitudes towards other nations is a case in point, for children develop national attitudes without any such assistance. Without direct experience of other nations, information about them must come from *social* sources; and so the essence of this national attitude development is the process of *social influence*. This process may *build on* the 'generic' norm of discrimination against other groups, already discussed. There is every reason to believe that these influences are the crux of *racial* attitude development too.

The early studies of national attitude development in children tended to focus on the child's cognitive abilities; his capacity to handle the rather complex concepts of nations, countries, and so on. The emphasis lay on his evolving ability to understand the logical relations between these concepts and between the entities they denoted. Piaget was the main exponent of this approach, and in his earliest study[32] he investigated the child's attainment of part-whole relationships, and the concept of inclusion, as applied

to the relations between a town, a district and a country. For
example, he examined the child's progress from the stage where
he might deny that he could be (say) simultaneously Parisian and
and French, to his eventual grasp of the correct relationship.

In a later study[33] Piaget and Weil described the development
of the child's notion of nationality as a dual process of cognitive
and affective development: 'The cognitive and affective elements
may be said to be parallel or isomorphous.' In other words, at the
same time as the child learns to handle concepts of nations and
absorbs factual knowledge about them, he develops *affective* dispositions towards them also.

As Jahoda[34] has written:

... a child's intellectual grasp of his environment begins in his immediate vicinity and only gradually extends outwards. One can think
of this as a series of concentric circles with the child at the centre.

This process of understanding the spatial reactions between towns
and countries, and the conceptual relations of the self to class and
nationality groups is paralleled by affective development. In the
young child, his evaluations or attitudes towards other countries
(according to Piaget and Weil) are initially ego-centric or personal
to be replaced subsequently by acceptance of the family's values
about other nations, finally giving way to attitudes based on wider
societal values.

Now, implicit in those approaches which emphasize the factual
and cognitive aspects of attitude development is the suggestion of
rationality, which is entirely in keeping with our attitudes towards
attitudes. People like to think of attitudes as evaluations, based
on a rational appraisal of facts, the end-product of some delibera-
tion. To describe national attitude development as an almost
simultaneous absorption of fact about countries, and production
of feeling about them does not rule out rationality. In theory, it
allows the feelings to be a response to the facts. The emphasis on
cognitive development and factual knowledge is quite in line with
this idea of rationality and seems to suggest that 'facts' are pre-
requisites, necessary conditions for attitudes to appear.

However, recent research has exploded this idea. It is now
clear that the relation between the cognitive and affective elements

of national attitudes is not a simple isomorphism, as Piaget and Weil suggested, nor are the 'feelings' necessarily a rational response to the 'facts'. This emerged from a study by Tajfel and Jahoda[35] in which they investigated the development of concepts and evaluations of foreign nations among 6–7-year-old children. In particular they looked at the relation between the children's preferences for various countries and their factual knowledge about them, in this case, the size of the countries concerned. This was achieved by paired comparisons of the children's preferences for four countries (America, France, Germany and Russia), paired comparisons of these countries with regard to distance from the child's own country, and determination of the relative size of the child's own country and the other four countries;

> One aspect of the results can be described as follows: at the ages of six and seven children in Britain agree rather more about which countries they like and dislike than about practically anything else concerning those countries ... [they] agree rather more that they prefer America and France to Germany and Russia than that *both* America and Russia are larger in size than *both* France and Germany. There is no theoretical difference between the learning of these two kinds of 'facts'; *and, if anything the knowledge of facts about preferences crystallizes rather earlier than the corresponding knowledge of facts about size.*

Before this study, the possibility that the affective elements could emerge *before* the items of knowledge on which they were supposed (according to folk-psychology and common sense) to be based, had not been widely accepted. The child's development of national attitudes was now clearly seen as a process of social learning; and this consisted of learning various 'facts', some of which might be items of information about the countries themselves, but more importantly a variety of social 'facts' such as 'Britons don't like Germans'.

These findings blur the distinction between the cognitive and affective elements of national attitudes. The precise relationship between these two elements was the subject of a recent study by Johnson *et al.*,[36] with children of 7–11 years. They found that children knew most about the countries they liked and disliked strongly, and least about the ones they felt neutral about. The knowledge they demonstrated, though, was not necessarily the basis for their preferences, for it contained information about geographical position, population, and so on. One interpretation of this is that 'there may simply be more information "in the air" referring to the nations the child is expected to like or dislike strongly . . . the relationship . . . may tell us more about the "propaganda environment" in which the child lives than about intra-individual processes involved in the formation of attitudes.'[36] Together with evidence from an earlier study by Johnson,[37] they conclude that 'some evidence exists for believing that knowledge is not an essential prerequisite for the development of emotional reactions to other nations'. As Horowitz[38] puts it, 'Within the individual the sequence frequently is the development of a prejudice first and the perfection of the techniques of differentiation later. The results of the present study are certainly congruent with that view.'[36] So these studies call into question the notion that the child's knowledge and conceptual development need to be very far advanced before he is able to reproduce, if not understand, national attitudes. This is important for our discussion for it emphasizes the child's sensitivity to the emotional and evaluative nuances of adult attitudes at an early age.

At the same time as children develop attitudes towards other nations, they absorb evaluations of their own nation; these are reciprocal aspects of the same process. Simply,

. . . As a function of age, children develop an increasingly stable system of preferences for various foreign countries and a more consistent identification with their own country.[39]

and, as with attitudes towards foreign countries, 'children do come to "prefer" their own country to others well before they are able to form, understand and use appropriately the relevant concepts of countries or nations'.[40]

This emerges from a comprehensive study of children's national attitudes conducted in England, Scotland, Holland, Austria, Belgium and Italy.[40] One test in the study required children to assign photographs of young men to boxes labelled 'I like him very much', 'I like him a little', 'I dislike him a little', 'I dislike him very much'. In a session separated by two weeks from the other, the children were asked to sort the same photographs into boxes labelled (for example) 'English' and 'not-English' in the case of the English subjects, 'Scottish' and 'not-Scottish' for the Scottish subjects, and so on. The children had been told that some of the photographs were of people of their own nationality.

In most of the locations, children tended to assign the photographs they liked better to their own national group. That is, 'through an association of national verbal labels with preference sorting of photographs one can elicit from young children a clear index of preference for their own national group ... Children clearly prefer those photographs they classify as own nation to those they classify as not own nation.' Although this relationship weakens with age, '. . . it would be naïve to assume that this decrease is due to a decrease in nationalism'.[41] It seems likely that the younger children base both the preference judgement and the nationality judgement on the same criterion – simple liking. The child's choices could then be interpreted as *unconsciously* saying 'I like him *because* he looks English', or 'Because I like him, he must be English'. Either way there is this clear association between 'liking' and one's own national group. However, it may be that the older children approach the two tasks using different criteria – for example, basing the nationality assignment on some physical stereotype of the national group rather than just on the basis of liking, thereby reducing the correlation between the judgements.

The exceptions to this rule were the Scottish children. They did not show this pattern of national preference, that is they did not always prefer the photographs they identified as 'Scottish'. One possible explanation of this is that the category 'not Scottish' was interpreted by the children to mean 'English', and their preference for the photographs they assigned to this category reflects the relatively less favourable evaluation of 'Scottish' compared with 'English' that exists in Britain. At first this seems to be a rather far-fetched explanation for the devaluation of Scotland and things Scottish is relatively mild and more a matter of history than a contemporary issue. However, it was borne out in a subsequent study[41] which employed the same tests with English, Scottish and Israeli children. The English children discriminated in favour of their own group, and this decreased slightly with age, as before. The Scottish children did not discriminate in favour of 'Scottish' when choosing between 'Scottish' and 'not Scottish'. When further children were tested and given the choice between 'Scottish' and 'English' the children discriminated in favour of the English. In other words they demonstrated a preference for another nation, and an implicit devaluation of their own nation.*

Equally interesting results emerged from the sample of Israeli children; two groups were tested, some of Oriental origin and some of European origin. They were shown twenty pictures, half of which depicted young 'European' Jews and half young 'Oriental' Jews. In choosing between 'Israeli' and 'not Israeli',

... The national preference results which were obtained in other countries are – not surprisingly – strongly replicated ... the correlation based on the overall degree of liking of the photographs and their assignment to the category 'Israeli' is very high (among the highest of any of the national groups).[43]

Further, *both* groups of children preferred the 'European' photographs; and the difference between the frequency of assignment of these photographs to the 'Israeli' category and frequency of assignment of the 'Oriental' photographs to this category is highly significant.

There are several interesting issues here. First of all, the high level of preference for their own nation clearly reflects the heightened national consciousness of Israelis, as a result of their historical experience and of current tensions in the Middle East. Secondly there is evidence among the 'Oriental' children of some devaluation of their own group and preference for the 'other' group in the society, that is, Jews of European origin. This is thought to be a reflection of the more dominant role played by European Jews in the Israeli state, further evidence by the children's assignment of the European photographs to the 'Israeli' category. The Oriental children, then, combine side by side a pronounced preference for their own *national* group over all others, and a devaluation of their own 'ethnic' group within the

*Note: Clearly, there is some doubt as to whether these results would now be replicated, since the advent of Scottish Nationalism.

society, through their preference for the more dominant group.

*

The burden of all these studies is that the development of attitudes towards the child's own country and other countries is primarily a result of processes of social influence. The child is dealing with abstract entities – 'nations' – with which he has no direct contact (and whose members are not obviously distinguishable from one another by virtue of physical or other characteristics). His sources of both factual and evaluative information are therefore social sources – his parents, siblings, peers and teachers, together with some non-human equivalents like comics, books and television. Within this system the child acquires a preference for his own country and an enduring identification with it. At the same time he develops a pattern of preference for other countries in advance of some of the simplest items of factual knowledge about them. These preferences and dislikes derive from contemporary and historical national alignments; they mirror the portrayals of his own and other countries current in his social world. The strength and pervasiveness of these mechanisms of attitude formation is best illustrated by those children who belong to national or other groups which in some sense have an inferior status. These children may not show the same preference for their own group, a direct reflection of its devalued portrayal in their social world. And this operates even in situations where no overt intergroup tension or strife is evident, and where the group is not substantially disparaged. The child is apparently sensitive to the most subtle nuances of social influence and incorporates them in his attitudes.

The development of racial attitudes

In this light, the emergence of rudimentary racial feelings in very young children is easily understood. The development of national attitudes serves as a baseline for comparison; here the child has no cues to assist the process other than adult attitudes, but as we have seen, these are sufficient. Racial attitude development is almost the opposite extreme, for over and above adult teaching, the process is assisted by direct experience of contact between the races, obvious physical differences – like colour – which distinguish them, and often strict rules governing conduct between them.

Contact ensures that the issues enter directly into the child's experience in a concrete way; wholesale physical differences, and hence high visibility, make discrimination between the groups and labelling them extremely easy; rules of behaviour establish patterns of responding to other racial groups which are consistent with adult attitudes towards those groups, whether or not the child has yet developed those attitudes for himself. But we must not lose sight of the fact that while these cues help to foster and to reinforce children's attitudes, they only complement the central role of adult influence.

Here we must anticipate the next chapter, in which a detailed picture of the course of racial attitude development is presented and of the various factors influencing the process. For the moment we need only an outline of this. In a multi-racial society the white majority-group child shows evidence of being aware of simple racial differences from a very early age, sometimes as young as three years old. In the following years he begins to show feelings about these groups; these are simple evaluations, which invariably take the form of preferring and identifying with his own group, and showing some dislike or rejection of the other racial groups. These evaluations are picked up from adults, brothers and sisters, friends, teachers, and from children's literature and the mass media, as we shall see later. Soon afterwards, around the age of 5, rudimentary versions of adult attitudes may be mouthed, and the first understanding of the social roles of whites and blacks appears. Versions of adult stereotypes are reproduced, and the process of absorption of the society's colour-values crystallizes into fully fledged racial attitudes.

For the black child brought up within the same society, things are rather different. He is surrounded by the same colour-values and attitudes, and they are made real to him; they pervade all the social life and the institutions of the society, and he cannot help but absorb them. They speak directly to him, for within those attitudes is a picture of his group, and by implication, of himself. The more derogatory is this portrayal, the more unacceptable is the 'identity' it imposes. Even without the more lurid sterotypes, which tend to accompany tense inter-racial situations, the inferior status of the minority underwritten by their colour, ensures them a devalued identity.

So as the white child develops a positive identification with his group and a preference for it over others, in line with the attitudes of the majority, the black child faced with the same climate of attitudes may develop a very much more ambivalent pattern of identification and preference. Obviously, it is difficult for the child to incorporate within his self-image a picture, apparently subscribed to by the majority of the community, which depicts him as somehow inferior. In inter-racial situations, as we have seen, 'race' is likely to be one of the most important aspects of the social reality, and so contribute centrally to the person's identity. For the black child, then, a crucial element of his identity – his race – is devalued, and in some cases it may be rejected.

This is the burden of the findings of any number of research studies, which will be reviewed at some length in the next chapter. 'Black' minority-group children in a variety of different countries have shown an orientation away from their own group and towards the dominant white majority in experimental test situations. In some cases this has extended to a denial of their black identity and a momentary escape into the fiction of a white one. Although this passes with age, there is no reason to believe that the conflicts which engender it do so. The socialization of racial attitudes in both black and white children undoubtedly form the foundations of adult racial attitudes.

3 Children's Racial Attitudes

Until now we have rather taken prejudice for granted. In the previous chapter we *assumed* the existence of a society in which prejudiced racial attitudes were common among adults, and described how these attitudes were passed on to children in the course of the socialization process. This of course begs the question of how racism arises in a society in the first place. That question is really one which falls outside the scope of this book. If we stop to consider the complex of factors which lie behind the emergence of racism in any one society, it becomes clear that the topic deserves several books to itself, not merely a small part of one book. For example, in the case of our own society, such an analysis would have to take account of our traditional cultural image of black people based on the history of our exploitative relationships with them, cultural colour values, traditions of nationalism and cultural ethnocentrism, and the history of competitive class and 'caste' attitudes towards 'others' deriving from class attitudes in a capitalist society. Then it would need to include an analysis of social and economic conditions at the time of the immigration – a decline in post-war expansion, contraction of demand for labour other than unskilled labour, selective strains in areas of the housing market, education system, social services, and the attitudes of those white people already affected by these strains (and this would be supplemented by an account of the political exploitation of these fears, and the imaginary fears of much wider sections of the white population, by politicians in pursuit of personal political capital). Finally, at the individual level, the analysis would include an account of personal dispositions towards prejudice among particular groups of the population due to personality organization, themselves the result of certain kinds of child-rearing practice and parental attitudes.

From this mass of factors three rough categories are separable: the *cultural* determinants, the *social structural* determinants and the *individual* or *personaltiy* determinants. As Porter[1] has pointed out, they correspond to Talcott Parsons's notion of the three principal elements of human action. Each has been utilized by various schools of thought to 'explain' prejudice. Any one on its own is inadequate to do so; but a combination of the three can account for the genesis of racism in a society, its proliferation through the culture, and its transmission to future generations. It is this last aspect which has been given the most emphasis so far. The reason for this continuing emphasis is as follows: once racism has emerged within a culture, has become widespread and established, then the *cultural* factors (of the three groups we have mentioned) become the most important agents in its continuance. When racism has taken root in the *majority culture*, has pervaded its institutions, language, its social intercourse and its cultural productions, has entered the very interstices of the culture, then the simple process by which a culture is transmitted from generation to generation – the socialization process – becomes the most important 'determinant' of prejudice. For then it reaches all sections of the population, including those who are neither objectively nor subjectively threatened by black people, nor stand to gain anything by discrimination against them – in other words, those who have neither 'social structural' nor 'personality' reasons for prejudice. This is why the last chapter laid such emphasis on the socialization of attitudes in children.

When, in addition, the culture contains a residue from past race relationships – any legacy of assumptions and attitudes about black people from the days of imperialism and colonialism – then we see that the introduction of a 'new' contemporary racism builds on some pre-existing foundations. These too, assist the transmission of prejudice to children, as we shall see.

The first part of this chapter deals with all these cultural factors – both the traditional foundations and the contemporary content of prejudiced racial attitudes. In asserting the primacy of cultural influences, the 'social structural' and 'personality' factors are not overlooked; rather, as far as children are concerned, they are discussed as 'intervening variables', factors which add to or subtract from the basic process of attitude transmission. They materially affect the incidence of prejudice within various groups of adults in the society, and therefore equally affect *their* children's attitudes in the first few years of life.

Cultural factors in prejudice

In the first chapter an issue was raised that gives some insight into the relation between culture and prejudice against black people. It was shown that in our culture, and in many others, the colours 'black' and 'white' have traditionally had very strong *evaluative* overtones. In our language, literature and art, white is conventionally used to depict good, pure things and black to denote badness and evil. These usages may affect the way we think of objects which bear these colours – and perhaps even 'black and 'white' people, too. Now although we can find any number of illustrations of this 'colour-code' at work in everyday speech, in books and in pictures, that is a far cry from explaining people's prejudiced behaviour towards 'coloured' racial groups. However, there may be *some kind* of link between the two, and this has been the subject of a whole series of studies by Williams and his associates in the USA.

Their first study looked at the different connotations of a series of colour-names – black, white, yellow, red, etc. – and particularly at the different *values* associated with each. Using a technique called the Semantic Differential it was possible to find out the *evaluative* connotation of each colour-name. Perhaps not surprisingly, 'white' and 'black' differed the most in this respect, connoting 'good' and 'bad' respectively.[2] (In a later study, these American results were replicated in Germany, Denmark, Hong Kong and India.[3] So not only are these colour connotations found in traditional art and literature of many different cultures, as was shown earlier, they are alive and well in the present day.)

The next step was to find out whether people's values about colours, like 'black', spilled over into feelings about *people* of different colours, like 'black people', and from there into names of racial groups, like 'Negro'. For the white subjects it was found that colour-linked groups of concepts (like 'black' – 'black person' – 'Negro') had greater similarity of connotative meaning (that is, were *evaluated* in a more similar way) than did groups of concepts which were not colour-linked. So in other words, there could be a translation of feelings and values about the colour black to people coloured in this way, and their associated group name, 'Negro', since all three were rated in the same way. Or, as the authors put it, 'racial concepts have connotative meanings similar to the colour-names with which they are linked by custom.'[4] Of course, to find that they have similar connotations does not prove any cause–effect relationship between them: one could cause the other, or vice versa, or they could both be caused by something else entirely.

The issue is whether *colour*-values in any way determine values about people of the same colour. The experiments described show that the two sets of values are congruent; they point in the same direction, as it were. People who rate the colour 'black' negatively also rate the concepts 'black person' and 'Negro' negatively; but that does not prove that they rate 'black person' and 'Negro' negatively *because* they rate black negatively. That would imply that the colour-values came 'first' and the values about coloured people developed later by association. Indeed, another of Williams's studies[5] showed how this process might work; it was shown that the connotative meanings of colour names can be *conditioned* to terms with which they are associated. When subjects learned to associate certain stimuli with particular colours, they later rated those stimuli in the same way as they treated the corresponding colours. In other words the stimulus that they had been made to associate with the colour black was rated negatively even though at face value it had nothing to do with blackness or any other colour. Is it not possible, then, that having learned the values our culture attaches to the colours black and white, we then learn to associate the same values with black and white people, giving us (respectively) negative and positive evaluations of them? The argument is the more plausible for the demonstration that these values can be so easily conditioned to *irrelevant* concepts, let alone concepts which even have words in common (e.g. black – black people).

Clearly, the issue of what gives rise to what can only be settled if we trace these processes back as far as possible until we find how, and in what order, these values originally develop in individual people. This entails studying children at the age when they are beginning to use language and to learn the conventional meanings of words like black and white. Renninger and Williams[6] conducted a study of pre-school children in which they tried to find a direct answer to this chicken-and-egg problem. In the words of the authors:

The principal purpose of this investigation was to study the degree of awareness of the connotative meanings of white as good and black as bad among Caucasian preschool children. A secondary purpose of the investigation was to attempt to determine whether the awareness of colour connotation develops prior to, concurrent with or subsequent to the development of the child's awareness of racial differences between Caucasian and Negro persons.

Two sets of materials were used with the children; one set to assess their awareness of the connotative meaning of black and white and one to determine their racial awareness. In the former the children were required to finish off stories that the experimenter began for them using cards with black and white figure drawings. Their score was the number of times (out of eight opportunities) that they completed the stories by using black to indicate a negative evaluation and white to indicate a positive evaluation. Six, seven or eight answers of this type were respectively labelled 'low', 'medium' and 'high' awareness. This seems rather a strict criterion, but even so, 7 per cent of the three-year-olds, 20 per cent of the four-year-olds and 43 per cent of the five-year-olds fell in the 'high' awareness category. Perhaps a more meaningful picture is given by combining these categories, in contrast to those children who made five or less responses of the prescribed type, thus showing little awareness. By means of this classification it emerges that 29 per cent of the three-year-olds, 73 per cent of the four-year-olds and 81 per cent of the five-year-olds showed some degree of awareness. These data were interpreted by the authors 'as indicating that most of these Caucasian children were learning the colour-meaning concept during the third, fourth and fifth years'.

The second test involved a kind of jigsaw puzzle with black and

T–C

white figures which the child fitted together, and about which the interviewer asked a number of questions; these questions explored (1) whether the child preferred the dark-skinned child or the light-skinned child as a playmate; (2) whether he could apply a racial name to the dark-skinned child; (3) whether he could connect the racial labels 'Negro', 'coloured' and 'white' with the appropriate figures when the labels were supplied by the experimenter; and (4) whether the child 'segregated' the families in the puzzle arrangement. On sections 2, 3 and 4 there was a clear tendency for racial awareness to increase significantly with age from a relatively low level among the three-year-olds to a much higher level in the five-year-olds. So clearly racial awareness is both present and increasing at ages three through five. More surprising were the answers to section one. Over 80 per cent of *all* age-groups preferred to play with the light-skinned child depicted in the puzzle; this is the clearest evidence from the study that pre-school children have both an *awareness* of race, and some kind of *preference* for one race over another, however unsophisticated.

Clearly this study does not give us conclusive evidence as to which develops first: colour values or racial values. Both are present to some extent even in the three-year-olds. As the authors conclude:

The results of this study indicated that Caucasian children are learning the evaluative meanings of black as bad, and white as good, during their preschool years, the period in which awareness of race is also developing.

The data clearly do not support the idea that colour-values precede racial values. As interpreted by the authors, the picture we receive from the data, is one of a concurrent or parallel development of the two sets of values. However, we should consider an alternative interpretation. As we pointed out earlier, the congruence of colour-values and racial values could have a number of explanations. We have really only explored the possibility that colour-values contribute to the development of racial values. But there are one or two indications from these data that, if anything, the process operates the other way round. While awareness of colour connotations increased from 29 per cent of the three-year-olds to 73 per cent of the five-year-olds, over 80 per cent of the three-year-olds proved to be aware of racial differences and to base their playmate preference upon such differences. In other words, racial values seem to be already very strongly established in this sample of three-year-olds, while pure *colour*-values are only slowly being learned. So we have to consider the hypothesis that adult racial norms and values instil into the child a very early awareness of racial differences and rudimentary values, *before* colour values are well established. Whether it is the case that the former contribute to the latter – rather than the reverse – is not clear. It *might* be that values about black people colour our values about 'blackness' rather than the other way round. However, this is pure speculation, and we can offer no further evidence on the matter. In any case, it is clear that there is not a once-and-for-all process: both sets of values continue to reinforce each other. This is important, because together they generate a persuasive emotional climate around these colours and the people and objects which embody them. Children subsequently learn very much more about black people than the simple items tapped in this study. It seems that by means of cultural colour-values and social influence they are provided with a dangerously simple scheme of things into which they can fit this information. As the authors of the study wrote:

If the pre-school child is learning that white things are good and black things are bad, it seems reasonable that these meanings could generalize to groups of persons designated by the colour-code as 'white' and 'black'. Thus, the 'convenient' designation of racial groups by colour names may provide the child with a general evaluative frame of reference, within which the more specific learnings of prejudice can easily be incorporated.'

So we should regard this whole area of colour-values *not* as an alternative explanation of the genesis of prejudice, but as, firstly, a possible contributory factor to prejudice and, secondly, providing an *evaluative context* into which prejudices about people's colour can be easily fitted, and which gives them credence.

These cultural influences operate chiefly through our language and the conventional usages of particular words. This is rather an indirect source of influence because it arises in situations (like conversations) which are not actually concerned with racial issues at all. Now we should look at other cultural media and the content of their direct communications about *racial* groups.

Parents and children

Parents are of course the prime agents of cultural transmission. It is a little difficult for researchers to 'catch them in the act' of directly teaching racial attitudes, and so the empirical evidence of this is rather thin on the ground. However, a number of studies have found a close correspondence between parents' and children's racial attitudes,[7] and behaviour,[8] and an early survey[57] found that nearly 70 per cent of the young people they questioned felt that they had been influenced by their parents' attitudes, or had taken them over, even if in slightly modified form. This process has been dealt with at some length in the previous chapter, and is mentioned here only to group this source of influence with the other cultural media.

Books

Until the advent of film and television, books were among the most influential carriers of culture. While this influence has diminished to some extent, they remain a telling mirror of current social values, including racial values. They are thus an important source of racial attitudes for both adults and children. In recognition of this importance, the topic receives an extended discussion in the final chapter of the book. We will anticipate the core of this discussion here.

Literature enjoys a privileged position in our culture. 'The book' as a source of information and knowledge has a mystique and an authenticity which is unrivalled by other cultural media. It is the means of communication which underpins our entire education system. This centrality is most evident in the priority we accord to 'learning to read', the necessary condition for participation in every other aspect of education. Inability or retardation in this sphere handicaps the child to an extent comparable to mental or physical handicap. Both the process of reading and reading materials themselves have a halo of value surrounding them that simply does not attach to films or television or conversation in the same way. The emphasis we place on reading is not lost on the child: many tangible rewards are offered for success, above all the manifest approval of his parents and his teacher. Now, while older children and adults can be more objective and critical of the *content* of books, for the young child with whom we are concerned the first glimpse of a new reality that reading offers him is likely to be potent and influential. He has no basis to discriminate between 'good' and 'bad' books, and he is more vulnerable to the message of the book, invested as it is with all the highly positive connotations we have described. For this reason we have to look rather closely at the reading material we offer to young children and divine the message it conveys. Whether fact or fiction, 'information' is seldom conveyed in a social vacuum; it often implies, or is conveyed in an atmosphere which implies, certain social values. The recognition of this has led, for example, to the production of children's books which depict aspects of working-class life, to offset the rather middle-class atmosphere of their predecessors.

When we look at the portrayal of racial minorities in children's literature, it is soon evident that black people are largely omitted. Clearly, this is an inaccurate representation of the real world, and in recent years, of our own society. It is arguable that children may conclude that black people are not a sufficiently large or significant group to warrant inclusion, which is patently not the case. There is an element of devaluation here, which tends to be underlined by the kinds of portrayal of black people that the child encounters when they are included. Until very recently black people have been depicted in a more or less derogatory manner. While contemporary authors might avoid this kind of portrayal, the racial stereotypes devolving from our colonial past survive in the writing of the period, in the children's 'classics' which are still widely read. The fact that these are now outdated values is not readily evident to the reader; and of course, in a sense they are not outdated because they square with a general negative feeling towards black people which is current in the society at large. So the racial content of children's books is an important issue, not as a central determinant of children's attitudes, but as an additional source of confirmation of the racial values we communicate to children.

Comics

Children's comics are usually thought of as frivolous but harmless reading matter. For the most part this is true, and the worst objections that educationists could raise to them are that the adventures of Korky the Kat and Desperate Dan are not very elevating for the child. Comics do have a more serious aspect, though. George Orwell realized this and in an article[10] on 'Boy's Papers' he argued that they relayed an outdated view of society. This, he was sure, was a conservative force because it encouraged a reactionary ideology in the minds of future citizens. This could only help to shore up that society against change. His faith in the powerful influence of comics over children's minds was purely intuitive, for there was no hard evidence to support his case when he wrote this in 1939. But his case can be made solely on grounds of exposure, for children in Britain currently buy over 10 million comics a week, and many like *Lion*, *Valentine*, etc., sell more copies than the *New Statesman*, *The Spectator* and the *Listener* combined.[11]

Broadly speaking, the comics for younger children are the most harmless. But as the comics stretch towards an older audience they devote an increasing amount of space to war stories. War we believe to be undesirable; and yet fictional war is presented to the child in comics as a scenario in which the nobler qualities of men emerge: courage, endurance, patriotism, self-sacrifice, comradeship, and moral purity – being on the side of Right, or at least on the right side. And this is the crux; for these are *our* qualities, not *theirs*. Wars are Us against Them; and in comics a complex social phenomenon is reduced to staccato sentiments in strip illustrations which can be easily absorbed by the just-literate reader. Loyalties must be left in no doubt, so that the enemy is invested with exactly the opposite characteristics to our lads, not only making the distinction clear, but justifying their slaughter. For example, in Nicholas Johnson's[11] fascinating study of war comics and their effects, he showed that 'The enemy is described, either by the comic itself or by British characters, as "deadly and fanatical; lousy stinking rats; brainless scum; swine; devils; filthy dogs; slippery as snakes; or slit-eyed killers."'

As Orwell found, the world-view and the alliances the reader is called upon to support, are years out of date, in this case dating back to the Second World War. Others, particularly American comics, include more contemporary enmities against 'Commies' in general and Russians and Chinese in particular. (Some which are set in the Second World War have a timeless quality about them . . . no doubt the Australian soldier who 'didn't fancy the idea of his country being overrun by yellow men' would still support the 'White Australia' Policy today.)

Johnson analysed comics for older boys and war comics, looking in particular at both the number and nature of references to different national groups. Countries involved in the Second World War were mentioned very much more frequently than other

nations; however, the *ways* in which the Allies were mentioned
was very different to the treatment of the Enemy nations. Taking
as an index the use of derogatory nicknames, pronounced differences were obvious. The Allies' nicknames, 'Limey', 'Yank',
'Aussie' (which are fairly mild anyway) were used in less than 6
per cent of the references to those countries, while the much
harsher 'Nazi', 'Jerry', 'Kraut', 'Boche', 'Hun', 'Jap' and 'Nip'
comprised over 38 per cent of all references to the Enemy nations.

Johnson was naturally interested in the possible effects of this
material on children's day-to-day attitudes towards the countries
involved. With a group of Oxford primary school children, he
obtained their ranked preferences for various countries, which
produced the following order of preference; England, Australia
and America, France, Italy, India, Germany, Russia and China,
and Japan. He then partitioned the children into those who regularly read Boys' and War comics and those who did not, and looked
at the nationality preferences of each group. While the rank order
of preference for the *entire* sample is as above,

... the enemy nations, Germany, Japan and Italy, are liked less by
the children who read War or Boys' comics (than by non-readers)
while the allies, America, Australia and France, are liked more.
Russia, India and China which do not appear in the comics as involved
in the war, show the smallest differences in preference between the
two groups of children. There seems also to be a stronger identification
with the children's own nation England in the case of the Boys' and
War comic readers.

Johnson rightly concludes that the effect on children of reading
war material as it is presented in comics is far from trivial, and that
it may also be long-lasting.

It is interesting that the Japanese were the most disliked group
among his sample of children. This may be due to their record of
atrocities, though it is arguable whether these were any worse than
German war-crimes, or those of any other nation, for that matter.
An alternative explanation is that the Japanese provide two reasons for antipathy; they are both an enemy and an alien racial
group. Both the author and the artist can play on the extra 'meaning' which attaches to such groups. It is easier to portray them as
enemies because they *look* different from us. And all the traditional

overtones of mystery, danger, inscrutability, barbarism and animality which surround our feelings about foreign races make it easier to invest Orientals (or Negroes) with the bestial qualities that the enemy must have.

This shades into the question of how comics treat racial as opposed to national groups, irrespective of whether they are involved in wars or not. Jennie Laishley[12] has recently looked at this issue by analysing some sixteen comics over a six-month period. 162 issues were examined, including comics for very young children, boys' comics, teenage girls' magazines and a general-knowledge magazine. When most comics contain at least five stories, it is significant that only twenty stories from the entire sample featured any non-white figures at all. Of these

. . . eight treated these characters in a wholly unfavourable fashion, that is, they were represented as evil, treacherous, violent or stupid. Three stories included some favourable and some unfavourable characters. Three stories included characters who, although not treated in a strongly unfavourable manner, were nonetheless represented as rather limited stereotypes. Two stories included a single non-white in the background of the story, who had little or no personality, and two further stories included characters who had a personality of their own but whose status was still subordinate to the white hero or heroine of the tale.

The precise way in which these effects are achieved are rather similar for both comics and children's books, and they are discussed in the final chapter. In comics, of course, the pictorial aspect is the most important; the illustrations overleaf encapsulate the different aspects of 'foreign' and non-white characterization.

Two conclusions are clear from these surveys of comics; they encourage outdated and dangerously hostile views of foreign nations; and non-white peoples are largely omitted from comics, and derogated in their few appearances. While comics are fantasy materials we have seen that they have real consequences. Their present treatment of black people can only foster ignorance and divisiveness in a multi-racial society. Perhaps some of the energies of the anti-pornography campaigners could be directed to other parts of our bookstalls; their zealous concern for the innocence of children could usefully extend to social, as well as 'moral' corruption.

Television

In the past twenty years television has grown from a luxury enjoyed by a minority to a mass medium. In many homes it is almost the only source of entertainment and information, and it provides this service for many hours every day. It is arguably the single most important purveyor and mirror of contemporary culture. Yet we have been singularly slow to acknowledge this influence and to assess its effects on young children. One of the only exceptions, Himmelweit *et al.*'s study of *Television and the Child*,[13] is now sixteen years old, and the programmes it mentions belong to another era. Since this time there has been no major analysis of television with respect to its racial content. We have to turn to the United States once again, and draw what lessons we can for the British experience.

Until recently American television was almost exclusively white. The tiny proportion of programmes which included black characters portrayed them as happy-go-lucky, unreliable 'coons', maids and manservants, or featured them as entertainers or athletes. In the mid-sixties a token move towards 'integrated' TV began when a few black actors were called upon to play comparatively major roles, as assistants to white detective heroes, like 'Ironside'. In 1968–9 the television industry announced that important changes in programming to include black people were to be undertaken. The net result of this was an increase in the incidence of blacks in commercials from 5 per cent to 7 per cent of all commercials; in dramas, 37 per cent of the total had at least one black character compared to the previous figure of 32 per cent. With regard to the kinds of roles blacks now enacted, it was found that there was virtually no increase in major roles, a significant increase (from 29 per cent to 46 per cent) in minor roles, and a decrease in the use of blacks as background figures.[14]

Even though the original exposure of blacks was small, and the increase in exposure not very great, some effect on children's perceptions of TV blacks or even blacks in general might be expected simply on the basis of sheer volume of television watching. For another study had shown that children of both races and all income groups averaged between four and seven hours viewing every day. It is not possible to talk about *changes* in children's reactions to TV blacks because there has been no 'before–after' comparison, and because the introduction of blacks has been slow and irregular. We only have data on children's present reactions to blacks; this comes from a study[16] by Greenberg in which he found that the more white children were exposed to programmes with black personnel (through greater TV watching in general, not selective exposure to 'black' programmes), the more likely it was that children would select 'black' shows as their favourites. More surprisingly, it was also more likely that these children would identify with, or want to be like a black TV character. This finding assumes much greater importance in the light of research findings (described later) which show that white children usually identify across racial lines very infrequently, and seldom express preferences for black figures. There is, of course, no guarantee that these more positive attitudes will generalize from the screen into real-life, but any influence they do exert is obviously in the right direction. Black actors also serve as models with which black children can identify and this undoubtedly boosts the status of the group in their own eyes, compared to the situation where no blacks featured in the media at all.

In Britain we are in an interim stage. The atmosphere that Himmelweit *et al.* described in the mid-1950s is no longer with us – one where children's views of other races were only of academic interest – for there was no substantial domestic black population. Then the issue was one of attitudes towards 'foreigners' of various types, the information coming from programmes like *Children's Newsreel*, which now have a pleasantly old-fashioned Reithian ring to them. In addition, as the authors pointed out, 'Negroes are often seen in dance-bands and variety shows.' Despite the events of the intervening years, and the American experience, there has not been any wholesale importation of black people into television. It is a grotesque indictment of our sensitivity and awareness that the single most regular exposure of 'black' people on our television screens has been the *Black and White Minstrel Show*.

The effects of programmes in which British blacks feature in some way, like *Curry and Chips*, *Love Thy Neighbour* and more indirectly *Till Death Us Do Part*, are extremely difficult to gauge.

In general, the effects of showing black people in everyday situations as opposed to their former stereotyped exposure may well be beneficial; but each of *these* programmes also gives a platform to at least one bigoted white character. Although their ludicrously extreme prejudices are played up for humorous effect, this is a two-edged sword, for it is the humorous atmosphere itself which allows the expression of these views, by making them more acceptable. This effect reverberates off the screen, too, for it becomes permissible to use Alf Garnett's language in ordinary conversation, because we know it's all a joke, don't we ? The philosophy of this approach seems to be that we should air prejudices, and perhaps laugh them away. A peculiar extension of this is the anti-black black comedian. This strange phenomenon allows the expression of the most racist sentiments, cushioned both by humour *and* by the fact that the raconteur is black. There is no need to feel guilty laughing at his jokes about blacks, for he's one of them – so neither he nor his jokes *can* be prejudiced, can they ? Again, it's a way of making the sentiments acceptable – if *they* say those things against themselves, why shouldn't I ? And the very popularity of these shows makes it possible for the jokes – and the sentiments – to be passed on socially.

There is no effective counter-balance to the expression of prejudice in these programmes. And even if there were, that which we think of as the opposite of prejudice, namely tolerance, is insufficient. In other words, you cannot balance off a highly negative sentiment with one that is merely neutral or passively accepting. The difference is frequently illustrated in studio discussions of race relations. The dramatic statements of the Powellite speaker have a much more compelling appeal to a popular audience than do the liberal appeals for tolerance, fair-mindedness and sometimes sacrifice. And here is the crux: the black coverage that is 'balanced' in this way has already unbalanced itself by conceding the terms of the debate to the racialists. It has conceded that black people are a *problem* and have to *be tolerated*.

This criticism can be extended to the whole of the news and opinion media, not just television. This factor acts in concert with another source of bias which helps to determine the presentation of black people in the media. This is a bias endemic to media which have an 'entertainment' function which is in turn related to the need to sell copies, in the case of newspapers, or boost audiences in the case of broadcasting. This is the bias towards 'negativeness', or the newsman's maxim that bad news is good news-copy. As Husband[17] has written: 'It is a

... Journalistic fact that bad news – e.g. murder, rape, disasters, deviance, etc. – makes 'good news'. Even a superficial perusal of the press, or other news media, will provide ready evidence of the frequency with which negativeness is reflected in news copy. If we look at the possible consequences of negativeness as a news value in relation to race relations we begin to see that it is likely to be harmful. At its simplest it means that stories of racial conflict are likely to predominate over stories of harmonious race relations. Similarly the negative behaviour of minority groups becomes a more frequent item of news content than do their positive achievements. Stories of criminal acts ... become more accessible than stories of socially meritorious behaviour ... The fact that negativeness also applies to the reporting of the host population does not detract from the seriousness of this bias. For the generally negative image of the ethnic minorities created by such coverage is likely to be consistent with stereotypes already held about minority groups. Pressures towards selective perception are therefore likely to amplify the negative image presented in the news media.

So that black people in this country tend to receive news coverage either by virtue of their group, as a whole, being 'a problem', or by their individual misdeeds. The former is the most serious source of bias, for it is an assumption which is implicit in nearly all coverage of black people, and of course lends credibility to the latter bias, too. It operates to confirm the popular stereotypes of black people, whereas a different kind of selectivity could help to rebut them. Husband[18] has given some concrete examples of this process at work over the immigration of Ugandan Asians:

... the Home Office was much quoted as saying 'We are already a crowded island and immigration must and will remain strictly controlled' – the implication being that immigration is the cause of over-population. Yet a feature of this country for a decade and more has been a net *emigration* rate. In the midst of the panic over the Asians official Government statistics became available which confirmed that in 1971 emigration exceeded immigration by over 20,000. This statistic was remarkable for its relative invisibility in the Press ... The reliance of the British medical services on Asian doctors has similarly not been regarded as a significant fact in the debate about Asian immigrants; and the findings of Jones and Smith [19] that coloured immigrants are less of a demand upon the social services than the indigenous population still remain one of the submerged facts about immigration.

Few of these nuances, of course, are directly detected by young children, but they certainly contribute to their parents' attitudes. And even young children could scarcely develop a positive picture of black people from their coverage in the media.

*

While the influence of individual media over the child may be small, the aggregate effect of all the media is considerable. The media reflect majority culture. As a result, the majority of children absorb a picture of the world from the television and newspapers which is very like their own and their parents' reality. This congruence assists the socialization process, for although the media are far less influential than the parents in this process, they are an independent source of confirmation of this version of the world.

When racism takes firm root in a culture it is very difficult for the child to escape its influence. As we have shown, it taints the picture of the world that is presented to the child by the parents, by books and by the mass media; beyond the home, to the extent to which peers and teachers share similar pictures of the world, so will these values receive confirmation. The very young child has little choice but to absorb this; for these agencies are the only sources of information available to him.

It seems an appropriate point to move on from the forces which form children's attitudes to the attitudes themselves – in other words to describe the actual course of racial attitude development in children as it is observed. We will deal with majority-group (i.e. white) children in societies pervaded by prejudice and discrimination against black 'minorities', and therefore subject to the kinds of 'cultural' pressures just described. Later we will discuss the influence of various factors on these developmental patterns, some 'social structural', like the effect of socio-economic status, some 'individual', like the effects of various child-rearing practices on the child's personality and attitudes, and some which fall happily into neither category. The most important of this last group is the factor of minority-group membership itself; a major emphasis of this discussion will be the racial attitudes developed by black children.

The course of racial attitude development

Mary Ellen Goodman[20] developed a simple schema for this process which identified three main phases, *racial awareness*, *racial orientation* or 'incipient attitude', and thirdly true *racial attitudes*. They are not discrete phases, and overlap to some extent, but they always occur in the same order: each is necessary for the next to appear.

One of the most remarkable discoveries in this area is precisely how early in a child's life he or she begins to develop racial awareness. By this is meant an awareness of differences, between racial groups, the ability to recognize and label these differences, and also to identify oneself in racial terms. A number of studies [21-23] have identified this phase in children from three to five years old. The lower limit of this phase has not been firmly established but it is clear that for some children it begins at a very early age. Ammons,[24] for example, found that 20 per cent of the *two*-year-old subjects in his study, and 50 per cent of the three-year-olds were able to discriminate skin-colour and facial differences between Negro and white dolls. Kenneth Morland, a distinguished worker in this field, has conducted a number of studies of this age-range. In an early study[25] he found that this ability to recognize racial differences improved rapidly over the period from three to six years, the improvement being most marked in the fourth year. And in a later study[26] he found patterns of self-identification in three-year-old children which did not differ significantly from those of older children, suggesting that they were already well established at this age.

Morland's method of testing for racial-recognition ability was typical of many in this area. He simply showed a series of multi-racial pictures to the children in the study, and asked 'Do you see a white person in this picture?' and 'Do you see a coloured person in this picture?' If the child answered either in the affirmative, he was asked to point to the figure concerned. The terms 'white' and 'coloured' were agreed to be the most common racial designations in this area where the study was run. So this racial awareness not only involves the ability to distinguish between different skin-colours and facial features, but also to recognize and use the labels which are applied to each racial group.

The measure of *self*-identification in racial terms involved showing children pictures of white and black children of their own age and sex, pointing to each in turn and asking, 'Do you look like this child?' 'Do you look like this child?' and 'Which child do you look more like?'. Not surprisingly, as white children's racial awareness increased, so did the ability to identify themselves correctly, and 71 per cent of the subjects identified themselves correctly, the remainder being equally divided between those who identified themselves wrongly and the 'don't knows'. Misidentification and uncertainty decreased with age.

Racial awareness, then, is the phase in which the child learns to perceive and label racial differences. It soon gives way to the next phase, *racial orientation*, in which the first positive and negative *feelings* about racial groups are apparent – the first feelings of like or dislike, of preferences for one over another. Because this involves an evaluative disposition towards the groups, which is a rudimentary version of a true attitude, Goodman sub-titled this phase 'incipient attitude'.

Numerous studies[21,27,28,29] have shown these embryonic racial attitudes to be present in three- to six-year-old children. Ammons[24] found that these attitudes became more widespread among the children as they got older; while only 10 per cent of three-year-old children showed negative feelings towards Negro figures, by the age of four this proportion had grown to 40 per cent.

The methods used in this kind of study are mostly variants of the same basic technique. Because it is impossible to use verbally sophisticated measures with young children, the questionnaires used for adult attitude scales are impractical. Instead an interview is held with the child in which the researcher presents the children with a variety of dolls or pictures representing the various racial groups in the child's environment, and uses these as the basis for a series of questions to the child. For example, in testing racial orientation, the child might be presented with a series of pictures of black and white children, and simply asked which he would prefer as a friend, playmate, classmate, and so on. When Morland[30] put questions of this type to young white American children he found that some 82 per cent of them showed a clear preference for their own race over the black figures.

Of course, preference for one's own race over another does not automatically imply rejection and hostility towards the other race, simply a greater amount of favourability towards one's own group. Morland conducted some tests to see whether black children would be accepted in a situation where there was not an either/or choice to be made between black and white figures. He found that relatively few of the children made an outright rejection of black figures, citing their race as the reason.[31] A larger proportion were not prepared to accept black playmates for 'other reasons', some of which may have been excuses; in all, 20 per cent of the children would not accept black playmates. It seems then that the vast majority of white children express a clear preference for figures of their own race in these situations, but would theoretically accept black figures as playmates; a sizeable minority will not accept black figures, even when there are no white alternatives, which seems to indicate a far greater degree of hostility towards blacks. It should be stressed that these findings have been replicated in any number of similar studies.

The phases of racial awareness and racial orientation, then, are the foundations of racial attitude development, The two phases should not be regarded as entirely separate, particularly in view of what we said earlier about the simultaneous learning of 'facts' and 'feelings' about groups. As Kenneth Clark[35] has written:

The child's first awareness of racial differences is ... associated with some rudimentary evaluation of these differences ... the child cannot learn what racial group he belongs to without being involved in a larger pattern of emotions, conflicts and desires which are part of his growing knowledge of what society thinks about his race.

So that although we find empirically that racial orientation is evident slightly later than racial awareness, there is a good deal of overlap between the two. It may simply take longer for the orientation phase to be overtly expressed.

The essential significance of this period has been described by Harding et al.[36] as follows:

In what sense then, can we speak of an ethnic attitude, inchoate or otherwise in the very young child? The fact is that his ethnic awareness is by no means affectively neutral. He reveals clear preferences for some groups while others are rejected. Thus a fundamental ingredient of an inter-group attitude is present: an evaluative orientation that is expressed in ingroup versus outgroup terms.'

This 'attitude' is expressed very simply: in preference for his own group and strong identification with it, and in rejecting or hostile feelings towards the outgroup. The sentiments the child will utter are equally simple; for example, children's spontaneous remarks about black figures during tests of racial orientation are often of the following kind: 'He's a stinky little boy, take him away', 'He's a blackie, I don't like him', 'He's no good', 'He kills people'. Or as described in the last chapter, the child may 'model' sophisticated adult attitudes and retail them without fully understanding the concepts involved, but with the feeling behind them faithfully reproduced. The sophistication of these utterances or lack of it is not important. What is crucial is that the child has absorbed a simple polarized evaluation of the groups involved, so that one is positive: good and liked, the other negative: bad and disliked. Into this evaluative frame of reference can be fitted all the more complex information the child will subsequently encounter. But selective processes may operate to absorb only the information that is congruent. In other words, the existence of this simple evaluative scheme – white/good, black/bad – provides a foundation for the whole superstructure of prejudice, and the reasons and rationalizations which are supposed to justify prejudices are absorbed later, selectively, to consolidate this basic disposition.

It is precisely when this process starts to happen – that is, the absorption of the more complex information about racial groups, their stereotyped characteristics and their social status, that we say the child is entering Goodman's third phase – of true racial attitudes. This generally occurs between six and eight years of age. In Trager and Radke-Yarrow's research with children of this age, they found that

concepts and feelings about race frequently include adult distinctions of status, ability, character, occupations, and economic circumstances ... Among the older children stereotyping and expressions of hostility are more frequent and attitudes more crystallized than among the young children.[37]

An index of this was the children's allocation of poor housing and menial employment to black people (and superior environments to whites) in doll and picture tests. Once again, recognition of the real-life social status of black people does not constitute prejudice against them, but it has been shown that 'There is a tendency for hostile feelings towards Negroes and a perception of Negroes in inferior roles to appear together; however, many children who show a dislike for Negroes show no awareness of the status factors studied.'[38] Among the reactions to the black dolls in this study were the following: 'He is coming out of jail', 'They are gangsters', 'He would be digging dirt', 'He doesn't have no work'. 'All ladies who are coloured are maids', 'He's a coloured and he carries knives'. Clearly there is an intricate mixture of social-status references and outright hostile stereotypes in these remarks.

During the first few years of life, then, the child absorbs the colour values of his community. At first he simply learns the social valency of skin colour, and later, as his intellectual world broadens he absorbs the more complex concepts involved in adult racial attitudes. As he works out the differences between his own and other racial groups – or more exactly, the social significance of these differences – so does his identification with his own group and preference for it increase.

Older children

Beyond the age of seven or eight years there is a continuation of the trends we have described, that is, a gradual intensification of prejudice.[39,40] However, there is not as marked an increase as in the preceding years, and in some respects it levels off in early adolescence. During this time, too, the organization of the child's racial attitudes undergoes change, in the direction of greater *differentiation*, *integration* and *consistency*. We conceive of attitudes as having three components: the *affective* or emotional component, the *cognitive* or 'intellectual' component, and the *behavioural* or action component. In the case of racial attitudes these three components are our feelings, beliefs, and behavioural dispositions towards another racial group.

The process of differentiation may occur within each one of these components. For example, the affective component may become differentiated to allow that a child likes one particular black child, while disliking the black groups as a whole. Or the cognitive component may be differentiated to admit both the bad and good attributes of the group or the individual. Blake and Dennis found precisely this process operating in their adolescent subjects.[41] Or the behavioural component may be differentiated as children comply with the demands of the de-segregated classroom while deliberately segregating themselves in the playground. In other words, the components become less 'global' and more fitted for rationally handling the more complex information about groups that the child is now encountering. While the admission of discrepant 'positive' items may 'tow' the attitude in the direction of greater tolerance, this does not automatically happen as the item can be perceived as exceptional, atypical of the group and its stereotype. It must be recorded that only a few studies have given concrete evidence of differentiation, but that most writers have assumed the process to be at work in the transition from simple 'childish' to adult attitudes.

At the same time, the three components undergo *integration*, so that there is greater consistency between them. Thus the child who has always disliked black children as a group but has previously accepted them as playmates if not friends may begin to alter this. The behavioural component may fall into line with the affective component as he begins to withdraw from inter-racial contacts and spends his time exclusively with his own group. Horowitz found increasing correlations between the three components of attitudes, with age, in his five- to fourteen-year-old white subjects.[22]

Radke, Sutherland and Rosenberg's[42] study of seven- to thirteen-year-old children well illustrates the form that racial attitudes take during this period. When confronted with pictures of Negro and white children and asked to assign a variety of favourable and unfavourable descriptions to them, the white children 'show clearly their acceptance of the attitudes of their culture toward the Negro . . . in each grade (i.e. at each age-level) the white children assign many more undesirable than desirable characteristics to Negro photographs.' However, among the older children there was a greater tendency to attribute a few good characteristics to the black figures. Overall, though there was not a single case in which a good characteristic was more frequently attributed to a Negro figure than to a white one; and the proportion of white children making pro-white, anti-Negro assignments averaged across all the picture presentations was 80 per cent.

The investigators also measured the children's preferred choice of 'friends' from the same photographs. Around 90 per cent of the white children chose friends from within their own race. However, from measures of the children's real-life friendship choices, inside the class, within the school and from the community at large an interesting picture emerges. A majority (76 per cent) of the younger white children choose black friends within their class; this declines sharply among the older children to 53 per cent. It should be stressed that the school concerned has a white population of only 15 per cent, therefore the choice of white friends within any one class is severely limited. When this constraint was removed and the children were free to choose friends from other classes within the school, the proportion of younger children choosing white friends jumps to 92 per cent and to 100 per cent for the older ones. And 100 per cent of both age-groups choose white friends when they are allowed to choose them from the wider community. In other words, there is consistency between the rejection of black figures in the picture tests and the children's real-life friendship choices, which increases with age.

So the period from childhood through adolescence is characterized by a consolidation of attitudes. There is a slight increase in hostility which later seems to level off, a greater differentiation within the attitudinal components, and a greater consistency between them. This makes for a more stable attitudinal structure.

'Social structural' determinants of attitudes

Having surveyed the cultural influences on children's attitudes, and the 'typical' developmental pattern they follow, we turn to the 'social structural' and 'individual' determinants. Very few studies have successfully isolated 'social structural' factors in a controlled way. More often comparisons have been made between different geographical and social areas, on the assumption that they differ with respect to the variable in which the investigators are interested, say 'socio-economic status' or 'inter-racial contact'. As a result few clear-cut findings emerge, partly because of the influence of other factors which have not been controlled for, and which may interact with the variable in question. Take the case of *socio-economic status* as an influence on children's racial attitudes. Now despite the rather consistent finding in studies[43] of *adults* that there is a correlation between higher socio-economic status and less prejudice towards blacks, it is only just possible to discern this relationship from equivalent studies of children drawn from these same social groups. Thus, some studies have found no differences in racial attitudes between different status-groups;[44] and Morland's studies [26,31] showed both that lower-status whites were more prepared to *accept* black children (chosen from pictures – 'Will you play with this child?') than higher-status whites, but that on preference measures, where the child had to choose between the races, more of the lower than the upper status group preferred the whites and rejected the blacks. The latter finding was confirmed in a different context by Landreth and Johnson;[45] and Chein and Hurwitz[46] identified more positive outgroup attitudes among their higher status Jewish subjects. Another confirmatory study, by Chyatte, Schaeffer and Spiaggia,[47] illustrates the difficulties in interpreting these studies. They found that children of professional fathers showed significantly less 'prejudice verbalization' than did children of non-professional fathers. This points to the whole complex of differences which go hand-in-hand with socio-economic status differences, in this case 'education'. This factor alone could account for all the differences so far described which have been attributed to status differences. 'Intelligence' is a related factor which may also contribute to these results. For Singer[48] found higher intelligence to correlate with decreased prejudice.

When we consider the extent of *de facto* residential segregation in America, or in Britain for that matter, it is clear that differences in status among whites also ensure differences in the amount of contact with blacks. '*Inter-racial contact*', then, is another fellow-traveller which could account for the findings described above. A number of studies have considered the influence of 'contact' on children's attitudes, though seldom with adequate controls for other related factors. Singer's[48] study looked at this problem by comparing children's attitudes in segregated and desegregated schools. Her white subjects from integrated schools were more accepting of the outgroup compared to the segregated school children. Tolerance was shown to correlate with both 'contact' and 'intelligence', but of the two, contact was the more important.

Mussen's[49] study of an inter-racial summer camp is one of a number of studies which suggest that it is not contact *per se* which determines racial attitudes but rather the *type* of contact. Contact, after all, provides opportunities for people's prejudices to be contradicted *or* confirmed; it is the quality of the contact that will help to decide which of these happens. Here we should draw a lesson from studies of adult attitudes, for several of these[50,51] have shown that frequent inter-racial contact in equal-status situations helps to diminish prejudice and foster more positive racial attitudes.

An early study by Horowitz[22] seems to confound some of the other findings concerning 'contact' and prejudice, but underlines the point that it is not a simple matter of frequency of exposure. He compared the racial attitudes of schoolchildren in New York, Tennessee and Georgia, in both segregated and mixed schools. The children in New York from an all-white school showed neither more nor less prejudice than those from a mixed school, who would have more contact with black children. More surprisingly, 'The Southern groups tested showed no more prejudice than that shown by the children in New York City.' Further, 'Comparison of the Southern samples showed no difference among them, in spite of differences in mode of living represented by sampling urban and rural living.' Clearly, this is a case where many more factors are being varied in the course of the comparison between different areas than simply contact 'alone'. Nevertheless, it is surprising that in spite of the variation of a number of factors between each situation, this uniform picture of hostile attitudes persists. Horowitz's conclusion reinforces the argument that it is the qualitative aspects of inter-racial situations that are more important: 'attitudes towards Negroes are now determined not by contact with Negroes, but by contact with the prevalent attitude towards Negroes'. The implication, of course, is that an overall climate of hostility exists towards black people in the United States, and it is absorbed by children uniformly, that is, irrespective of their direct experience of black people, and of the institutionalization of racism through segregation in particular areas.

'Individual' factors in children's racial attitudes

Of the individual differences that might be expected to affect attitudes, the sex of the individual is potentially one of the most important. However, while the vast majority of studies have involved subjects of both sexes, very few have published data on sex differences. The reason for this may be less neglect than a reflection of the same situation described in those studies which have included such data – simply that very few investigators have found consistent sex differences in children's racial attitudes. While Koch[52] describes a slight trend for her white girl subjects to choose own-race figures as friends more frequently than do white boys, and Goodman[20] refers to sex differences in racial awareness, Springer,[53] Morland,[25] and Chyatte et al.,[47] for example, found no such differences, and the latter are much more common findings. As Vaughan[54] concludes, 'Significant attitudinal differences by sex, then, are yet to be demonstrated'.

The earlier emphasis on the role of parents in forming the child's attitudes directs us to the most obvious source of individual differences: the kind of parents with which a particular child is blessed. We know that children's racial attitudes [7,55–8,63] and behaviour[8] often show close similarity to those of their parents. What is at issue here is whether there are other reasons, over and above the simple existence of prejudice or tolerance in the parents, which help to determine the attitudes of their children. Are there other factors, like more general social attitudes, child-rearing practices and so on, which assist in the process? The major research initiative in this area remains the classic 'Authoritarian Personality' study[59] which investigated a whole complex of attitudes and personality characteristics thought to be associated with prejudice. Having identified highly prejudiced subjects, the researchers attempted to isolate the kinds of family styles, child-rearing practices and parental beliefs that characterized the childhood of these people. Harding et al.[60] have described the findings as follows:

... highly prejudiced subjects, in contrast to those who were tolerant, showed a more rigid personality organization, greater conventionality in their values, more difficulty in accepting socially deviant impulses as part of the self (for example, fear, weakness, aggression, and sex) a greater tendency to exernalize these impulses by means of projection and more inclination to be status- and power-oriented in their personal relationships. These personality attributes as well as others (for example, idolizing one's parents, impersonal and punitive aggression, dichotomous thinking) represented the defining features of the authoritarian personality. These attributes in turn were found to be related to early childhood experiences in a family setting characterized by harsh and threatening parental discipline, conditional parental love, a hierarchical family structure, and a concern for family status. The unconscious conflict involving fear of and dependency on parents, on the one hand and strong hatred and suspicion of them, on the other, seemed to be contained by an authoritarian personality structure tuned to expressing this repressed hostility toward members of socially sanctioned outgroups.

The controversy engendered by the study gave rise to a great deal of research.[61,62,87] An issue which remains unresolved is how far children's prejudices reflect this whole complex of parental beliefs, child-rearing practices, etc., or simply represents the direct transmission of attitudes in the socialization process which go along with these other parental characteristics. However, the fact that home backgrounds of this type tend to produce children who are disposed towards prejudice is now well established.[57,63]

Attitudes versus behaviour

A central issue we have not yet resolved is the question of what these attitudes tell us about the children's *behaviour* in everyday life. Do prejudiced children (or anyone else, for that matter) necessarily behave in a discriminatory way in practice? After all, we have only presented evidence of children's expressed *attitudes*, in a possibly artificial experimental situation. Unfortunately researchers have too often presented their data on attitudes as though they were predictive of behaviour, even though we have known that the situation is not that simple, ever since the classic study by LaPiere[88] in the 1930s. There are sound 'economic' reasons why attitudes rather than behaviour have received the most attention from social psychologists, as I have argued elsewhere.[89] Vernon summarizes it this way:

> Words are actions in miniature. Hence by the use of questions and answers we can obtain information about a vast number of actions in a short space of time, the actual observation and measurement of which would be impracticable.[90]

Isaac Deutscher, among others, has pointed out the many fallacies involved in this kind of inferential jump from one sphere to another. He argues cogently that in many situations it is a 'dubious assumption that what people say is related directly to what they do'.[91] Why not? Quite simply it is because reality imposes all kinds of restraints on our behaviour that *can* be ignored in situations where we are simply expressing our attitudes. To take an extreme example, a South African black *might* have a very positive attitude towards whites and wish to integrate and socialize with them; in reality, *apartheid* proscribes any such behaviour. Ascertaining his attitudes would not, in itself, tell us very much about his everyday behaviour and the legal limitations on it; similarly, in deducing his attitudes simply from his observable actions, we would be misled.

In other words, the *situation* in which behaviour takes place will decide whether that behaviour is a reflection of the individual's attitudes, or whether it is an accommodation to other influences – like social pressures. Minard[92] provided an example of these kinds of processes at work in his study of race relations in an American mining community. While generally segregated in the social life of the community 'above ground', blacks were largely accepted by whites in the working situation below ground. Sixty per cent of whites managed a complete reversal of behaviour by accepting blacks while working *and* rejecting them in the outside world, while 20 per cent rejected them in both situations, and the remaining 20 per cent rejected them in neither. The behaviour of the 'consistent' 40 per cent may be said to accurately reflect their attitudes: it is not altered by changes in the situation. The real attitudes of the other 60 per cent are disguised by their willingness to comply with the demands of social pressure in *both* situations.

Wicker[93] has emphasized how both 'situational' and 'personal' factors affect the attitude–behaviour relationship. Amongst the latter he includes the presence of other, perhaps related attitudes, the presence of competing motives (as when a prejudiced tradesman may lose money by discriminating against blacks), and also the verbal, intellectual and social abilities of the individual. Some of the situational factors at work are the 'actual or considered presence of certain people' (e.g. the experimenter, or group pressures) normative prescriptions of proper behaviour, the availability of alternative behaviours, unforeseen extraneous events, and the expected and/or actual consequences of various acts.

So it is not possible to make a simple statement about how children will actually interact with children of other races, based on the attitude studies described in this chapter. To say that 'it depends on the person and the situation' is not an equivocation or a lame excuse, but the best possible account of what happens in reality.

The school environment is the 'situation' in which many of these studies have taken place. Within schools there is often a norm of 'tolerance' and 'integration', so this could be one restraint on the expression of hostile attitudes through antagonistic behaviour. Nevertheless, studies of real play-behaviour[8] and friendship choices[32-4] of schoolchildren have often shown considerable cleavage between racial groups, which is consistent with the rejecting attitudes shown by white children in many of the attitude studies we have cited (but not with the black children's attitudes, as we shall see shortly).

The author has encountered many teachers who find it difficult to accept the validity of the findings of these attitude studies, because of the apparent integration of their own classes. There is a tendency to see observable everyday behaviour as somehow more 'real', and therefore more important than the invisible world of attitudes. One purpose of this book is to redress this imbalance, for to frame educational policy on the basis of appearances, would be erroneous; it ignores the deeper level of children's emotions and beliefs about other races.

Black children's racial attitudes

The single most important determinant of children's racial attitudes is race itself. For although the attitudes of white and black children take a similar form – in which whites are often valued more highly than blacks – the significance of these attitudes is different for each group. Black children do not automatically develop the preference for and identification with their own group, and hostility towards the other groups that characterizes white children's attitudes. Rather, many seem to internalize almost the *same* attitudes as do white children. The similarity points to an explanation of the process behind it: that this pattern of attitudes is due to membership of an oppressed minority which has absorbed some of the values of the dominant majority culture, including devaluation of blacks. We shall see that this is a feature not only of American race relations but of other cultures where minorities with subordinate status are devalued by the majority. The conventional use of 'majority' and 'minority' is misleading here, for the crucial factor is the *status* relations between the groups, not the relative numbers; the same attitude patterns exist where the devalued group is actually in the numerical majority, for example, in South Africa.

It was from America, however, that there emerged the first evidence of the intrusion of these evaluations into children's attitudes. As early as 1939, studies of black children indicated that a minority of them were unwilling to specifically identify themselves *as* black.[64,65] In a classic experiment by Kenneth and Mamie Clark[66] black children were asked to choose between black and white dolls in response to various questions, designed to measure their racial awareness and identification. When asked to 'Give me the doll that looks like you' some 33 per cent of the black children chose the white doll. It was clear that this mis-identification was not simply a perceptual mistake, as 94 per cent of the children had labelled the black and white dolls correctly in other questions. Mary Goodman came to a similar conclusion, again using doll-choice tests of identification; only half as many 3–4-year-old Negroes as whites correctly identified themselves in her earliest study.[67] She suggests the reason for this: 'The relative inaccuracy of Negro identification reflects not simple ignorance of self, but unwillingness or psychological inability to identify with the brown doll because the child wants to look like the white doll.'

Indeed, if anything the evidence suggests that black children are *more*, rather than less aware of racial differences and their significance than white children. Several studies[20,68,69,70] have shown an earlier development of ethnic awareness in minority group children than whites; and Landreth and Johnson surmise that 'environmental influences directing attention towards skin-colour may be effective earlier in Negro than in White groups'.[45] So it is clearly not a question of *inability* to perceive racial differences, but more probably a *heightened* awareness of the negative connotations of the black figures. To identify with the disparaged figure is to disparage oneself, and those that made this 'correct' identification in Morland's study 'did so reluctantly and with emotional strain'.[25]

These self-attitudes are completely congruent with the children's expressed attitudes towards whites. Goodman's black subjects, aged $3\frac{1}{2}$ to $5\frac{1}{2}$, made more outgroup preferences than did the white (64 per cent cf. 7 per cent) showed less antagonism towards the outgroup (9 per cent cf. 33 per cent) less friendly responses towards the ingroup (56 per cent cf. 93 per cent) and more antagonism towards the ingroup (24 per cent cf. 0 per cent).[71] Morland's studies[25,26,30,31] showed very similar results and a majority of the black children he interviewed went as far as to say they would 'rather be' white than black.

The evaluative climate which surrounds black people seems to be subjectively real to these young children. So too are the more subtle nuances concerning gradations of colour. This much is clear from a study[45] which used picture-and-inset matching tasks with both black and white children. Interestingly, whereas the white children perceived them as intended, that is, *as* matching tasks, many black children perceived them as *preference* tasks. Having done so, they tended to choose white in preference to black, white over brown, and brown over black. The form and content of the black children's attitudes is predictably similar to those of white children. For example, in one study[27] rejection took the form of ascribing inferior roles to black characters in story-telling tests. In another,[21] black figures where chosen less by black children for playmates, companions to go home with, and guests for a birthday party. In completing unfinished stories involving black characters, the black children more frequently placed own-race figures in negative positions, and said they were more likely to be the aggressor, 'the badman', or the loser in a contest, and less likely to give aid.

There is not a great deal of data on the development of these attitudes with age. The few relevant studies suggests a decrease in outgroup orientation as the black child gets older. For example, the Clarks'[66] seven-year-old subjects chose the white doll as 'nice' and black doll as 'looking bad' *less* often than did their younger subjects. However, it may simply be that the orientation is less overt, for there are some indications that the emotional correlates of outgroup orientation and self- or own-group devaluation continue into adolescence and beyond. Deutsch,[72] for example, studied nine–eleven-year-old children of both races and found that

a relatively high proportion of the white lower-class children in this sample have negative self-responses, but not nearly as many as in the Negro group ... The Negro group as a whole is affected by lowered self-esteem.

As a result of this negativity in their self-conceptions they were also more passive, morose and fearful. Lowered self-esteem among black children has also been identified by Butts,[73] and some confirmation of the overall picture offered by Deutsch is suggested by the findings of Palermo,[74] that black children experience more anxiety than whites, and Mussen,[75] that they perceive the world as more threatening and hostile than do their white counterparts. Clearly there is much more at issue here than the incorrect choice of a few dolls; in so far as a positive sense of self and identity is almost a prerequisite for mental health, the phenomenon of mis-identification assumes considerable importance. However, it should also be stressed that many of these studies date from before the growth of black consciousness in the United States, so that the picture may be changing. These issues, the significance and con-sequences of misidentification for mental health are discussed at length in Chapter 5.

Cross-cultural replication

All the studies described so far have come from America, but this pattern of racial attitudes is not an exclusively American pheno-menon. Moving away from studies of black American children, we find that similar patterns have emerged from investigations with other minority-groups in other cultures. Graham Vaughan has conducted a number of studies[28,29] in New Zealand with Pakeha (the white majority) and Maori children. Using similar kinds of methods to those described, he found a situation analo-gous to the American one. That is, while Pakeha children showed a preference for and identification with their own group, this was much less evident among the Maori children. A significant mino-rity of them identified with the outgroup (on doll and picture tests) but this declines around age nine, as does other-race favouri-tism. But until then Maori children:

(a) tend to favour other-race figures when assigning stereotypes that refer to desirable or undesirable attributes; (b) tend to prefer other-race figures as playmates, and (c) tend to prefer other-race dolls to 'take home'.

Although the New Zealand racial situation is not as severe as in America, Ritchie[76] has shown how very derogatory stereotypes about Maoris have a wide currency in some sections of the white population. The 'good' stereotypes are based on the 'noble sav-age' concept, while the bad ones depict the Maori as 'wilfully poor ... breeds irresponsibly, dirty ... children moronic and undisciplined, virtually unemployable and grossly irresponsible if not plainly criminal'. However Thompson's analyses (e.g. Thompson – 1953)[77] of newspaper items concerning Maori affairs suggests a wider circulation of bad stereotypes, not just restricted to low-status whites. He found that a high percentage of the themes implied unfavourable attributes, for example that the Maoris are 'lazy', 'irresponsible', 'ignorant' and 'superstitious'.

The children's attitudes do not prove that the racial situation is as tense as in America, but rather that a much less explicit racism can still penetrate into childhood to distort the child's attitudes, identity and self-image.

The same applies to situations where the minority is both less visible and less obviously disparaged than are black Americans. Werner and Evans[78] showed this to be the case with young Mexican-American children. In structured doll-play interviews the children showed the 'usual' preference for the white figures, and light skin was generally evaluated as good and dark skin as bad. The socializing role of the school was brought out by the finding that these responses were much more prevalent among children with school experience. The children also showed a substantial amount of outgroup identification. An interesting finding was that 25 per cent of the sample indicated that the white man-doll was larger than the dark one, even though they were actually equal in size. These remarks were quite gratuitous as no questions about size had been asked. Werner and Evans comment that the phenomenon is reminiscent of the classic Bruner and Goodman[79] experiment in which working-class children over-estimated the size of coins of high value, as compared with middle class children.

Outgroup orientation is not an automatic consequence of belonging to a minority-group. Some studies of ethnic groups, perhaps less disparaged than the minorities we have dealt with so far, show no such orientation, for example Springer's[53] work with Caucasians and Orientals in Hawaii, and Johnson's study of Spanish children in the US. However a lot of work with Jewish children,[46,81-4] although using a variety of methodologies, generally support the previous findings concerning minority-group attitudes.

Of course it is very difficult to make precise cross-cultural comparisons because of variations in methodology, sample characteristics and cultural contexts. However, if we tried to predict a cultural milieu which embodied all the necessary conditions for the familiar pattern of majority–minority attitudes to emerge, South Africa would very quickly spring to mind as an obvious candidate. Gregor and McPherson circumvented some of the methodological problems by using an almost identical method to the Clarks'[66] in their study of white and African children. Not surprisingly, the white children tested showed an unequivocal orientation towards the ingroup and rejection of the outgroup. 83 per cent liked the white doll best, 90 per cent indicated that it had a nicer colour, 93 per cent thought the brown doll was the bad one, and 100 per cent correctly identified themselves with the white doll. These are even higher proportions than among white American children. The African children, correspondingly, 'give evidence of marked outgroup orientation'. On the preference questions their responses were similar to the white children's, that is, 76 per cent like the white doll best, 79 per cent thought the brown doll 'looks bad', and on the crucial identification question, 'Show me the doll that looks like you', 34 per cent chose the white doll. This is a very substantial minority, but not as large a proportion as has been found in some studies. It is interesting to speculate whether there might be a curvilinear relationship between outgroup identification and racial hostility of a culture. In other words, where the status gap between the groups is enormous and the hostility directed towards the minority is very intense, the 'unrealistic' act of outgroup identification may be deterred, both because it is so totally unrealistic and may involve personal danger.

The last study we shall consider in this section is a particularly interesting one. It embodied both a cross-cultural comparison and an attempt to test the notion that racial attitudes are a function of dominant–subordinate status relations between groups. Morland[30] achieved this by gathering data in Hong Kong and comparing it with his American studies, which had employed the same methods. The island of Hong Kong is one in which, Morland says, 'The most appropriate description of the social structure . . . [is that] the Caucasians and Chinese might be said to hold parallel positions . . . a multi-racial setting in which no race [is] clearly dominant.' He compared three groups of subjects, Hong Kong

Chinese, American Caucasian and black American, on tests of racial acceptance, preference and identification.

There were no significant differences on tests of racial acceptance, but on tests of racial preference all three groups differed significantly. 82 per cent of the white Americans and 65 per cent of the Chinese preferred their own group, compared to 28 per cent of the black Americans. Morland writes:

... a plausible interpretation of the differences between the American Caucasian and Hong Kong Chinese subjects is that race differences carry more importance for status in a multi-racial society that has dominant and subordinate races than they do in a society in which races have parallel positions.

On the tests of racial self-identification ('Which doll do you look more like?', 'Which child would you rather be?') the white American children chose the white figure 77 per cent and 77 per cent of the time, respectively, the black American did so 45 per cent and 62 per cent while the Chinese chose the Chinese figures 36 per cent and 54 per cent of the time. (The low Chinese figure on the first question does not indicate that a majority identified with the outgroup; exactly half of the sample were 'not sure, or insisted that they looked no more like one than they did the other'.)

In other words, the Chinese children preferred and identified with their own group less than white Americans, and more than black American children. As Morland claims, the data

... uphold the assumption that race awareness varies with the social structure, for it reveals a different pattern of race awareness in a society with dominant and subordinate races from that in a society with parallel races, for in the latter, there is no dominant race to maintain its superior position and no subordinate race to show unconscious preference for and identification with the dominant race.

Social status then, lies near the core of racial attitudes; and when political, economic and cultural subordination are underscored by skin-colour, the divide between the high status majority and the low status minority is almost absolute. In 1965 Kenneth Clark explained how these gross social forces are translated into individual experience, and with what consequences:

Human beings who are forced to live under ghetto conditions and whose daily experience tells them that almost nowhere in society are they respected and granted the ordinary dignity and courtesy accorded to others will, as a matter of course, begin to doubt their own worth. Since every human being depends upon his cumulative experiences with others for clues as to how he should view and value himself, children who are consistently rejected understandably begin to question and doubt whether they, their family, and their group really deserve no more respect from the larger society than they receive. These doubts become the seeds of a pernicious self- and group-hatred, the Negro's complex and debilitating prejudice against himself ... Negroes have come to believe in their own inferiority.[86]

These are the conditions which have given rise to the patterns of racial attitudes in black children described in this chapter. The last decade has seen black Americans attempt to contest that notion of inferiority, both in the minds of the white majority and in themselves. Before we discuss those developments in Chapter 5, we move to a consideration of racial attitudes in Britain.

4 Racism and Black British Children

Much of this chapter is devoted to a recent study of children's racial attitudes in Britain. The study set out to answer a number of questions, some of them raised by the American research described in the previous pages: how far, for example, will black British children show the same reactions to prejudice and discrimination as their American counterparts?

But first, to understand the effects of racism on children in this country we need to appreciate both the intensity and the pervasiveness of that racism. At the beginning of the last chapter, the historical and contemporary determinants of racism in Britain were described; while they convey the pressure of cultural traditions and current social conditions in creating racist attitudes, they tell us little of the *extent* to which those attitudes have come to be held amongst British people.

The assertion that British society is racist has been difficult to accept for many people. It contradicts an image of ourselves and our ancestors which has been assiduously fostered in us since childhood, an image of democracy, equality, tolerance and justice. Black immigration has been an exacting test of those principles with the result that the image has been thoroughly tarnished. For some time there has been ample evidence of various kinds that prejudice and discrimination against black people pervades our institutions and our social behaviour.

There have been relatively few attempts by social scientists to quantify this picture – that is, to measure the extent of British racism. Two of these in particular have attracted a lot of attention. The encyclopedic survey of race relations in Britain, *Colour and Citizenship*,[1] included within it a study of the incidence of race prejudice in Britain. It was concerned with the white community's *attitudes* towards 'coloured immigrants' and did not investigate behaviour. In other words, the survey collected verbal statements of white people's opinions about immigrants rather than collecting evidence of the way they *behaved* towards them. This is a perfectly legitimate objective for a survey and the assumption that a person's attitude and verbal statements are a guide to his behaviour is the principle behind all market-research opinion polling that uses survey techniques.

The authors of the study devised a prejudice–tolerance scale on which they could locate people according to the answers they gave to four key questions (which 'provided an opportunity to express unconditional hostility to coloured people') and to ten others scattered through the questionnaire, 'where an unfavourable attitude towards coloured people could be expressed'. Overall, they found that only 10 per cent of their respondents were 'prejudiced') (when three or four hostile replies to the key questions was the criterion of prejudice'), 17 per cent were 'prejudice-inclined' (having given two hostile replies), 38 per cent were tolerant-inclined (one hostile reply) and 35 per cent were 'tolerant' (having given none). The incidence of prejudice was highest among the middle-aged, lowest among the over-65s and under-35s. Women were more consistently tolerant than men, and people with further education were more tolerant than those who had left school at fifteen. The highest incidence of extreme prejudice was found among skilled manual workers and their wives in the lower middle-class.

This survey was the subject of a lot of criticism (e.g. Lawrence, 1969),[2] which pointed to a number of methodological inadequacies, and threw some doubt on both the validity and reliability of the study. One of the main criticisms centred on the (apparently) arbitrary labelling of the four categories of attitudes. Why, for example, should a person who replies to one question in a way that shows 'unconditional hostility towards coloured people' be described as 'tolerant-inclined', whatever his replies to the other three questions? The question of how much prejudice a certain number of hostile replies signified came down to a matter of opinion, and it was certainly the opinion of a number of social scientists at that time that the criteria used to define prejudice and tolerance in the survey were inappropriate.

When the survey was re-published in an abridged form, different criteria were employed. The authors[3] simply re-named the four categories of responses in the following way:

... people who gave no hostile replies can be regarded as exhibiting tolerant attitudes – or perhaps more accurately as showing no overt prejudice; those offering one hostile response as mildly prejudiced; those with two hostile responses as prejudiced; and those with three or even four hostile responses seemed to be wholly rejecting in their attitudes towards coloured people and may be regarded as intensely prejudiced.

This change in terminology was effectively a change in the criteria of prejudice–tolerance. By this definition 35 per cent of the white people interviewed could be said to have given no verbal evidence of prejudice, while 65 per cent of the sample had shown some degree of prejudice.

Despite this adjustment, and the slightly different interpretation of the findings that it gave rise to, the raw material of the survey obviously remained the same. By the same token, the issue of how accurate this data was as a guide to the incidence of racism in Britain remained unresolved. The situation where an interviewer asks a respondent for his opinions and attitudes is vulnerable to all kinds of biases and distortions over which we have no control. This is particularly true when the subject at issue is a controversial one like race relations. Whereas a person may have no compunction about voicing his prejudices to work-mates who he knows to share his views, he may not reply with the same degree of candour to a stranger asking him questions on his doorstep. Few people at the time of this survey could have been unaware that the Government and the mass media were, at one level, trying to encourage the growth of racial tolerance. The fact that this principle was simultaneously being undermined by official immigration policy, and by the media's coverage of racialist speeches by right-wing politicians, was less obvious. It could reasonably be argued that the majority of respondents would, as a result, identify their interviewers with the more liberal view of race relations and 'coloured' people. 'Official' policy appeared to many people to favour tolerance over prejudice, and 'official' surveys and interviewers could be assumed to share this perspective. One influence

on a respondent's statements is the social acceptability of his sentiments, and so in this context it is more likely that the attitudes
recorded in the survey were biased more in the direction of tolerance than prejudice. It is much less likely that the respondents
voiced more prejudice than they actually felt; and so there are
grounds for thinking that the results of this survey could be an
under-estimate of the degree of prejudice in the white community.
Even if we accept them at face-value, they show quite clearly that
two thirds of the British population admit to holding prejudiced
racial attitudes.

What does this tell us about the way white people will behave
towards black people in day-to-day situations ? The authors of the
study themselves acknowledge that

... The evidence from other studies suggest that expressed attitudes
predict behaviour only to a very limited degree and that changes in
the social situation or roles that individuals perform over-ride the
pre-dispositions which may be expressed in answers to questions
about opinions.

There is much to be said for directing our attention to white
people's behaviour towards blacks; for if we wish to understand
the black person's reaction to racism then we need to know how
it affects him directly in face-to-face situations, not just how he
experiences it from the climate of attitudes around him. The PEP
report[4] overcame many of the objections to conventional attitude
surveys by examining the issue of racial discrimination practised
by the white community in real-life situations. To investigate
racial discrimination in housing they sent equally qualified white
English, white Hungarian and black West Indian applicants to try
for the same advertised accommodation, whether privately advertised or through an estate agent. Similar tests were set up for
employment vacancies, and for public services from shops and
hotels to mortgage facilities and hire purchase companies. These
tests were supplemented by interviews with the black people and
white people concerned in each instance.

In the area of housing, the West Indian in the situation tests
encountered discrimination in the letting of rented accommodation on 75 per cent of the occasions he tried for it. 'Such discrimination was in most cases overt in the sense that the West Indian

was just told that the accommodation had gone when it had not.'[5] The figure did not include the occasions when the white applicant was told, 'Come round quickly, I've got a West Indian coming at 7 p.m., so get here by 6·30.' When the landlords were interviewed later, they all confirmed that they had in fact discriminated. In addition, the West Indian experienced discrimination at nearly 75 per cent of the accommodation bureaux and estate agents tested. 'There was no less discrimination against the West Indian when he was applying for accommodation in a professional, educated role . . . than when he was applying as a bus conductor'; if anything, there was more.[5] On 64 per cent of occasions he was discriminated against in the field of house purchasing; in council-house allocation, while 'no discrimination' was invariably official policy, it was found that a variety of complex processes operated to prevent black people getting council housing as easily as white people.

Very much the same situation was found regarding employment; three quarters of the time West Indian applicants were refused jobs that were offered to an equally qualified white applicant. Similarly, substantial discrimination was found in public services, particularly in motor insurance, where black applicants experienced difficulty in getting insurance cover and were often charged considerably higher premiums.

Again, this does not automatically mean the people who discriminated were prejudiced. It is possible for a person to be 'forced' into discriminating, by social pressures or the employment policies of his employer without the person *necessarily* being prejudiced himself. It is as wrong to *automatically* assume prejudiced attitudes from a person's discriminatory behaviour, as to assume the reverse. Nevertheless one will *tend* to produce the other. Indeed, one of the principles behind anti-discrimination legislation is precisely this: if we can compel people to behave in an undiscriminating way this will tend to influence their attitudes in a tolerant direction.

Taken together, the evidence from the attitude survey and the behaviour tests adds up to a convincing indictment of our society's treatment of black people. Though our immediate concern is with children's attitudes and behaviour, it matters little that they are not in a position to perpetrate and suffer the forms of racial discrimination described here. For one thing there are childhood equivalents: exclusion from groups of friends, name-calling and bullying. Equally importantly, they are the sons and daughters of the adults who have figured in these studies, whose own experiences are communicated to their children in the socialization process.

In their different ways, the PEP report[4] and *Colour and Citizenship*[1] 'measured' British racism. Employing the techniques of social science, they have provided us with some *indices* of discrimination and prejudice. And yet, the reader experiences an inescapable sense of unreality, of abstraction. There feels to be a gap between the sterile presentation of survey data and the real social context from which they are drawn. Something all too definable has been lost in the translation. We *know* that however accurate and well documented are these facts, they simply do not convey the reality – the flavour, however unpalatable – of people's experiences. The situation is like a rather monotonous reading of the football results, so little and so clinical a relation does the message bear to the events it describes. This is endemic to social science and its reportage, and no more true of these studies than any others. But it means that we must look beyond empirical surveys for a larger view. Despite the burgeoning literature on 'immigrant' life in Britain (see Sivanandan[36]) there are very few books which give the kinds of insights we have received into black American life. The best of these are Ann Dummett's sensitive and humane book *A Portrait of English Racism*[37] (once described as 'the kind of book which gives liberals a good name'[34]) based on her experiences as a Community Relations Officer, Derek Humphry's account of immigrant–police relations,[38] and Humphry and John's 'existential' collage of black people's experiences, *Because They're Black*.[39] To these we should add Rex and Moore's[42] study of the immigrant-housing situation, and Sheila Allen's general survey, *New Minorities, Old Conflicts*.[43] In a more immediate form, the monthly magazine *Race Today* published by Towards Racial Justice gives an authentic view of the reality behind the statistics.

Black children in Britain: the cultural backgrounds

This social climate suggests that there may be parallels between the situation of black Americans and black people in this country, both for adults and children. But there are important differences too; black Americans are now an indigenous minority, while the West Indian and Asian people of this country are recent arrivals, many of whom have been here for scarcely a decade. The culture of their homelands is an integral part of their attitudes and life-styles, long after the migration, and is an important part of the context in which their experiences here – and their reactions to them – must be seen. Only a thumb-nail sketch of the cultural backgrounds can be provided here; for an adequate account the reader must turn to other sources (e.g. Lowenthal,[8] Holroyde,[40] Searle[41]). And in portraying the backgrounds of the immigrants it is necessary to convey a slightly dated picture. For while many of the children who concern us were born and brought up in this country, the adults who socialize them were themselves socialized in the homelands in the 1940s and 1950s; and it is their experience of the sending societies during that period which are relayed to the children and which help to shape their upbringing.

The West Indies

'The West Indies' refers to the islands of the Antillean archipelago, namely Jamaica, the Leeward Islands, the Windward Islands, Barbados, Trinidad and Tobago and Guyana. Of course there is wide variation between the islands in geography, natural and human resources, and social organization and custom, but also sufficient similarities to allow a general description. Jamaica is central to this, for it is from there that the largest group of West Indian immigrants to Britain originates.

The West Indian economy is largely dependent on agriculture, and although there is increasing industrialization in Jamaica and Trinidad, the greater proportion of the population live in rural rather than urban areas. Despite, or because of, their long histories of capital investment from outside, they remain essentially poor, underdeveloped and overpopulated countries. They are multi-racial societies whose members are descended from immigrants, imported from Africa as slaves, and exploited by competing European colonists anxious to develop the economic potential of the area. People born within the West Indies are referred to as 'Creoles', but this term is not applied to the sizeable East Indian minority. Other minorities like the Chinese have managed to preserve their own cultural identity and are referred to in appropriate national terms. The Creoles are persons of Negro, white or Negro–white ancestry born within the Caribbean. Creole culture has always varied between the British Caribbean and the islands colonized by the Dutch and the French. All of these cultures are products of colonialism, slavery and the plantation system, and so contain both European and African elements. However, the two elements do not contribute equally; Smith[6] describes how 'the ideal forms of institutional life such as government, religion, family and kinship, law, property, education, economy, language, etc., are of European derivation'. They have undergone considerable adaptation, interacting with those parts of African culture that the immigrants maintained, so that they only approximate to the original metropolitan models. The African residue is most apparent in language, diet, folklore, magic and religion.

Family life

Under slavery, marriage between the slaves was forbidden on many plantations, for this allowed a completely mobile pool of labour which could be shunted from one place to another when the need arose. Men were also excluded from land or property ownership and therefore could not give permanent support to a wife and children. This situation, together with the residue of the African heritage, gave rise to forms of conjugal union and family organization based on concubinage. With the Emancipation, a land-owning coloured middle class was created who were able to adopt white values concerning marriage. But for the majority of people, while marriage was now legally possible, it was still unattainable without the necessary resources to support a family. Four types of family unit have persisted to the present day. The ideal has always been European-style legal marriage, but faithful concubinage, unstable concubinage and disintegrated concubinage predominate. Clarke[35] maintains that some of the conditions which made it impossible for men to perform the roles of husband and father still prevail, so that these styles of family organization persist too. Stable concubinage, while more vulnerable to break-down than legal marriage, is more enduring than the less formal sporadic cohabitation. While in concubinage the father assumes responsibility for the support of the children, including those of previous unions; if the union breaks down, the family centres on the extended family of the mother.

Generally, the higher the socio-economic status of the group, the more nearly their mores approximate to those of British society. The various forms of concubinage predominate among working-class West Indians, while marriage is more frequent among the higher-status groups. Because so many children are born outside marriage, 'illegitimacy' bears no stigma, in contrast to the British situation. In concubinage it is rare for childless relationships to endure, and for the majority, equally rare for marriage to take place before children are born to a union. Another pre-condition for marriage is that the man must own a house and be able to sup-port a wife and family. As a result cohabitation is the usual pre-liminary to marriage, which then 'legitimizes' a proven stable union.

The European culture of the white ruling-class was the most highly valued element of Creole culture and served as an index of high status. This implied a devaluation of all the African com-ponents of the culture, including racial traits, so that the high- and low-status sections of the society were distinguishable both cul-turally and racially: 'The Creole cultural and social organization was a graduated hierarchy of European and African elements, crudely visualized in a white–black colour scale.'[6] The economic system has always maintained a division of labour on a racial/cultural-group basis. Negroes occupy the lower-status manual positions (e.g. sugar-plantation labouring), 'coloureds' (mixed Negro–white ancestry) hold many of the clerical positions, while whites predominate in management and executive roles. The categories are not entirely homogeneous, and are becoming less so, but, as Lowenthal points out, despite the progress of de-colonization the 'black or brown men [who] occupy the seats of political power . . . have maintained the status quo . . . 'coloured' West Indians have generally emulated whites . . . the Jamaican establishment is still dominated by a white and light-coloured elite that (in conjunction with expatriates) owns most local resources and runs the economy, the banks, the schools, the civil service, and even the trade unions.[7]

The racial organization of the society intrudes into all aspects of its life. The attribute of lighter skin-colour is a social advantage in almost all situations, and status differentials can depend on quite subtle gradations of colour. It has been the ambition of many darker-skinned West Indians to 'marry lighter' and so 'improve' the colour (and therefore opportunities for advancement) of their offspring. The correlation of colour and class is nowhere better illustrated than in an example cited by Rose *et al.*[1]

Colour in the sense of appearance as a key to descent has been of such importance in this society that colour terms are often used to indicate class and a man is spoken of as 'white' because he is rich or successful.

Lowenthal[8] argues that, in spite of emergent black consciousness all over the world, 'In the West Indies, black is not yet thought beautiful . . . few West Indians profess to admire the 'natural look'; their ideal-types are avowedly white-oriented.' However, it is clear that this picture is rapidly changing.

The child's situation in the West Indian family contrasts with that of the English child in the nuclear family. In all types of union the extended family plays a much more important role than it does in Britain, allowing for the care of both the young and the aged. Partners are probably more independent of each other than is usual in this country, and maintain strong links with their own families. Children, then, have a more diffuse network of both support and discipline. Similarly, neighbourhood ties through social units such as the 'yard' – communal areas for washing, recreation, and so on – ensure frequent contact with adults other than the parents. For these reasons the failure of a conjugal union does not result in a 'broken home' in the same sense that we understand it.

Fitzherbert[9] points to some of the negative consequences of this: 'The majority of West Indian children do not spend their

entire childhood in the same home with both of their parents . . .
Most children have a very unsettled childhood.' It is true that
concubinage is vulnerable to disruption at any time; and because,
in the event of breakdown, children invariably stay with the
mother, she is central to the organization of the family: Rose *et al.*
describe how, 'with so much instability, the man's authority
passes to the woman, and the role of mother and grandmother
are by far the strongest in the West Indian family system'. It is
said that the discipline of children tends to stress the virtues of
obedience and passivity, and to be exercised in a pragmatic and
inconsistent way: 'Children are shown a mixture of extreme per-
missiveness and extreme strictness . . . scolding and punishment
are not always meted out on a very logical basis . . . Nor are
children usually given a reason for things they are told to do or
punished for not doing.'[9]

On the whole, young children have little in the way of manu-
factured toys or play materials to exercise their mental and physical capacities, and parents give them little instruction apart from
essential general knowledge. It is not until the child goes to school
that any formal learning takes place. The West Indian education
system is based on the British model, with a network of primary,
secondary and grammar schools, (including 11+, 'O' and 'A'
level examinations) with higher education catered for in teacher-
training colleges and university. However, the resources available
to the education system are completely inadequate. Under-
staffing, inconsistency of attendance, and old-fashioned teaching
methods combine to depress the standards of education the children receive.

The immigration

The principal motive for West Indian migration was economic.
Widespread unemployment, poverty and a high birth-rate all
increased pressure on the limited economic resources of the area.
As well as these 'push' factors, 'pull' factors operated from this
country. The demand for labour in certain areas of the British
economy was such that employers (for example London Transport) made arrangements with West Indian governments to encourage the flow of manpower to Britain. It is ironic that one such

invitation, for hospital staff, was extended by the Minister of Health at that time, Mr Enoch Powell.

The immigrants had been taught to regard Britain as the Mother Country. They had been raised in a culture which bore a clear British trade-mark, had learned British history and folklore, and had absorbed many of our values. They expected to find a land of equal opportunity, and because of the cultural and racial values of the sending societies, aspired to integrate into the white community. These aspirations were rapidly discouraged by the host community. While the new immigrant naturally gravitated to the areas where kinsfolk had already established themselves, he soon found that economic and social pressures ensured he remain there. These were invariably dilapidated inner-city zones of low-cost housing; low rates of pay for the menial employment that they had to accept, racial discrimination in all areas of the housing market, and the need to insulate themselves from white hostility, all militated against upward mobility into the more desirable white areas. Although a minority of immigrants have moved beyond these areas, for example to new housing estates, the picture has remained relatively static. Neither have the immigrants' employment situations improved very much, the majority being concentrated in unskilled and semi-skilled jobs, while their employment rates, particularly among the young people, have remained substantially higher than those of their white counterparts.

In this country, West Indian family structure has changed considerably, towards a much closer approximation to the nuclear family. This probably causes some problems for the West Indian child who comes to re-join his parents having enjoyed the wider network of support provided by the extended family. The child, whether born in the West Indies or in this country, also has to resolve the conflict between a cultural background, embodied in his parents, but which he is no longer part of, and a culture which rejects him and his group.

India and Pakistan

It is impossible in this short space to do justice to the diversity within the Indian sub-continent. Both in this section and in the study that follows the Asians are grouped together, for there are many similarities in their backgrounds, family structures and orientation towards British society, the variables with which we are concerned.

The majority of Indian and Pakistani immigrants originate from poor rural areas. Nearly three quarters of the total population of the sub-continent derive their living from some form of agriculture. The fertility of the soil depends largely on the monsoon rains, and when these are inadequate vast areas remain uncultivated or yield no harvest, bringing widespread famine. The cultivation of the soil, principally by manual methods, occupies people of every class. The introduction of modern methods is impeded both by the capital cost of machinery and adherence to traditional practices. Principles like rotation are accepted as necessary, but poverty dictates that the ground simply cannot be left fallow for any period. Industrialization has been slow to develop; the greater proportion of exports consists of raw products as the industrial capacity for manufacturing from these materials is inadequate.

The great majority of Indian immigrants to Britain come from the Punjab or from Gujerat. They are Caucasian in racial type and are distinguishable by skin-colour from West Indians, Africans and Europeans, though varying from light to dark brown. Approximately 80 per cent of Indians in Britain are Sikhs, the remainder mostly Hindus. Sikhism originated as a reform movement within Hinduism, and therefore the two share some similarities. Pakistani immigrants however, are Moslem and originate principally from the Mirpur district of Kashmir, and Sylhet in East Pakistan (now Bangla Desh). The main source of differences in the cultural backgrounds of Indian and Pakistani immigrants lies in religious belief and practices, and language. These together with dress and diet mark both groups off from West Indian immigrants and the British host community – who share much more in common in these respects.

Family life

In certain important respects the Asian groups share similar family structures. The basic unit is the joint or extended family, which is an important part of normal family life centred on stable conjugal unions. The various members of the extended family participate in the division of labour and fulfil traditional roles; they are as crucial to the activities of the household as the nuclear family. In Indian families

. . . Land is held and farmed jointly on a cooperative basis . . . kitchens are communal, but there are separate sleeping quarters for each nuclear family or part. Family wealth is communally held and payments to individuals are made from the pooled resources.[10]

So the extended family includes married brothers and their families, and unmarried brothers and sisters, the head of the family being the oldest male member (the father or grandfather). It includes all dependants – orphans, widows and the aged – who are cared for by the others.

Thus the feeling of belonging to a group much larger than one's immediate family is ingrained in people with a rural background and they retain it even when they migrate to another province or country.[11]

People therefore experience a feeling of support and solidarity which encompasses distant kin, fellow villagers, and even provincial and linguistic groups.

The joint family evolved in an agrarian setting as an economically self-sufficient unit, providing for the physical, social and moral welfare of its members. The head of the family exercises complete authority over the other members, takes the major decisions, and controls the economy. In contrast to the West Indian situation, the father is the source of discipline and order in the family, and it is he who punishes the children, in later childhood. The woman's role is very much a subordinate one (although Moslem law recognizes the equality of women, which is reflected in the propriety of a woman's proposal of marriage to a man and her right to request divorce). She is largely restricted to running the household and caring for the children, particularly in infancy. Modest and restrained behaviour is expected of her and the virtues of conscientious motherhood are traditionally respected. Her upbringing is a training directed towards performing this role successfully.

Patterns of child-rearing in Indian and Pakistani families are quite similar; Goodall[12] writes of the Pakistani family:

Overall, learning in the early years of childhood is characterized by observation and imitation, little is expected of the child in the way of domestic chores, and attempts at deliberate instruction are few. Nevertheless, by the age of 5 or 6, the child, by his observation of the scenes around him and his imitation through play, has come to absorb many of the skills, customs and values of the group, especially the adult segregation of the sexes, and the respect that is due to other members of the family. After the age of 5 or 6, boys and girls are progressively treated separately and taught to identify with members of their own sex.

Much stricter discipline is now employed; girls are increasingly confined to female activities and their work and interests draw them more closely towards their mothers. This situation persists until their marriage. Boys now withdraw from female company and begin to learn the rudiments of their role in the agricultural process, spending much of their time with the men of the family.

With many people in the same family network, there is a wide web of support for the child: 'The child feels a sense of security in that there are many adults in the family with whom he can, or rather must identify.'[13] This helps to foster a strong sense of group identification in the child.

The education systems of both India and Pakistan show the influence of Britain. In India, since 1961, eight or nine years of education has been compulsory, through primary and secondary schools. However, Bell[14] points out that the whole system suffers from 'lack of trained teachers and slavish following of out-of-date methods', compounded by a shortage of facilities and funds. The residue of British colonial rule in Pakistan is an education system which retains a bias towards higher education, to the detriment of primary and secondary schooling. Both nations, as a result, have very high illiteracy rates.

The immigration

Like the West Indians, the primary motive for the Asians' migration was economic. In some areas the average annual income *per capita* was £25, compared with £400 in Britain at that time. Some of the immigrant homelands have traditionally been centres of migration because of the inadequacy of the land. In addition, the Partition of India in 1947 provided a great impetus to migration because it exacerbated overpopulation in some areas due to an influx of refugees, and there was enormous economic disruption.

The initial migration to Britain in the late 1950s and early 1960s consisted mainly of young male workers, to be followed a few years later by their wives and families. They made their way to the homes of relatives and fellow-villagers who had preceded them, from whom they had received news of employment opportunities and sometimes fare-money. Thus the extended family and tightly woven village communities served to connect and support their members even at a distance of several thousand miles. During the initial wave of all-male migration, the immigrants tended to live in male boarding-houses, which were cheaper and more congenial than living alone and allowed them to send the maximum amount of money back to their wives and children. The money was frequently used to send over the eldest son to join his father so that their combined income would eventually allow the rest of the family to join them. In this way, kinsmen laid the foundations for the re-creation of the family/village network in the new environment. With the arrival of wives and children it was necessary to acquire property, which was often achieved by cooperative mortgage schemes.

The life of the immigrants has remained essentially community-centred, revolving around adjacent dwelling-places, shopping areas and places of worship. This is only partly an accommodation to the hostility they experience from the white host community; it is largely an effort to maintain the social organization of the homelands, while protecting their cultural ways from dilution or corruption by Western standards. It is also partly a reflection of the immigrants' original orientation towards the society at large: they had intended to come, work hard, send as much money as possible to the villages from which they came, and return at the earliest opportunity. In contrast to the West Indians, then, they had no real desire or aspiration to integrate into white society. Although in many cases the immigrants have settled on a more permanent basis, they have maintained this detached and autonomous relationship to the host community, providing their own goods and services, and wherever possible, preserving their cultural distinctiveness.*

Racism and British children

The two themes we have developed so far – the effects of racism on black children in America and the existence of black minorities in Britain, subject to prejudice and discrimination – converged in a study of black children in Britain and the social climate surrounding them.

The central concern of the study, conducted by the author, was to investigate the effects of racism on the children of West Indian and Asian immigrants to Britain. While a number of studies (e.g. Pushkin[15]) had provided evidence of rudimentary racial attitudes and behaviour in English children, none had focused on black children. Given the incidence of prejudice and discrimination in this country, it seemed a plausible hypothesis that black children here would show similar reactions to the devaluation of their racial groups by the white majority as do young black American children.

In the discussion of the immigrants' cultural backgrounds it was clear that major differences distinguish the principal immigrant groups; differences in culture, in their orientation towards British society, and in their experiences since immigration. It seemed likely that the British component of the West Indians' culture, and the ' white bias '[45] in the racial ordering of West Indian society, would enhance their children's orientation and positive feeling towards whites in this country. In addition, the West Indians' original aspirations to integrate ensured more contact with the

*Note: There have recently been some indications that the adult immigrants' desire for autonomy is causing inter-generational conflict within the Asian family. This is acutely felt by their older children who have to reconcile the contrary pressures of traditional beliefs and customs, on one hand, and adolescent peer group pressures on the other. Their understandable desire for the fashions and freedom of their English counterparts causes anxiety for their parents; in a few cases this has happened to an extent where the children have been withdrawn from school to arrest this moral decline, as it is seen.

white community – and its hostility – than was experienced by the Asian community. Not only did the Asian's detached stance *vis-à-vis* the host community insulate them to some extent, they also had entirely separate cultural traditions which provide a strong sense of identity. In the American studies many black children internalized the racial values that were imposed on them by the dominant white group, such that they had difficulty in identifying with their own group, and were very positively disposed towards whites. For the reasons discussed, it seemed likely that this response to racism would be more prevalent among West Indian children than among the Asian children.

The study was conducted in two large English cities, both with substantial 'immigrant' populations. In one, West Indians constituted the majority of the immigrant population and Asians the minority; in the other these proportions were reversed. The research was carried out in local schools. Pilot experiments had suggested that the concentration of the various groups in an area might be an important factor in determining attitudes, and so a variety of schools were selected for study, in such a way as to include all possible combinations of high and low concentrations of the various groups. If more than 50 per cent of the pupils in a particular school belonged to one immigrant group, this was taken to be a 'high concentration of that group', while the criterion for a 'low' concentration was set at 10 per cent or less of the school population. Naturally the 'high' concentration schools were situated in the very centre of the immigrant areas in each city, while the 'low' concentration schools were on the outskirts of these areas. The schools in the two cities were matched as far as possible, as had been the areas themselves. Although the 'immigrant' children were the main focus of the study, a sample of white English children was also drawn from these schools. Not only would they provide a further index of host community attitudes, but it was necessary to avoid the appearance of discriminating in the execution of the study by only withdrawing black children from each classroom.

The age range selected for study was from five to eight years old; the American studies had shown this to be a particularly crucial period in the development of children's racial attitudes, and it allowed direct comparison with the many other studies of this range. In addition it included the critical sixth year in which Pushkin[15] had found a sharp increase in hostility among white English children.

In the main study, some three hundred children were involved, drawn equally from the West Indian, Asian and English groups within the schools. They were all interviewed individually, away from the classroom, by a young white male interviewer, who tape-recorded the sessions unknown to the children. After a period of conversation to establish rapport, the children were given doll- and picture-tests of racial attitudes, similar to those described in previous studies.

The tests

Four aspects of the children's attitudes towards racial groups were investigated, each via a separate group of questions. Every question involved the same basic situation, namely that the child was required to make a choice between two dolls or two pictures, in response to a question put by the interviewer. In each case, one figure represented the child's own racial group while the other figure represented the other principal racial group in the child's immediate environment. That is, the West Indian children were presented with questions which required them to choose between a figure representing a West Indian and one representing a white English person; for the Asian children, the choice was always be- tween an Asian figure and and English figure, while the English children were asked to choose between an English figure and a figure representing whichever immigrant group predominated in their area. Although the basic choice situation was the same in each question, a different set of dolls or pictures was used for every question to minimize the association between them. The materials used in the study were specially prepared for the purpose. The pictures were painted by a professional artist, based on photographs of children from each racial group. The dolls were produced to order by a firm specializing in costume dolls of his- torical figures. Starting from their basic 'naked' figures, the dolls were sprayed, wigged and dressed to specification. In this way it was possible to achieve a good approximation to the correct facial features, skin-colour, eye-colour and hair-type for each racial group. The finished products were very much more life-like than commercially produced 'coloured' dolls which tend to be over-glamorized or stereotyped. The children were clearly engaged by both the dolls and the pictures and needed no encouragement to respond to them as though they were real people.

The first set of questions dealt with the child's racial *identity* or self-attitudes, and related identifications. This included the crucial self-identification question ('Which doll looks most like you ?') that has been used in so many studies, since the classic study by the Clarks.[16] This was followed by a question to elicit the child's *ideal* identity: 'If you could *be* one of these two dolls, which one would you rather be ?' Two other questions completed this group, requiring the child to identify the figures which 'looked most like' their mother, and sister or brother, respectively.

The second group of questions probed the child's straight-forward *preferences* for one racial group over another. After first being asked which of two dolls he 'liked best', a series of questions was asked about the child's preference for companions in various situations: 'to play with in the playground', 'to sit next to in class' and 'to share your sweets with'. Finally the child was asked to indicate which figure looked most like his best friend, in order to get some index of his real-life racial preference.

A third section of questions dealt with the extent to which the children might hold rudimentary stereotypes about the characteristics of each racial group, in simple evaluative terms. The children were asked to indicate the 'bad' doll of one pair, the 'nicest' one of another, and the 'ugly' one of a third. This was an entirely projective process as the children had no information on which to base these attributions, other than the racial differences between the figures.

Finally an attempt was made to gauge the children's social aspirations in the future. The child was encouraged to imagine that he was grown up and had a house and family. He was then asked which of two families of dolls he wanted to live next door to, which man would be his best friend (which woman in the case of the girls), and which he would go to work with (go shopping with, for the girls.)

It was also necessary to administer a test of the children's ability to distinguish racial differences between the dolls and identify the groups they represented, without which none of the other tests would have been meaningful; all the children did this correctly.

The findings

The burden of the results can be stated very simply; black British children are showing essentially the same reaction to racism as their American counterparts, namely a strong preference for the dominant white majority-group and a tendency to devalue their own group.

The most dramatic evidence of this out-group orientation came in the Identity section of the tests. In response to the question which tapped the child's notion of his *actual* identity ('Which doll looks most like *you*?') a significant proportion of both immigrant groups misidentified, that is, maintained that the *white* doll looked more like them. None of the English group misidentified themselves. It was really only on this section of the tests and this question in particular that the predicted difference between West Indian and Asian children's reactions was clearly evident. The following table shows precisely how the children from each group responded to the question:

Table 1: Children's responses to the test of 'actual' identity

	% choosing own-group figure	% choosing other-group figure
English	100	0
Asian	76	24
West Indian	52	48

A similar pattern emerged from the other questions in the Identity section, for example those concerned with Family Identification. Some 35 per cent of the West Indian children and 20 per cent of the Asian children misidentified either their mother, or sibling, or both. Again, none of the English children misidentified family members. Perhaps the clearest pointer to understanding these results was provided by the test of *ideal* identity ('If you could *be* one of these two dolls, which one would you rather be?'). Once

again 100 per cent of the English children chose the white doll;
and no fewer than 82 per cent of the West Indians and 65 per
cent of the the Asians made that choice too, apparently signifying
that they would prefer to be white than a member of their own
group.

Clearly there are very substantial differences in identity and
identification between the 'immigrants' and the English children,
the latter showing a much stronger and more positive identification with their own group. Many of the immigrants, in contrast,
seem drawn towards identification with the white group, and this
is much more prevalent among the West Indian children than the
Asians.

The differences *between* the responses of the two immigrant
groups disappeared on the Preference tests. But both groups
showed a consistently high level of preference for white playmates,
companions, etc., over members of their own group. Only a tiny
minority of the English children reciprocated this feeling. This
was the pattern for the remainder of the tests, as we can see from
the following summary table:

*Table 2: % of each ethnic group making predominantly out-group
choices, on each section of the tests.*

	Identity	Preference	Stereotypes	Aspirations
English	0	6	0	9
Asian	17	74	65	63
West Indian	30	72	68	72

The figures represent the proportion of each group making predominantly *out*-group choices on each section of the tests. For
example, on the Preference section 72 per cent of the West Indian
children made a majority of choices which favoured the white
figures over figures representing their own group. The message
which emerges clearly from the table is that on three out of the
four sections of tests, the vast majority of the children in both
immigrant groups predominantly favour the white group over
their own.

In other words, the majority of black children ideally *prefer* to
have white friends and playmates, and *aspire* to have white neigh-

bours and companions when they grow up. The third section of tests underlines the real significance of these results. It could be argued, of course, that there is nothing wrong in black children having these attitudes, indeed that they are both desirable and necessary in the creation of a harmonious multiracial society. But the responses to the Stereotypes section of the tests show that this out-group orientation involves a corresponding *rejection* of the child's own group. That is, the positive feelings towards the white figures are a complement to the negative image of black figures that our society presents to the child; it is clear that he has internalized some of these images and finds them unacceptable, preferring instead to orient himself towards whites.

Take the case of the West Indian children: 58 per cent and 82 per cent of them respectively maintained that the black doll was the 'bad' doll and the 'ugly' doll of the pair, 78 per cent said that the white doll was the 'nicest' of the two. The Asian children's responses were not very different, 45 per cent, 77 per cent and 84 per cent attributed the same unfavourable characteristics to the brown dolls and favourable characteristics to the white figures. Again, it should be stressed that the child had no cues as to which dolls were bad, ugly or nice, other than the simple fact that they represented different racial groups.

Sometimes the interviews gave other indications of these feelings. Many children made spontaneous comments about the dolls or about racial groups, and the interviewer occasionally asked them why they had made particular choices. Of the two 'immigrant' groups the West Indians were the most vocal in this respect. There were many examples of the children projecting imaginary characteristics on to the figures to explain their choices. For example, the black doll was the bad one 'because he fights', 'because he tries to kill people', 'because he shoots people', and so on. Others seemed grounded in the child's own experience at home or at school: 'because he do things wrong', 'he fights rough in the playground', 'he gives his daddy lip'. The simplest and most frequent reasons for the choices are perhaps the most worrying, for they suggest that the figures are disliked and rejected for the sole reason that they have certain racial features: 'because he's black', 'he got rough hair', etc.

The data as a whole was examined to discover whether other factors like age, sex differences or the concentration of immigrants in the schools had had any influence on the children's responses. The first factor to be looked at in this way was 'skin-colour', a variable that we had not originally intended to study, but which suggested itself through the presence of a minority of lighter-skinned children in the West Indian group.

SKIN COLOUR There is, of course, considerable variation in colouring among West Indians. In looking at the effects of skin-colour within the group only the very 'lightest' children were selected out, for comparison with the remainder of the group. None of these children were half-caste.

They all sustained a consistently higher level of out-group orientation throughout the tests than the rest of the West Indian group. For example, on the 'actual' identity test, 70 per cent of the light group identified with the white doll, compared to 40 per cent of the darker group. The explanation of this lies partly in the relatively closer approximation of their skin-colour to white than is true of the darker children. Nevertheless all the light group identified the black doll as 'the Jamaican man' in the test of ability to discriminate racial differences, so that there was no doubt that they knew which kind of figure was supposed to represent them and their group. A further explanation lies in the status of light skin within the West Indian community. Lighter skin has always been a passport to greater opportunity and wealth; lighter children have often been favoured within the family and encouraged to think of themselves as more like whites, in preparation for their superior social position. And so it is much more credible for the light child to identify with the white figures and aspire to social contact with whites than it is for the dark child.

CONCENTRATION There were no consistent differences in the data from schools with different concentrations of black children. Of course the concentration in a particular school may be less important than the concentration in the area as a whole, and the former is not always an accurate indication of the latter.

AGE No general age-trends emerged from the data, apart from the tendency for out-group identification to decline with age in certain cases. This is to be expected as the 'fiction' involved for the black child in choosing the white doll becomes more difficult to maintain. However, the overall lack of age-differences in the children's responses had not been expected.

SEX Neither were there consistent differences between the boys' and the girls' attitudes; however, this correspondence had been expected on the basis of other studies.

The consistency of the children's responses, despite variations in their age and the concentration of immigrants in the area, held good across the different localities in which the research was conducted. Different immigrant groups predominated in the two cities involved in the study, and yet the responses of the children were remarkably similar in the two locations. Perhaps this is not surprising, and the experience of 'being a coloured immigrant' is rather similar throughout our society, and relatively independent of local factors. For in one sense white attitudes towards blacks – which have determined the black children's responses – are undiscriminating. As we have pointed out, virtually all discussion of racial issues in the news and opinion media has been couched in terms of 'coloured immigrants' as if they constituted a single homogeneous group. There is no evidence that the white community really distinguishes between the West Indians and the Asian groups, to the extent of feeling more or less prejudice against one group over another. The attitudes of the host community children, as they emerged from the study, give some credence to this interpretation.

THE ENGLISH CHILDREN It is worth looking more closely at the English children's attitudes because they give some indication of the attitudes held by their parents and other white adults. While the children's attitudes are not the sole reason for the black children's reactions that we have described, they are *one* of the means by which the white community's attitudes are made real to the black child. As such, they do contribute to the experience of 'being black' for the 'immigrant' children.

If we look back at Table 2, it is clear that the great majority of English children consistently favour white figures in the tests, and rarely prefer the black ones. Of course those choices do not, in themselves, necessarily imply prejudice against blacks. It could be that while they liked the white figures more in most cases, they nevertheless still liked the dark figures – but *less* than the white ones. But there is evidence from the Stereotypes section that they *do* have very negative, rejecting feelings towards black figures, which makes this interpretation less plausible. Some 63 per cent of the children indicated that the black figures were both 'bad' and 'ugly', while a further 31 per cent made one or other of these assertions. Again, the children's comments and reasons for their choices filled out the picture, one of considerable hostility towards blacks. They frequently showed distaste for physical features – colour, facial characteristics, hair, body smell – and projected a number of crimes on to the inert black figures – 'he shoots people', 'he takes money away from the white man', and so on. A few children were unwilling to give reasons for their choices, or took time to 'think them up'. Others clearly showed the effects of parental influences: one six-year-old maintained that the black doll was the bad one, 'because he should have learned the language before he came over here'. Others were even less circuitous about the source of their attitudes: on the Identity section one boy said he would 'rather be' the white figure 'because he's white, and my mum and dad don't like the black ones, so I don't either'.

This picture was essentially the same for the two catchment areas involved in the study. If indeed the white community creates a similar atmosphere of hostility around the immigrants in the two milieux, despite the very different characteristics of the principal immigrant groups, the largely similar reactions of the West Indian and Asian children are wholly explicable.

Real life behaviour

Essentially this study dealt with children's racial *attitudes*. It is just as important for us to know how they behave towards children of other groups, in day-to-day situations, and while attitudes may be some guide to behaviour, it is not possible to make a simple equation between the two. For example, while a white child may himself feel friendly towards West Indian children, or one in particular, he may be unable to express this in his behaviour because of disapproval from others in his group. No direct measures of actual behaviour were made in this study, but one question in the

Preference section got rather nearer to this issue than the others. This was the question in which the child was asked to indicate the doll which looked like his real-life 'best friend'.

Once again both the West Indian and Asian children chose white figures much more often than English children chose black figures. Obviously there may be an element of wishful thinking in these choices, but there is no doubt these responses were more reality-based than the straightforward attitude-questions. It is significant that there was a much lower level of outgroup choices on this question than on any others in that section. To indicate someone as a 'best friend' clearly involves at least an element of reciprocation; as only 17 per cent of the entire English sample indicated a black 'best friend', this was obviously not forthcoming. It was found to be more forthcoming in schools where there was a high concentration of black children, but even here it was not very common. When it did occur, West Indians were indicated as best friends much more often than Asians, which is probably a reflection of the Asian's perceived exclusiveness; that it may be only 'perceived' is suggested by the Asians' own choices, which favoured white figures quite as much as the West Indians' choices. This ties in quite well with the sociometric studies of Rowley,[46] Kawwa,[30,47] Saint[48] and Durojaiye,[49] which indicated a marked cleavage between children along ethnic lines in both junior and secondary schools. Saint found that 'the ingroup feeling of the majority English group was in every case markedly greater than that of the Punjabi group'. When we compare the results of the doll tests of attitudes and these tests of actual friendship choice, it is clear that the white children's attitudes can find expression in their behaviour, while the black children's wishes for white friends must contend with the *realpolitik* of the playground and classroom, and are often frustrated.

The race of the interviewer

In recent years there has been a certain amount of controversy over the issue of whether the race of the interviewer may influence the subject's responses in these doll-test situations. There is evidence both for[17-21] and against[22-6] these unintentional influences;

where they have been shown to occur, they seem to produce somewhat greater favourability towards the experimenter's own racial group in the responses of the subject. However, after reviewing most of the relevant studies, Sattler (1973) concludes that 'Young black and white children do not appear to be affected by the experimenter's race in their preferences for dolls which vary in skin-colour.'[29] The issue is not clear-cut, however, and Sattler's conclusion is more emphatic than the evidence justifies. The present study should therefore be viewed in the light of this issue, as it is *possible* that greater outgroup orientation was shown as a consequence of using a white experimenter with black children. However, it should also be stressed that even when a black interviewer is used, the phenomenon of outgroup orientation by no means disappears, so the difference in response is one of degree rather than kind.

Some British studies

What of other attitude studies in this country that might throw some light on the picture presented in this chapter? Pushkin's (1967) study of children in three London boroughs was the first to deal directly with British children's racial attitudes. He conducted his experiments in one area in which few immigrants lived, and two areas with a high immigrant population, one of which had been the scene of some racial incidents. His subjects were mostly white children, between the ages of three and seven years, to whom he administered a number of doll and picture tests. Another dimension was added by his structured interviews with the children's mothers, which produced information about their ethnic attitudes, their child-rearing practices and those of their parents, and their social mobility aspirations. He found that the white children's preferences for their own group were present in the nursery-school age-range, increased with age, and frequently increased in hostility to a noticeable extent during the sixth year. He found no relation between the children's attitudes and the child-rearing practices of their mothers. But a substantial proportion of the racially 'hostile' children had mothers who were also rated as very hostile. So the central role of parental influence is demonstrated here: so too is the role of wider social pressures, as the greatest hostility amongst both children and mothers was found in the area where there had been marked racial tension. As Pushkin[15] concluded, his results point to:

... (1) the reflection of strong ethnic attitudes of mothers in their young children, and (2) the importance of the kind of contact (between races), through attitudes prevalent in the area, in the formation of young children's attitudes to the ethnic outgroup.

In Jennie Laishley's study of nursery-school children in areas which were not racially tense, it appeared that the children had not yet internalized any negative evaluation of black people and were relatively unaware of skin-colour differences.[31] She stresses the low age-range involved in the study and suggests that children only a little older than these may well show different reactions. That this is sometimes the case is shown by Brown and Johnson's[32] study of three- to eleven-year-old white children. While their youngest subjects did not show consistent preferences for one racial group over the other, 'children between the ages of 5 and 8 years showed a marked increase in the attribution of negative statements to shaded figures and positive statements to white figures'. These findings were largely confirmed in Richardson and Green's study,[33] where the majority of English children preferred white skin-colour to dark in pictures they were shown. The researchers added an original, if somewhat macabre, dimension to this kind of study by assessing whether this preference was still upheld when the white figure involved was visibly physically handicapped. Only the white boys in the study showed a significantly greater preference for the white handicapped figure over the dark figure; however, 'on the average, boys and girls, coloured and white, preferred light to dark skin-colour' when neither of the figures was handicapped. There then follows evidence of orientation towards the white outgroup among the coloured children; around half of both the boys and the girls preferred white figures, this pattern being slightly less frequent among the girls. In both cases the proportion is quite high in view of the age of the children (10–11 years) and the finding in the American studies that expressed outgroup preferences often decline considerably around this time.

Jahoda, Thomson and Bhatt's study (1972), conducted con-currently with the major research reported earlier in this chapter, provides both some confirmation of the general picture described there, and some discrepant findings. In comparing the preferences of Asian immigrant and Scottish children, 'the Scottish children aged 6 exhibited a balance of preferences towards their own phy-sical features, which increase sharply and significantly by age 10. The younger immigrants did not differ from the younger Scots, but at 10 there was a dramatic reversal of preference towards the outgroup.'[21] In a follow-up study in which an Indian psychologist conducted the tests, 'all Scottish children showed a slight and uniform bias towards the outgroup. The immigrants, on the other hand, significantly preferred their own physical make-up at the age of 6. By age 10 they had shifted somewhat towards an out-group preference'. Overall, the 'racial experimenter effects' here seem greater than those reported in any other study, particularly as regards the Scottish children. Of course, in varying the experi-menter, there is a danger of altering variables other than just the experimenter's race. Jahoda writes that his results suggest 'that the presence of a charming and attractive Indian experimenter (another variable calling for control) completely reversed the pat-tern of preferences in this group'. It is not altogether clear whether charm and attractiveness are the variables in question, but they may have been influential in the results. It is relatively unusual for white children to encounter Indian women in professional roles, and in combination with an evidently attractive personality the children may well have 'suffered' some (hopefully permanent) disconfirmation of negative stereotypes.

Jahoda and his co-workers also investigated the children's ethnic identification; they were able to conclude that 'these Asian chil-dren had no particular tendency to distort their physical self-image in the direction of that prevalent in the host community', in contrast to the frequent misidentification found in other studies. It should be said that quite a different methodology was entailed here. Rather than a choice between dolls, the child was presented with celluloid sheets on which were printed a variety of skin-colours, eye-colours, hair-colours, and face-, nose- and mouth-shapes. The child was asked to build up a picture of himself by super-imposing different components of this 'identikit'. Perhaps we should not be surprised that different results emerged from this procedure; it does, after all, break the identification (or mis-identification) response down into several separate tasks. It is clear from the doll tests that misidentification can be a difficult response for the child to make (witness the tendency for some black children to withdraw their hands under the table after identifying themselves as white) because of the fiction involved. Clearly this fiction will be much more difficult to sustain across a more analytical and protracted test.

Misidentification and everyday life

Finally we want to discuss the meaning of misidentification for black children. What is the significance of this phenomenon, and what does it tell us about the everyday experience of the child? The experimental situation is rather an artificial one, after all, and it is conceivable that misidentification is an artifact and signifies nothing at all about the child's real identity. Indeed, Greenwald and Oppenheim[22] have argued in this direction, on the basis of a study in which they added intermediate 'mulatto' dolls to the white and the black dolls in the test situation, and found considerably less identification with the out-group among black children than other studies had found. However, there are a number of methodological criticisms that could be levelled at this study; in addition, their results could be interpreted quite differently. The authors divided their sample of children into dark, medium and light groups on the basis of their skin-colour. A majority of all these groups indicated the *dark* doll to be the one who 'looked most like a Negro'. In fact 22 per cent of the 'light' children and 50 per cent of the 'medium' children actually selected this figure as 'looking most like them' on the identification test. In this context it could be argued that the other children, who identified with either the mulatto doll or the white doll, were misidentifying to an extent. So that although the sheer numbers of children identifying with the white doll was less than in other studies, the proportion of children *not* identifying with the figure, who they had maintained was most like a Negro, was very much the same.

At the opposite extreme of interpretation, no one has quite argued that misidentification represents a pathological belief on the part of all the children who make this response that they *are* white, though clinical studies of disturbed children show this is the case with a tiny minority. However, as we have seen, Goodman argues that: 'The relative inaccuracy of Negro identification reflects not simple ignorance of self, but unwillingness or psychological inability to identify with the brown doll because the child wants to look like the white doll.'[27]

This may be so, but it is only an inference and is not tied to any information from outside the experimental situation that would confirm it.

Neither explanation seems wholly adequate; the first throws away the baby with the bathwater, and the second lacks support because we have no information about the everyday identifications of the child, outside the test situation. An alternative explanation seems better able to cope with both the experimental phenomenon and its real-life correlates. Suppose that in an identification experiment 50 per cent of the black children chose the black doll as 'looking more like them' and 50 per cent chose the white one (which is very close to the actual results of the West Indian children in the study). The explanation would run this way: in real-life the children are ranged along a continuum, from those who are adjusted to their skin-colour and accept it, that is, know themselves to be black and see themselves as such, at one end of the continuum, to those for whom the negative social valuation of blackness is intolerable to accept for themselves, and who take refuge in a fantasy notion of themselves as being white, at the other end. These are the two extreme groups, both 'sure' of their identity, the former group with the more realistic identification, and therefore probably much larger than the latter group. Now *between* these two groups are ranged the majority of the children, those for whom the issue is not so clear-cut, and who are in varying degrees of conflict about their identity. For these children the negative connotations of the skin-colour and racial characteristics are too important to ignore, or to accept completely, while at the same time they are aware that it is unrealistic to identify with whites. In other words these children have not resolved the two conflicting pressures concerning their identity in one direction or the other. These pressures are, simply, that objectively they are black which is a realistic but undesirable identity in our society, while subjectively, many would like to be white, which is an unrealistic but desirable identity. So either choice has both a positive and a negative aspect to it. Those children for whom this conflict is very evenly balanced will be found near the centre of the continuum; those who incline *more* towards one identity or the other will be located rather nearer to two extreme groups. Perhaps this is easier to visualize if we portray it graphically:

see themselves as black (say 30%)	in conflict (say 60%)	see themselves as white (say 10%)

But in the experimental situation, the identity test requires them to choose either a black or a white doll as signifying their identity.

choose black	choose white

In other words, the real-life *continuum* must be expressed in the experimental situation of one or other choice of a dichotomy. Several groups with rather different feelings about their identity are compressed into two groups. Now in theory the central 'in conflict' group could choose either way. In the situation where an intermediate coloured doll is offered, as in the Greenwald and Oppenheim experiment, many will opt for that doll to resolve the conflict. But reverting to the two-choice situation, where a minority-group is the subject of virulent racism and devaluation of identity, they are more likely to veer to the right-hand side of the continuum, swelling the group who 'choose white' in the experimental situation. Or particular situations could arise, like the presence of a black interviewer, which make it 'easier' to identify with blacks. In other words, the cut-off point between those who choose white and those who choose black is not a hard-

and-fast one, but dependent on both the children's life-situation and aspects of the experimental situation.

In a sense this interpretation is less dramatic than one which maintains that 50 per cent of the children are wholeheartedly identifying themselves as whites; but really it is much more so, because it suggests that a much higher proportion are in greater or lesser conflict about their identity, 60 per cent in the diagram; in other words 70 per cent (including the extreme right group) are not fully identified with their own group. It distinguishes between the 'black' and 'white' choosers less in terms of 'identifying themselves as black' or 'identifying themselves as white' in real life, with an inexplicable barrier between them, and more in terms of a real-life continuity between the two groups, with the precise cut-off in the test situation determined by situational factors both surrounding the tests and in the outside world. The interpretation implies that a much higher proportion of the children than simply the outgroup identifiers have a positive orientation towards the outgroup, have a desire to be like them, but may be inhibited from expressing this by the fiction involved in saying they *are like* them in the identity test.

If this interpretation is correct, then questions to the children on this very issue – which race would the child like to be – should yield more 'white' choices than the 'actual' identity question. For while the choice of a white doll on the 'ideal' identity question *implies* rejection of the child's true identity, it involves no misrepresentation by the child, no outright *denial* of identity. It is much easier for the child to *express* his orientation towards the white group than on the actual identity question. If we turn to the studies which have included both of these questions, we find that the prediction is borne out. Sixty-six per cent of Morland's[24] black subjects said they would rather be the white figure, while 54 per cent had maintained that it looked most like them. In our English study, whereas 48 per cent and 24 per cent of the West Indian and Asian children had chosen the white doll on the actual identity test, 82 per cent and 65 per cent respectively did so on the ideal identity test. An indication of the relation between the two responses – and of their meaning – is that 100 per cent of the West Indian children who identified with the outgroup also said that they would 'rather be' the white figure, and 92 per cent of the Asian outgroup identifiers also did so. In other words, the children who choose white figures on the two questions are the same people, not separate groups.

The identification experiments, it seems, display the conflicts the black child experiences within his social reality. That reality focuses on the racial aspects of his identity, and renders his blackness a highly negative attribute, while at the same time idealizing the white majority group and conferring on whiteness a highly positive value. The identification experiment requires the child, momentarily, to resolve this conflict between the available but devalued black identity and the unavailable but valued white one. We find that a substantial number of children opt to deny objective reality and choose the latter.

In this chapter a new interpretation of this phenomenon has been offered, characterizing two extreme groups, on a 'continuum of identification', whose identification in the experiments exactly matches their real-life one; each one is strongly identified with blacks or whites, the latter containing a tiny 'pathological' minority. Between these groups lie the majority, in conflict about their identity both in the experiments and in everyday life. However, this is simply a hypothesis, and is going some way beyond the evidence we have. After all, this evidence is simply that in an identification experiment roughly half the black children misidentified themselves. That 50 per cent figure could represent either a very stable situation or a very volatile one, more stable or more volatile than any of the interpretations have suggested. Simply, is it the case that half the total group misidentify all the time or that all of them do so half the time? Clearly we would arrive at a very different interpretation if we found that a different group within the sample misidentified when tested again. In other words, to give any credence to our interpretation it is necessary to introduce another dimension, namely the persistence of these responses over *time*.

A further study

With this in mind, a follow-up study was mounted. It entailed a second series of identification tests with some of the West Indian children tested in the original study, after a period of one year. Other tests were also repeated, but it is the identity tests we are concerned with here. The picture that emerged from these tests showed a remarkably close correspondence to the predictions that follow from the interpretation of misidentification proposed in this chapter. Half of the sample maintained the same choice of figure from the first test to the second; the other half changed their choice from the first to the second test; some in one direction, some in the other.

Table 3: Consistency of choices over two identity tests

identified with blacks on both tests	black to white	white to black	identified with whites on both tests
31·25%	6·25%	43·75%	18·75%

The 'black to white' group contains those children who identified with blacks on the first occasion and white on the second, the 'white to black' group contains those who made the reverse change between the two occasions. In so far as these repeated tests give a better indication of the child's enduring notion of his identity, it does seem that there are two groups who are consistent in their identification (with either blacks or whites) and a central group whose choices are much more unstable. And the extreme groups are also distinguishable in terms of their Preference responses, a much higher level of white preference being found among the consistent outgroup identifiers. It cannot be said on the basis of this further study that our interpretations of the significance of misidentification is *proved*; however, it is certainly true that the data from the two studies taken together are entirely consistent with that interpretation.

Black identity and cultural insulation

Before we go on to consider the consequences of this situation, in the next chapter, one issue remains to be discussed, namely the similarities and the differences between the West Indian and Asian children as they have emerged from this study. The discussion of misidentification may have distracted attention from the equally important findings on the other sections of the tests. While a minority of both West Indians and Asians misidentified, *the majority* of both groups showed a consistently strong orientation towards whites on the other tests. There is overwhelming evidence that minority-group children in England have internalized the racial values of the society and the accompanying pecking-order. As a consequence they respond to the tests in a way which is highly favourable to the dominant white majority and derogatory to their own groups, a mirror-image of the evaluations of these groups current in the host community.

The close similarity between the West Indian and Asian children on all except the Identity tests was not expected. The hypothesis of differences between the groups was derived from the differences between their parents' cultural backgrounds and orientation towards this society – the 'white bias'[45] and aspirations to integration of the West Indians, and the defensive autonomy of the Asians. Clearly, these original orientations have undergone a great deal of change. The West Indians have been forced to revise many of their illusions about British society, and have been prevented from achieving the integration they sought. The Asians, on the other hand, have been unable to avoid the natural proliferation of ties with the host community, and the effects of its values on their children. Both groups, then, have retreated from their original intentions, and the distinction between them in this respect has become less clear-cut.

More importantly, as a result of their common designation and treatment by the host community, the *two groups have come to share an 'identity' of predicament*, in both senses of the word. As Rose[1] has described it: '. . . however diverse their origins, (they) are lumped together as coloured immigrants and are rejected because of their colour . . .'

The social reality of immigrant life is an *homogenizing* reality; its colour-scale and value system is dichotomous: white and 'coloured', positive and negative. As Ramchand[44] wrote:

Leaving the West Indies and coming to Britain is like entering a land where the natives suffer from a curious form of colour-blindness in the contemplation of human groups. This . . . manifests itself in an insensitivity to racial discrimination and variant shades within the category 'black'. It registers two crude categories, black and white.

We have seen many reflections of this in the English children's attitudes, where the obvious colour and cultural differences between the immigrants seem to have little influence on their evaluation.

What seems to distinguish the West Indian children is the extent to which these images have been internalized. As Klineberg and Zavalloni[28] have pointed out, it is possible for the individual to accept these views of his own group and still maintain self-esteem by distinguishing himself from his group. This could underlie the immigrant child's responses to the questions which involve favourability or unfavourability towards his *group* as a whole, without direct reference to him. He can express preference for one over another and attribute good and bad characteristics to them, without this being automatically self-disparaging. It is only on the Identity questions that the child cannot avoid direct self-reference. On these questions outgroup identification represents the ultimate extent of the introjection of host community values, for the child is effectively denying his own identity.

It seems that while the Asian and the West Indian children equally reproduce white values about their groups, they do not equally accept the implications for themselves. Although all the evidence suggests that the pressure of prejudice is the same, the reaction is rather different; the derogatory personal identity is less easily imposed on the Asian children. It is as though the same pressure simply meets with more resistance. The most plausible explanation is that the Asian child has more alternative *positive* resources of identity which counter-balance this pressure. His domestic life is one in which he plays well-defined traditional roles within the family structure. He practises religious worship which influences his attitudes and conduct, in fact most aspects of his life. In the home, his language and behaviour mostly derive from a reality quite different from that he encounters in the street and at school, the reality of his cultural heritage. His instruction in these roles, religious observance, traditional customs and practices, language and dress, tell him not only 'what to do' but also 'what he is'. In the process of learning he comes to construe himself *as* a composite of these facets, *as* an inheritor of these traditions. In other words he acquires a strong and valued identity, a positive notion of himself, locating him securely in his family, religion and culture. It is this, we would argue, that insulates him from the *most* destructive effect of society's attitudes – self-devaluation. But it is a measure of the strength and pervasiveness of those attitudes that even this protection is inadequate in a minority of cases.

5 Black Identity and Mental Health

One of the central problems the black child faces is that of establishing for himself a viable identity. He is socialized into a world in which the social valency of his skin-colour is highly negative. His parents and others communicate to him a reality in which his group is disadvantaged and devalued, and consigned to an inferior material environment. Later he will encounter prejudice at first hand, through actual social rejection.

The social depiction of his group 'de-identifies' him by rendering his real identity untenable. And the adults with whom he should identify bear the same social stigma. As a result of their own difficulties they may not either be able to provide the warm, stable background that could counteract these feelings in their children. So that, for black children in America, 'before the child is aware of being a Negro himself, he is affected by the tensions in his parents over *their* being Negro',[1] completing a self-perpetuating vicious circle.

Given that the child cannot unequivocally accept an important aspect of himself – his race – it seems inevitable that he must experience acute identity conflict. In other words he may have difficulty in creating a stable, positive sense of himself. As self-esteem is an important part of adjustment and mental health, the black child appears particularly vulnerable. Carrying these conflicts within him, the black person is prone to anxiety, maladjustment and personality disorder.

This has been the accepted view of black mental health for a considerable period. It is supported by a great deal of evidence, but the evidence is far from conclusive, is partial in some respects, and much of it is out of date. In this chapter we shall try to evaluate this view. First of all, what are the grounds for thinking that black minorities are any more prone to emotional disturbance than any

other groups ? Evidence from childhood of these identity-conflicts and the emotional problems they are said to engender
would give some support to the account. Of course, there is all
the evidence concerning self-attitudes cited in Chapter Three,
but we have tended to *assume* that these cause emotional problems
for the child; how justified is this ? There *is* empirical evidence
that many black children show symptoms of emotional difficulty
from quite early on. On projective tests, compared to whites
Negro children tend to perceive the world as more hostile and
threatening, less often see themselves as able to establish and
maintain friendly relations with other people, and tell more
stories in which the central figure is hated or reprimanded.[2]
Black children have also been found to be more anxious,[3] 'had
more negative self-concepts, and were more passive, more morose
and more fearful',[4] and more aggressive and severely neurotic.[5]
But when we turn to relative rates of mental illness for adult
blacks and whites, we find a very confused picture. This is not
only because different studies have produced quite different
results, but also because *actual* incidence rates for mental illness
are notoriously hard to discover.

For some time estimates of mental-illness rates for particular
populations were made from a simple statistic, namely mental-
hospital admissions. On this basis, the incidence of psychoses
among black Americans appeared to be approximately twice as
high as among whites.[6] However, these figures were culled from
state mental hospitals; as the white population can more frequently afford private treatment, these statistics seriously under-
estimate white rates for psychosis. A study[7] which took account
of private hospitals as well found the admission rates for Negroes
to be lower than for whites. Add to this self-selection factors which
might differentiate between the races, like attitudes toward
mental illness, recognition of symptoms, willingness to report and
confine oneself, and it becomes obvious that the statistic provides
an inadequate basis for comparison of the races. These considerations apply with even greater force to the milder psychoneurotic
disorders. In this area there has been even less differentiation
between black and white incidence rates but if anything tending
to show higher rates for whites.

Inter-racial comparisons on the basis of admission rates have, then, become somewhat discredited. As Dreger and Miller have pointed out:

Such comparisons have very appropriately decreased, being obviously of limited value ... attempts to talk about the 'true' incidence of mental disturbance among races on the basis of those in treatment is questionable even without considering the many definitional problems which exist.[8]

However, from their survey of the entire literature concerning mental health differences between the races, including research with personality tests, clinical studies and survey techniques, 'it does appear that Negroes more frequently experience psychiatric difficulties, particularly of a severe nature'.[9] They more often receive diagnoses of

schizophrenia, alcoholism, paresis, mental deficiency, drug addiction. The following diagnoses are more likely to occur among whites: senile psychosis, chronic brain syndrome, arteriosclerosis, psychophysiological and autonomic visceral disorders and the various depressive reactions. Again these differences are associated with lower socio-economic groups regardless of race ... [although] overall there are some consistent differences between Negroes and whites ... it is our opinion that the evidence over the last five years suggests that these differences are primarily related to class and caste.[8]

Despite the confusion over *reported* mental illness rates, it would be remarkable if there were no differences in actual incidence rates, in the general population. Given the intense conflicts and material privations of black people's lives, the potential for maladjustment seems enormous. In other words, there seems to be a discrepancy between a set of living conditions which are undeniably pathogenic and their 'visible' effect in terms of reported mental illness.

Perhaps the discrepancy hinges on different criteria for mental illness within the black and white communities. So that as well as different rates of reportage, the criteria for diagnosis of mental illness in whites are inappropriate for us with blacks. For example, it has been suggested that a personality organization, 'which clinicians would ordinarily consider to be schizoid ...

[constitutes] . . . an adjusted personality organization for Negroes in American society . . . since it serves to protect the core or ego aspects of personality'.[10] This appears to be something of an exaggeration; on the other hand, perhaps a slightly 'disordered' way of thinking and behaving may be the only effective way of coping with conflicting demands. This is in line with the way Bateson,[11] Laing[12] and others have conceived of schizophrenia: as a possible consequence of double-binds on the individual enmeshing him in incompatible demands. And when a government publicly encourages the advance of a minority, while privately endorsing a policy of 'benign neglect', we can see how double-binds can operate on a society-wide basis. It seems quite plausible that a degree of 'splitting' is necessary to accommodate this sort of contradiction, particularly when they are a part of face-to-face relationships.

If what white clinicians would think of as 'maladjusted' is actually an adjusted mode of thinking and behaving it will not be considered abnormal in the community and will not be reported. So that H.V., one of Kardiner and Ovesey's[13] subjects, who is preoccupied with violence in all his thought and behaviour, is described as 'about as "normal" an individual as it is possible to be. He has effected a successful adaptation to his social situation . . . His pre-occupation with assertion is not neurotic. It is entirely a projection of the social realities which confront him.' So what would normally be labelled as 'abnormally' violent, even 'disturbed' behaviour is seen as a realistic and viable response to his situation. But this 'abnormal' reality may also conceal many people who suffer painful psychological difficulties but who are never assisted simply because their predicament is common.

To put all this in perspective, it is not that the minority is somehow more *prone* to anxiety and personality disorder, simply that this is an inevitable result of degrading and miserable conditions of life. It is not 'abnormality' or 'inadequacy' but a natural response to 'abnormal' and 'inadequate' conditions of existence. To classify it as mental illness only disguises the causes, by emphasizing the individual rather than the society.

The quality of black life, both in the US and in this country, is undoubtedly inferior in its material aspects to that of most whites.

Add to this the various psychological conflicts connected with caste and race, and it seems a plausible hypothesis that black people simply have *less happy* lives than their white counterparts. Now that is a very simple construct, but we may need explanations of that order to account for the adjustment of large numbers of people to appalling conditions of life, but who fall far short of mental illness. Happiness, strangely, is not a construct which is used very much in psychology. It is not easily quantified, and is altogether more difficult to work with than, say, hospital admission rates. Because of our foundations in the scientific method, we tend to prefer statistical comparisons of populations based on numerical indices of their characteristics. In this case, those indices (like admission rates) are inadequate, so we must look to descriptive materials – clinical reports, life histories, even biography – for our evidence.

Claude Brown's[14] description of a Harlem childhood, *Manchild in the Promised Land*, conveys the reality of ghetto life particularly vividly. The title refers to the mistaken ideas of the North held by many Southern Negroes before they actually went there, often as a result of the idealized picture painted by earlier migrants:

It seems that Cousin Willie, in his lying haste, had neglected to tell the folks at home about one of the most important aspects of the promised land: it was a slum ghetto. There was a tremendous difference in the way life was lived up North. There were too many people full of hate and bitterness crowded into a dirty, stinky, uncared-for closet-size section of a great city.

Brown describes it as going 'from the fire into the frying-pan'. His own youth and adolescence is a chronicle of petty crime, violence, juvenile courts, reform schools and drug addiction, but above all poverty. In one passage he describes an embittered fight between a brother and sister over the possession of a single egg to eat. The sister is all but choked in the process and the egg broken. His own solution is to go out and steal a loaf and a dozen eggs, which is the only way to get them; but continual misdemeanour, however altruistic, leads to eventual retribution, beginning a self-perpetuating cycle of crime and punishment. Claude Brown was obviously a resourceful ghetto-dweller and his vitality tends to glamorize the picture we receive. But he understood that the reality for most of the inhabitants was miserable:

I remember telling Nick that there was no greater place in all the world than Harlem. We almost got into a fight one time because he started telling me about people in Harlem suffering and that sort of thing. I was hurt when he told me that. I guess Nick knew it was the truth of it all that hurt me.

The context of this is an area in which the 1959 Civil Rights Commission[15] found that 'if the population density in some of [the] worst blocks obtaincd in the rest of New York City, the entire population of the United States could fit into three of New York's boroughs'. But Harlem is just an extreme example of the quality of urban life for black people in any number of major cities. In the early 1960s the overall rate of Negro unemployment was double the rate for whites, while the average wage was around half the white average, and this differential has been increasing since then. In the under-21 age-group, 50 per cent of the unemployed are Negroes even though they represent only 10 per cent of the population. The unemployment rate for black high-school graduates was higher than the rate for whites who had not attended high school. In 1964 it was estimated that automation was wiping out 40,000 unskilled jobs a week, the section of industry with the highest concentration of Negroes. Black Americans on average get three years less education than whites and live seven years less.

In making a distinction between material conditions and psychological difficulties in their contribution to black suffering, we must be clear that it is only an arbitrary division. The two aspects are indissolubly linked, and each must be understood in the context of the other. But here we are concerned primarily with the psychological aspects, and in particular, conflicts over identity, to which we now turn.

Identity-conflict

The conventional view of the Negro's psychology can be stated as follows: living within a culture dominated by white people

and their values, the Negro to some extent introjects white attitudes which hold him to be inferior. Feelings of inferiority are
entirely natural, for the role of the black American as it is conceived by the majority and depicted in literature and the mass
media simply *is* an inferior one. Moreover, the social and material
environment to which racism consigns him is further cause for
such feelings:

... many Negroes ... accept in part these assertions of their inferiority ... when they employ the American standards of success and
status for judging their own worth, their lowly positions and relative
lack of success lead to further self-disparagement.[16]

This image of his race makes for difficulties in identification with
a despised and rejected group. He may identify with his own group
but then it is difficult to escape the implications of their derogatory
identity for his own self-image. Alternatively, he may identify
with whites, which denies his true identity, is unrealistic, and
fraught with anxiety. The problem presents itself as a choice
between two evils. He may resolve it in one direction or the other,
or he may stay in conflict over his identity; in each case, he
suffers anxiety and lowered self-esteem.

Identification with blacks

When we talk about 'identification with blacks' we include not
only those who unequivocally identify themselves *as* black and
see themselves as such but also those who are less certain of their
identity but are more inclined towards this identity than the
alternatives. Similarly when we talk of 'identification with whites'
we include not only the 'pathological' minority that see themselves
as white, but also those in conflict who tend more towards that
identity than their 'correct' one. In other words 'identification'
is here used in a rather broad sense: *namely the way in which the
person feels towards the group, his tendency to orient his behaviour
towards them and seek acceptance by them.*

Identification with one's own group is the 'normal' pattern, as
we have seen in Chapter 2; however, this is said to cause problems for black children, and in particular for the black boy, both

in terms of his identification (in a wider sense) with a socially rejected group, and in his specific identification with masculine models. For not only is his normal model for identification, his father, sometimes absent or passive, not only does he bear the same caste-mark, his colour, but his very masculinity is undermined by white society, too. In oppressing him it emasculates him, for he is powerless on his own to fight against it. 'Effective retaliation is impossible'[17] and it has been suggested that the aggression generated within him but prevented from discharge against its proper target is turned back in on the self, powering self-hatred.

An oppressed minority has few resources, psychological or material, with which to resist the imposition of a derogatory identity; identification with his own group necessarily involves him in absorbing some of that identity. The journalist I. F. Stone has characterized the black American's condition as 'a unique case of colonialism, an instance of internal imperialism, an underdeveloped people in our very midst'.[18] The analogy is a profound one, for colonial and neo-colonial societies involve similar privations to those described, both mental and physical. Frantz Fanon has described the psychological oppression of the colonized thus:

> The feeling of inferiority of the colonized is the correlative to the European's feeling of superiority. Let us have the courage to say it outright: it is the racist who creates his inferior. This conclusion brings us back to Sartre: 'The Jew is one whom other men consider a Jew; that is the simple truth from which we must start . . . It is the anti-Semite who makes a Jew.'[19]

This was never more powerfully nor more eloquently expressed than by Fanon himself when he wrote:

> All round me the white man, above the sky tears at its navel, the earth rasps under my feet, and there is a white song, a white song. *All this whiteness that burns me* . . .[19]

Indeed there is some empirical support for these ideas: Jahoda, writing of Ghanaians before independence described how elements of inferiority enter into the African's conception of himself. Through European-inspired schooling the African encounters a system of values which in many ways contradicts his own. There are strong pressures to accept these values, for in doing so, both the social prestige of education and the material benefits it makes available accrue to him. As a result

... He now comes to look at Africans and African culture to some extent through the eyes of those European educators who determined the manner and content of the teaching he received; but the price he often pays for this partially enlarged vision is psychological inferiority.[20]

Other parts of Africa and the Third World underwent the same experiences. There is ample evidence of the derogatory stereotypes of the 'native' held by the dominant groups throughout the history of colonialism and many survive to the present day.

   Even in inter-racial situations which are relatively free from overt conflict hostile stereotypes persist; in New Zealand, as we have seen, Ritchie[21] noted that some sections of the white Pakeha community described the Maoris in terms that were quite as derogatory as the familiar Western stereotypes about Negroes or Africans. They were considered 'wilfully poor ..., dirty ... children, moronic and undisciplined, virtually unemployable and grossly irresponsible if not plainly criminal'. In some instances, as elsewhere, these views are internalized by the 'natives' themselves, and as we have seen in the studies of Maoris and Africans, continue to mould the attitudes of their children.

Group-devaluation and self-devaluation

If the individual black American or Maori or West Indian absorbs the values of the dominant majority, and develops negative feelings about his group, will he automatically develop negative feelings about himself? Logically, of course, the correlation should be perfect, and derogation of his group should automatically entail derogation of himself, as a member of that group. Psychologically, this can be avoided. While disparaging his group, the individual can protect his own self-esteem by distinguishing himself from the rest of his group, at least in his own eyes. In this way he distances himself from the others and avoids the opprobrium heaped upon them. Jahoda found evidence of just this process:

... one of the most remarkable mechanisms was that people were apt to talk about the faults of 'Africans' in a way which implied that they were excluding themselves. Sometimes it was evident from the context that they were referring to another group, literates would be speaking about illiterates; but occasionally it seemed to mean 'all Africans except myself'.[20]

Obviously, then, there is not a simple one-to-one correspondence between group-attitudes and self-attitudes. But in interview situations like that we are dealing with *expressed* attitudes which may or may not represent the person's real feelings. In reality, group- and self-attitudes may correspond rather more than the person is prepared to admit in an interview. In the absence of information about his actual behaviour we can only conjecture about this, for avowed beliefs are rather less reliable than evinced beliefs. For example, among Kardiner and Ovesey's[13] adolescent interviewees, S.A. claimed to identify with Negroes and that his colour did not constitute a problem for him. However, he also attributed superiority to whites on a number of occasions, 'castigates his brother for deriding whites' and often showed 'unconscious rejection of Negro-identification . . . [he] would prefer to believe that he were really white'.

So that although there is no *necessary* relation between attitudes towards one's group and attitudes towards oneself – some individuals manage to psychologically distance themselves from the rest – only in a few cases like these will there be *no* relation between them. For the most part, holding negative attitudes about one's own group is likely to involve *some degree* of self-disparagement, even if these conceptions are not wholly self-derogatory. For the black person, then, identification with his own devalued group is certain to introduce some negative elements into his conception of himself. One opportunity for him to distance himself from this is to reject his blackness and identify with whites.

Identification with whites

Brody's[17] interviews with young Negro boys and their mothers confirmed

that many of these Negro boys do have significant conflicts involving anxiety or guilt-laden wishes to be white rather than Negro . . . Some seem to have little ambivalence or uncertainty, and clearly noted their wish to be white and their depressed feelings about being dark-skinned.

In the same vein, Dai[22] has written of Negro children like 'Tom', from whose interview data and self-description it was possible to see

how a child took over the white majority's evaluations of skin-colour from his own group, and how these evaluations created a sense of inferiority or unworthiness that became increasingly unbearable as time went on. In other words, the colour of one's skin, which does not occupy the consciousness of children of other cultures, is here made an issue of primary importance, and the personality problems thus created are almost as difficult to get rid of as the dark skin itself.

Or Alice, whose

transformation from black into white through the process of identi-fication is certainly an ingenious psychological manoeuvring, but it only enhances [her] lack of the sense of belonging; she strives to be acceptable to both white and coloured groups, but ends by belonging to neither.

In short, when the majority group is politically, economically and culturally dominant, and every aspect of this superior position is reinforced by social or legal sanctions, the racial minority-group cannot remain immune from it. The dominant culture pervades the subordinate culture and transforms or co-opts it. Through ideologies like racism the minority-group's identity is debased and dehumanized to a point where some find it emotion-ally intolerable to accept. Then the identity may be rejected as far as possible and the individual strives to attain the attributes of the dominant culture. It is only comparatively recently that Black movements have infused a positive pride in skin-colour and black identity. Until this time, lighter skin was a passport to higher status; 'white' hairstyles, fashions and accoutrements were adopted with the same intention, and Negro magazines contained more advertisements for hair-straighteners and skin-bleaches than perhaps anything else. Malcolm X, one of those most re-sponsible for the growth of black self-esteem, describes how he himself aped the white ideal in his earlier hustling days: 'I endured all of that pain, literally burning my flesh with lye, in order to cook my natural hair until it was limp, to have it look like a white man's hair.'[23]

Later he described how this denial of blackness and wish to be like whites is transmitted from parent to child within the black family:

As anti-white as my father was, he was subconsciously so afflicted with the white man's brainwashing of Negroes that he inclined to favour the lighter ones, and I was his lightest child. Most Negro parents in those days would almost instinctively treat any lighter child better than they did the darker ones. It came directly from the slavery tradition that the 'mulatto', because he was visibly nearer to the white, was therefore better.

James Baldwin describes similar experiences:

One's hair was always being attacked with hard brushes and combs and Vaseline: it was shameful to have 'nappy' hair. One's legs and arms and face were always being greased, so that one would not look 'ashy' in the winter time. One was always being scrubbed and polished, as though in the hope that a stain could thus be washed away – I hazard that the Negro children of my generation, anyway, had an earlier and more painful acquaintance with soap than any other children anywhere. The women were for ever straightening and curling their hair, and using bleaching creams. And yet it was clear that none of this effort would release one from the stigma and danger of being a Negro; this effort merely increased the shame and rage ... One had the choice of 'acting just like a nigger' or of *not* acting just like a nigger – and only those who have tried it know how impossible it is to tell the difference ... And the extraordinary complex of tensions thus set up in the breast, between hatred of whites and contempt for blacks, is very hard to describe. Some of the most energetic people of my generation were destroyed by this interior warfare.[24]

It is hardly surprising then, as Kleiner and Parker have pointed out,[25] that 'Almost every clinical study of psychopathology among Negroes indicates that the Negro who is not identified with other members of his group is relatively more prone to manifest various forms of mental ill-health.' For however hard he tries, he cannot be successful, except for those very light-skinned individuals who can 'pass' for white. It leaves him vulnerable to the people of his own race whom he implicitly rejects but desperate to gain the approval of whites. It is a difficult identification to make and maintain, for it involves a degree of 'splitting' of the personality: 'one is "himself" with other Negroes but transforms his behaviour to meet the expectations of whites'.[26] Understandably this is often accompanied by anxiety, hyper-activity, and sometimes mild dissociation. 'Commonly, Negroes are unable to maintain the split effectively, and their confusion of self and role shapes their personalities into the narrowly prescribed mould of the deferent, shy, dependent human being.'[16]

Sartre[27] has described a similar predicament – that of the 'inauthentic' Jew, the Jew who has allowed himself to be persuaded by anti-Semitic propaganda, and therefore lives in fear that his actions will conform to this despised portrayal of his race. He poisons the spontaneity of his actions by attempting to contradict his notion (absorbed from his oppressor) of the Jewish nature. 'For him it is not a question of recognizing certain faults and combating them, but of making clear by [his] behaviour that [he does] not possess these faults.' This deliberate self-consciousness destroys his authenticity; it arises because 'he knows he is watched . . . [and therefore] takes the initiative and tries to look upon himself with the eyes of others.'

In this way he can check his behaviour against the stereotypes of his group. The price he pays for this is anxiety at the possibility of rejection by both his own group and the majority group; for his actions imply a denial of his own group which must antagonize its authentic members, while his view of himself through the eyes of the majority presents him with a picture of a Jew or Negro trying to 'make it'. It is clear that the role is a peculiarly vulnerable one, and fraught with guilt and anxiety.

Complete 'identification with whites' and complete 'identification with blacks' are not the only alternatives. The individual may identify to a degree with one or the other, or he may not make a firm identification in either direction, but remain with a foot in both camps, leaving the conflict unresolved. Nor are these necessarily static dispositions: the person may change his identification as a result of his experiences. If the man who identifies with whites perpetually finds himself in situations where he is rebuffed, he may be forced to re-appraise whites and his feelings towards them; frustration and an aggressive identification with blacks may result. Malcolm X underwent a similar development; while not actually identified with whites, he was a 'light' Negro and enjoyed his higher status as a result. In prison he educated himself and arrived at an analysis of power-relations between the races, both from books and his very situation there. As a result he developed a deep identification with his race and emerged as one of its most forceful champions.

*

We have devoted a considerable time to synthesizing various conventional accounts of the psychological predicament of the black American. According to these accounts, he finds himself in a heads-you-win-tails-I-lose situation. By identifying with whites he is insecure, vulnerable to anxiety and mental illness; by identifying with blacks he incorporates within his own self-image disparaging elements which damage his self-esteem and may lead to emotional disturbance. This simplification verges on parody, but when reading the literature it is difficult to avoid the impression that the entire black race is embroiled in this Catch-22 situation, where to identify in either direction almost ensures psychological difficulty.

But where in all this are the normal, well-adjusted black Americans, who are identified with their race but have sufficiently resilient egos to withstand the imposition of inferiority on them? Very little has been written about them, the main emphasis having fallen on those with identity-conflicts and emotional difficulty. That is a necessary emphasis in describing the destructive effects of minority-group life, but it is a partial picture. However, it has been the accepted view of the black person's psychological experience for many years. In the last two or three years black psychologists, in particular, have begun to contest the conventional view, in terms of its veracity in the past and in the present. Some, like Baughman,[28] have raised similar objections to those just raised: that the emphasis on pathology and maladjustment has all but ignored the 'normal' black who may in fact be typical of the majority of his group. A key issue is that of self-esteem, which has been said to be lower in blacks, on the basis of relatively little empirical support. Baughman argues that although some blacks undoubtedly do internalize the definition of them as inferior beings, 'On the other hand, the fact that so many blacks learned to *act* subservient or inferior in the presence of whites cannot be taken as conclusive evidence that they *felt* this way about themselves.' He doubts whether blacks, on average, have a lower level of self-esteem than whites and points out that 'the discrimination that blacks have endured enables a black man to point "out there" to explain his frustrations, failures and so on, rather than to deficiencies in his own self', an option not available to white people. Indeed, he cites studies of black and white self-esteem in children which contradict the conventional view (e.g. McDonald and Gynther;[29] Wendland[30]). While some studies have found no differences in the levels of self-esteem of black and white children (e.g. Carpenter and Busse[45]), others, like Zirkel and Moses,[46] have even suggested that black children's self-esteem may be higher than whites. A recent study by Floyd[47] indicated 'basically positive self-concepts' among black children.

Really there is more evidence to support Baughman's contention than the alternative. This was Rosenberg and Simmons'[31] conclusion, and in their own study they found that 'black children as a group do not appear to have lower self-esteem than whites'. They list the psychological pressures and material deprivations of black life and add the comment, 'One can easily understand why so many writers have simply taken it for granted that black children would have lower self-esteem'. However, they point out that self-esteem depends on the context in which it is evaluated. In their study, black children in black schools had higher self-esteem than those in integrated schools, because they evaluated themselves against 'others' in a similar situation, as opposed to others who enjoyed superior conditions and achievements. Given *de facto* segregation, the majority of black children fall into the former category.

But of course, self-esteem is only one aspect of psychological development and adjustment and it would be as foolish to write off the entire conventional view of the effects or racism on the black personality as to accept it uncritically. Certainly it has been selective and somewhat ethnocentric: hypotheses have been accepted as fact without adequate empirical support, simply by frequent repetition. In effect, the argument has run: ' Given these antecedent conditions of poverty and deprivation, prejudice and discrimination, surely the black person *must* be prey to psychological disorder '. Undoubtedly a section of the black population has suffered disorder and will continue to do so, but they have been represented as though they were typical of the whole group. In other words, much of what has been written on this issue can be accepted as valid and representative; but of a *proportion* of black people not of the whole group.

The longevity of the conventional view is both its strength and its weakness, for it has allowed a substantial amount of evidence to be gathered to resolve some of the areas of uncertainty, for example, the issue of self-esteem; but it has also remained an almost static picture and this is the most serious criticism. Nowhere is there acknowledged any of the revolutionary *changes* in the conditions of black people in the last ten or fifteen years. In short, the account not only seems partial, as we have argued, but above all, dated. For the period has seen an unprecedented development in black people's lives, a 'great leap forward', which cannot have failed to influence this picture. As important as the tangible gains of de-segregation, Civil Rights legislation and economic development are the *psychological* gains. As the Civil Rights movement emerged, so too did the beginnings of a new identity; and all the successors of that movement have fostered black consciousness in different ways such that the contemporary ' image' of black Americans, both to others and themselves bears no relation to the deferent, slave-like stereotype that preceded it. Who would have agreed that black is beautiful twenty years ago ? Who would have predicted that black people would *choose* to identify with their African roots ? As Baldwin wrote:

At the time when I was growing up, Negroes in this country were taught to be ashamed of Africa. They were taught it bluntly, as I was, for example, by being told that Africa had never contributed ' any-thing' to civilization. Or one was taught the same lesson more obliquely, and even more effectively, by watching nearly-naked, dancing, comic-opera, cannibalistic savages in the movies. They were nearly always all bad, sometimes funny, sometimes both. If one of them was good, his goodness was proved by his loyalty to the white man.[24]

Friedman[32] suggests that this denigration of Africa was in itself an important component of the Negro's negative identity:

... the Negro's acceptance of the white man's image of himself has been inextricably intertwined with the Negro's acceptance of the white man's image of Africa ... the first in the long series of the Negroes' denials and self-denials was the denial of the African heritage.

These images were not remote from the American Negro, for they were retailed by their churches (raising funds to 'civilize' the African savages), by the mass media and by their schoolbooks:

In the fourth grade those pictures of the races of man ... with a handsome guy to represent the whites, an Indian with a feathered hat, a Chinese, and an East Indian, and then a kinky-haired specimen. That was me, a savage, a cannibal; he was at the bottom. That picture in the book was the picture of where and what I came from. I carried that idea around with me for years.[33]

Graphically:

If you can imagine inverting the biases consciously or unconsciously at work in this process, you might then see the white race represented ... by ... a mugshot of Al Capone, or, to make the selection on more purely aesthetic grounds, someone with the looks of Charles Laughton.[33]

Friedman argues that the world-wide development of black people now provides the black American with an alternative *positive* identity:

With the emergence of Africa on the world scene, the rewriting of African history, and especially the re-evaluation of pre-European African cultures, the place of Africa in the Negro's mental landscape is in the process of slowly moving from the negative to the positive pole.

As a result black people have prominent models like African leaders, have an alternative cultural identification, and the significance of colour is changing within the community. Blackness and everything that goes with it has a positive connotation, leading to different concepts of beauty and style. The Negro, Friedman argues, is in the process of exchanging 'a domestic for an international identity'.

Certainly, while dashikis and Afro hair are by definition superficial things, they have a very profound significance. What could be more diametrically opposed to button-down collars and short-back-and-sides, or sharp suits and conked hair, the old Negro equivalent? Their very superficiality – their outwardness – denotes their purpose, a proud and aggressive affirmation of an identity. The visible symbols of race – skin-colour and hair – which were once a source of shame and disguised and denied, are now accentuated; they are badges of a new identification. But this is not the whole story; Friedman seems to pass over the changes during the same period which have a far greater immediacy for black Americans, changes which they have effected themselves. Certainly emergent Africa has given them a history, a cultural heritage and racial pride; but emergent black Americans have given *themselves* a new identity, forged from their own experience, here-and-now.

Above all, this is an identity of self-respect, that comes from standing up and asserting oneself. The bus boycotts, sit-ins, freedom marches, the organization of black voters in the teeth of violent opposition and intimidation by whites, even the rioting and looting in the urban insurrections, all were experienced at first hand or via the media as psychologically liberating – liberation from a notion of black people as passive, fearful, even co-operative victims of oppression. This has been the aggressive aspect of the developing black consciousness – the assertion of manhood, in conflict with whites who had always emasculated them. The Black Panthers have been the most prominent expression of this; but while publicity has been devoted to their para-militarism and their victimization by the police, their other activities within the community have been largely overlooked. These well illustrate the new cohesion within black communities, the growth of organization for self-help. The Panthers' attempts at political and social education, welfare provision and breakfast

programmes for ghetto children have contributed to this feeling
of solidarity over and above their direct material benefits.

When we consider the extraordinary revolution in black
people's experience over the last decade or so, it would be surprising to say the least if it had had no effect on their attitudes
towards themselves. To take just one example, the sheer amount
of news-media coverage devoted to black people in the last ten
years probably exceeds the total for the previous four hundred.
In addition, the *type* of portrayal has altered equally dramatically;
figuratively, we might say that this has developed from Amos
'n' Andy, through Martin Luther King, to Angela Davis. Both
omission from cultural materials like television, newspapers and
books, and occasional portrayal in stereotyped roles is held to be
damaging to minorities; hopefully black people will have benefited from this new exposure in the media.

Any analysis of black identity must now take account of all
these elements; the 'conventional' view of black psychology is
now infused with reflections of the Third World and the evolving
domestic struggle. That is why the conventional view on its own
is no longer acceptable, for practically nowhere in that literature
concerning black personality and adjustment can be found any
mention of these developments. A static model cannot possibly
'fit' a dynamic process; Friedman puts this cogently: '... social
science was caught flat-footed when the "mood-ebony" appeared
... Now theory must follow newspaper headlines.'[32]

As yet there is little published research which gives evidence of
the new black identity, but it cannot be long coming. There are so
many indications from other sources that these changes are
happening; it would be a dreadful example of social-scientific
myopia to ignore the evidence all around us while we wait for the
researchers to deliver the goods. One of the first studies to point
in this direction was an investigation of black American children's
racial attitudes in 1970 which found rather less preference for
white figures and less misidentification than was found in earlier
studies. The authors discuss a number of possible interpretations
of this, including the following:

First, times may be changing. That is, Negroes are becoming
Blacks proud of their race. If change is occurring, previous research

indicates that it is not at a universal rate across the country . . .
[Another] interpretation is that conditions indigenous to Lincoln
have mediated the impact of the 'Black Movement' . . . We note that
during the past two years a black pride campaign, sponsored by
organizations which are black conscious, has been directed at adolescents and young adults in Lincoln. Black children through interaction
with kin and friends may be modelling these attitudes.[34]

Similar results have been reported by Harris and Braun[35], Paige[43]
and Brigham,[44] although it should be said that some current
studies have still found the 'old' pattern of attitudes, that is,
preference for white figures (e.g. Morland[36]) at least among
pre-school children. Morland's research with older children,
however, also shows the clear development of identification with
blacks and rejection of whites in 12–18-year-old black children.

Clearly, there are so many different sorts of information which
provide us with evidence of these changes that it is difficult to
integrate them into a simple picture of contemporary black
identity. The changes are evidently proceeding at different rates
in different groupings, both social and geographical. At best we
can only describe the direction of these changes, not the extent to
which they have progressed. There is, unmistakably, a movement
towards a re-definition of 'blackness' in a positive, accepting way.
To the extent to which this identity becomes more and more
attractive, so will conflicts over identity tend to be reduced. From
all that has been written here it is clear that a strong identification
with his own ethnic group makes the individual less vulnerable to
psychological difficulty than when he is in conflict or identifies
with whites. The white community's anxiety over the growth of
black political movements has distracted attention from their
contribution to this psychological liberation, which is quite as
important as their social and political actions.

Identity, mental health and immigrants to Britain

Obviously there is no question of making a direct comparison
between black Americans and 'coloured' immigrants to Britain
on these issues. Aside from any differences in gross social conditions, there is the fundamental fact that black Americans are

effectively an indigenous minority, while the black population in this country is a migrant one. Unravelling the strands which go to make up the immigrant's identification is thus even more diffi- cult than with the black American.

The question of mental illness illustrates this well. As we have seen reported, mental illness rates are one, very crude, index of maladjustment and emotional disturbance within a group of people. Just how crude this is in the case of immigrants becomes clear when we look at the number of factors involved and try to isolate the causes of these rates. Let us suppose for a moment that a given group of coloured immigrants do have a higher rater of mental illness than an equivalent group of white English people. Firstly there is the possibility of genetic differences; but it seems that schizophrenia, for example, has a rather uniform incidence rate across a variety of settings, which tends to discount that explanation. Then there is the possibility that people who migrate are different in some way from people who stay. Migration is a voluntary process, after all, so that the group who decide to go are self-selected; those who are already 'maladjusted' may be the most likely people to want to leave, for example. But as Bagley points out, in this case:

There are stringent regulations restricting the entry of coloured people to Britain, and emigration for such individuals requires con- siderable long-term planning, the accumulation of capital, and the acquisition of skills – precisely those qualities which the schizoid personality lacks.[37]

Then, of course, there may be something in the migration process *itself* which disposes migrants towards mental illness. Although some migrants become mentally ill soon after arrival, it seems unlikely that experiences in transit could account for many of the cases. Such cases could be related to early anticipation of difficul- ties to be faced on arrival. This brings us to the whole complex of possible explanatory factors, bound up with the immigrant's immersion in a new culture. Then difficulties can arise from 'cul- ture-shock' – because of the discrepancy between the old culture of origin and the new, alien culture with its totally different standards, ways of behaving, in fact, completely different reality. Or psychological difficulties can arise because the immigrant's predicament is not only new, but also *bad*. If, by virtue of being a *coloured* immigrant, he is discriminated against in all the most important aspects of life, he must be very strong to remain unaffected by it. It is really only this last set of factors which have any relation to the situation of black Americans and allow any translation between the two. The remainder are all connected with the fact of migration.

West Indian immigrants are probably less 'culture-shocked' on coming here than Asian immigrants because of the British influences within West Indian culture, discussed earlier. Indian and Pakistani immigrants, on the other hand, deliberately protect themselves and their cultural ways from collision with British culture, so they may experience less difficulties than if they wished to thoroughly integrate. Both groups, however, are equally burdened by prejudice, discrimination and social rejection.

There has been very little research into immigrant mental illness, and so it is difficult to point to the causal factors. However both Hensi[38] and Bagley found rather higher rates among immigrants (particularly West Indians) than among English people. Hensi studied admission rates for mental illness among West Indians and locally born residents in Camberwell and Lambeth, London. Whereas the first admission rate for the latter group was 10·9 per 10,000 the immigrants' rate was 31·1:

... the rate for schizophrenia was higher among the immigrants [as was the rate for] ... depression and allied conditions, 14·2 compared with 3·9 ... Character disorder and severe neurosis were twice as common among the immigrants.[38]

In Bagley's study the rates for schizophrenia, and mental illness in general, among West Indians, Africans, Indians and Pakistanis were considerably higher than the rate for British-born individuals. As Bagley points out:

The fact that schizophrenia is a relatively frequent diagnosis in West Indian and African patients suggest that there may be a similar excess of milder psychiatric states (depression, anxiety, etc.) which do not come to the notice of the psychiatric services.

He also notes that the immigrants' rate may be an underestimate because of their reluctance to submit themselves for treatment.

Now while we cannot eliminate the contribution of 'migration' effects to these rates, we can shed some light on the contribution of stressful factors in the immigrants' predicament here. Bagley compared matched groups of West Indian schizophrenics, English schizophrenics and West Indian 'controls' – immigrants who had never had any psychiatric consultation. He found that 'environmental stresses', like overcrowding, poverty, long working hours, were more common among *both* West Indian groups than among the English group, but that they were no more common among the schizophrenics. Measures of 'goal-striving stress' were also made; these derived from a study of Negroes by Kleiner and Parker,[26] and provided data on the person's own aspirations and his aspirations for his children's education and occupation. Given that the opportunity structure for immigrants in Britain is far from open, such aspirations are potentially stressful as they are unlikely to be fulfilled. When compared on this basis,

... West Indian patients have significantly higher scores on this index of goal-striving than either the English patients or the West Indian community controls ... Many ... are then in what might be described as a 'double-bind' relationship with society, which like an eccentric parent offers inducement for a particular kind of behaviour, while at the same time punishing or at least discouraging, the logical outcome of such inducements. He must strive, but he may not succeed.[37]

So that with the factor of 'having migrated' held constant, there is clear evidence of mental disorder correlating with a particular aspect of the immigrant's relation to the larger society: the fact that laudable aspirations are frustrated by individuals and institutions through the operation of wide-spread discrimination.

We do not have *direct* evidence that ties immigrant mental illness rates to other aspects of their life here; it is difficult, for example, to trace the effects of the whole climate of prejudice 'in the air' on immigrants' psychological experience. Empirical evidence is not available, simply because the necessary research has not been conducted – it may be there for the finding. So if we want to see whether our analysis of black identity in the US has any relevance to immigrants in this country, we have to look to all manner of suggestive evidence while we wait for empirical research to fill the gap.

We know, for example, that immigrants occupy the very lowest position in the social heap, as do blacks in America. We also know that prejudiced attitudes[39] and discriminatory practices are widespread in the white community.[40] From this we can only surmise that black people suffer psychological stress and that *some* become mentally ill as a result, and the evidence from America makes this seem very likely.

One example illustrates the black person's position in this country particularly vividly. Not long ago a native white Welsh man contracted chronic nephritis, a kidney disease, which caused his skin-colour to change from white to dark brown. Thereafter he was insulted in the street, ostracized in his normal social activities, and was unable to find a job; even his relationship with his wife was adversely affected. He was offered help by two coloured people who felt they could give him some hints on how to deal with prejudiced white people, for of course his experience was identical to that of many coloured immigrants. His experience, like Griffin's[41] deliberate colour change, was unusual in that he was made aware of both sides of the coin – first as a member of an apparently prejudiced community, then as a recipient of that prejudice. This is a very rare event, a naturally occuring 'controlled' experiment. For throughout the process his cultural similarity with the white community did not alter, a factor which is sometimes invoked to explain prejudice, on one hand, or 'maladjustment' on the other. When we consider that he was socially rejected despite this cultural similarity and despite his numerous personal ties with white individuals, it becomes clear that this colour-prejudice is extraordinarily powerful. It is the seemingly automatic devaluation on crossing the colour-line which crystallizes the issue. Perhaps inevitably the man suffered emotionally:

Since the change of colour I can feel a change in my personality. I have become more wary and withdrawn. I have to be on my guard all the time. Because of my colour I go as little as possible to London . . . I've read about this Paki-bashing. I hate going on tubes and buses just in case there's a skinhead ready to put the boot in.[42]

The story has a particularly tragic sequel. So intolerable was this situation that he underwent a kidney transplant operation in the hope that it would restore his original colour, and he died shortly afterwards.

Of course this is a single case-history, but in a very simple way it brings out all the forces at work – and demonstrates some of their consequences for the individual. Now let us look at the problem from another angle. We saw in the previous chapter that some immigrant children show a very similar pattern of racial attitudes and identification to black American children. Many of these children were born in this country and have little or no experience of the sending societies, except second-hand from their parents. They have been socialized within this society and so they are more nearly comparable with black American children. In other words, we have some evidence that the *subjective* experience of 'being black' is rather similar in the two countries, among the most comparable sections of the two populations.

This is perhaps the most powerful evidence that there may be common identity problems. For we have seen where there is outgroup identification, or 'identification with whites' as it has variously been called, the whole syndrome of conflict and anxiety is much more likely to occur than when the person is identified with his own group. Among black Americans those who are not strongly identified with their own group tend to have lower self-esteem and be more prone to mental illness. And to complete the circle, we have indeed found that mental illness appears to be more common among black people here than among whites. In other words, there are a number of indications that our analysis of black identity-conflict may be equally relevant to the experience of immigrants in this country, particularly the second generation. But is it also true that the radical *changes* in black Americans' identification are occurring or will occur here?

Developments in Africa and the rest of the Third World are equally real to immigrants here as to black Americans, giving the same sense of pride. In an even more immediate way, television relays the urban confrontations in the States directly into British living-rooms, almost as they are happening. Both these influences can be detected in black youth in Britain – on one hand, a cultural identification with Africa and negritude, on the other a militant identification with 'liberated' black leaders like Eldridge Cleaver and Angela Davis. More recently still, there are clear signs of a young-black-British sub-culture emerging, centring on reggae and distinct black styles of clothes, language, etc.

But despite this and despite the exploited position of black people here, there is not yet anything approaching the strength of black consciousness that exists in America. At the same time, there is no reason to believe that the picture is any more static here than there, and various black movements have established themselves in the last few years. As the original hopes of easy integration have faded, so the realization has grown that the black community has to fend for itself from its own resources. Community organization for self-help has been the main activity but militant political organizations and local defence groups have also attracted support, particularly among young adults.

It is impossible to predict future developments, but while black people remain an oppressed minority we should expect the emergence of black consciousness to continue and to intensify, conforming more and more to the American pattern. Probably there will be a greater (and to some extent more genuine) emphasis on cultural roots than in America, for they have not been left so far behind. They provide an alternative identity which is more acceptable than that imposed on them by white attitudes. Here a distinction should be drawn between the West Indian and the Asian groups. The Asian communities have fostered this cultural identity from the very beginning, and there are clear pointers to the success of these practices in the research reported in the last chapter. It will be recalled that the Asian children identified with whites much less than did the West Indian children, as though their own culture had protected them against the most damaging effects of prejudice. Hopefully the growth of black consciousness in the West Indian community and the fostering of cultural ways will tip the balance of identity-conflict in much the same way as is happening in America. But this, were it to happen, cannot be the whole solution. There is evidence that young blacks are, rightly, less prepared to accept their imposed social position than their elders. The statistics of homelessness and unemployment among black youth depict a situation which is fostering increasing bitterness and disillusionment, but Howe[48] argues that it is a mistake to see black youth as passive and helpless 'victims' of the economic situation:

West Indian youths *refused* to follow their parents into London Transport and the various other traditional haunts of immigrant labour . . . Wherever immigrant labour has traditionally been placed there are numerous vacancies open – London Transport, nursing, the many small factories, particularly engineering, hospital cleaners, etc. . . . The entrance of youths into the class of unemployeds represents not only an increase in numbers but also a qualitative change in the composition of the class. They bring to the class a boldness and confidence which stems from the fact that they are not the demoralized strangers their parents were,

with the growing likelihood that this determination will be directed against the root-cause of their situation, white racism.

6 Education and Black Children

It has been argued that the identity-problems of the minority-group child derive directly from the valuation of his group in the wider society, and from the status accorded to it in the social structure. Race and status are here related in a complex way; race determines status so that it is often possible to estimate a man's position in society if he is dark-skinned, and both race and status contribute to the climate surrounding him and his group.

Many of the deprivations suffered by racial minorities are the deprivations of the urban poor, irrespective of race, but there is always another dimension, that of colour and its caste-status. Now we shall examine the educational experience of black children and look individually at the effects of 'race' and of poverty, in so far as they are separable. As before, we shall lean heavily on American research material.

Urban poverty and education

There is no shortage of research material on the educational problems of the poor; taken together it represents an encyclopaedia of deprivation and inadequacy but it is a partial one, as we shall see later. For the moment let us synthesize this material into a profile of the lower-class child as depicted in the literature.

From the very outset, the lower-class child is said to be at a disadvantage; it has been shown that nutritional factors may account for disorders of pregnancy, spontaneous abortion, and infant disability at low socio-economic levels.[1] There is also more prematurity[2] involving neurological abnormalities and subsequent retardation of development.

In infancy the child suffers handicaps in developing perceptual abilities:

The slum child is more likely than the middle-class child to live in a crowded, cluttered home . . . There is likely less variety of stimuli in the home, and less continuity between home and school objects. Where money for food and basic clothing is a problem, there is little for children's playthings . . . and for decorative objects . . . Where parents are poorly educated, there is likely to be less verbal interaction and less labelling of objects (or of the distinctive properties of stimuli) . . . There is less stress on encouraging the production of labels by the child, and on teaching him the more subtle differentiation between stimuli (for example, knowing colour names and identifying them) . . . as a result, he could be expected to come to school with poorer discrimination performance than his middle-class counterpart.[3]

Indeed, it has been demonstrated that lower-class children do perform less well on auditory discrimination tasks.[4] This may well contribute to both speech and reading difficulties.

The beginning of speech is more likely to be delayed in lower-class children.[5] Apparently the 'shaping' of a child's speech sounds through differential reinforcement by the parent is more persistently practised by middle-class parents than lower-class ones. In addition, the lower-class home provides a high level of 'noise' through which discriminations must be made and which distracts both parent and child from satisfying interaction. In Bernstein's[6] early work it was argued that the language the lower-class child acquires is different from middle-class language. It was called a 'restricted' code, signifying a more informal, concrete, immediate and need-oriented mode than the 'elaborated' code of the middle-class child. The latter was portrayed as more formal, abstract and concept-oriented; as a nearer approximation to grammatical written language, it put the child at a considerable advantage in dealing with reading materials and teachers in schools. As language and thought are in many ways interdependent, the lower-class child would experience more difficulty with abstract problems and with concept formation. Subsequently, this analysis has been modified in the light of further research by Bernstein and others to take account of situational factors in the production of language.

In what other ways is the lower-class home apparently deficient in preparing the child for school? Lower-class children, it seems, have less family activities than middle-class children;[7] they have less interaction with parents and seek information from them less.[8] They have fewer books in the house, are read to less, speak less with parents at meal-times. They also have more physical punishment.[9] Parental aspirations for their children are lower in the working class;[10] and the children themselves have less achievement motivation.[11] The expressive style of the lower-class child is concrete, 'motoric', 'thing-oriented' and non-verbal, in contrast to the conceptual, abstract-symbolic, 'idea-oriented', verbal style of his middle-class counterpart. They learn more quickly for material incentives than for non-material ones like praise or satisfaction, while the reverse is true for middle-class children.[12] Apparently, lower-class children also have a time-perspective which is more immediate than middle-class children. These last two factors fit them badly for school systems in which rewards are abstract and long-term.

Deutsch[8] sums up this background to learning in the following way: 'The lower-class child enters the school situation so poorly prepared to produce what the school demands that initial failures are almost inevitable, and the school experience becomes negatively rather than positively reinforced.'

After 2-3 years of age, social class differences on measures of intelligence appear and increasingly diverge with age, in favour of the middle-class children.[13] In school, lower-class children do worse on arithmetic concepts tests,[14] IQ tests, reading scores and problem solving.[15] 'High-status children score higher than low-status children on all tests of conceptual ability.'[16] On comparisons of overall IQ and achievement scores of lower- and middle-class children, 'groups of pupils from higher-income families scored higher on all cognitive measures, even when these were ostensibly "culture-fair"'.[17] Lower-class children receive a disproportionate share of lower grades;[18] and in one study of eight-year-olds, lower-class children were eight months behind middle-class children on vocabulary, nine months on reading comprehension, six in arithmetic, and eleven in problem solving.[19]

Lower-class children make more modest estimates of their ability than middle-class children;[20] show greater maladjustment;[15] are more aggressive and competitive;[21] participate less in extra-mural activities[15] and drop out more.[22]

Collating the empirical material in this way produces a profile of the lower-class child which gets perilously close to caricature. Similar generalizations about the lower-class child are usually tempered with some sort of acknowledgement that variations do exist within the lower class, but these aspects receive very much less emphasis. Generally it is suggested, at least by implication, that sufficient homogeneity exists within the class (and between different studies) to permit a 'summary portrait of the disadvantaged child' of the sort just provided. Typically these catalogues of deficiency all but neglect individual differences within the class and also the various strengths of the child and his environment. This is simply because the lower-class child is being evaluated within a certain frame of reference, that is potential for scholastic achievement, and in comparison to middle-class children (to whom this is more meaningful). It is not surprising that within that frame of reference and within educational institutions that embody it, the lower-class child appears inadequate. Rist[23] found that within their first fortnight in school the middle-class children in the class came to be perceived by the teacher as the most able and the most enthusiastic; and that, thereafter, teachers concentrated their efforts on helping these children.

What is particularly dangerous is that this portrayal *itself* hampers the progress of the lower-class child by instilling *expectations* about his performance in teachers and educators. The drastic effect of such expectations in depressing actual performance demonstrated by Rosenthal and Jacobson[24] will be discussed later. Moreover, this picture of deficiency tends to locate the 'blame' solely in the child and his background. Perhaps it would be more realistic and more helpful to include in the 'blame' the too-academic school programmes which are unresponsive to the needs and difficulties of a whole section of their constituency.

We must allow for the middle-class perspective of research findings, which, evaluating the child only for academic potential, must find him lacking. (Within the last few years, however, more realistic and objective assessments of the working-class child's abilities, and the schools' inability to realize this potential, have emerged; see for example Silberman[25] and Ginsburg[26]). By other criteria the lower-class child may even emerge as 'advantaged', an apparently unthinkable prospect to many theorists and educationists. Nevertheless there is some indisputable evidence in the preceding pages of the ways in which the lower-class child's experience, even from before birth handicaps him in the educational process. Those which derive from his material environment (rather than the more suspect 'inadequacies' of socialization and cultural ways) may be directly translated into other situations of poverty and deprivation, whether they involve black or white people. We shall return to this topic later, but now let us consider those educational difficulties of the minority child which derive primarily from his ethnic or racial group membership. These difficulties are not literally due to racial characteristics; rather they are the result of an inferior caste position imposed on a group which, incidentally, has certain racial characteristics.

Most important of all is the question of caste. The black child's inferior status enters into his school life in a variety of ways. Before the child even enters the school gates, certain pre-conceptions about him and his group await him and influence his educational career. The caste status of the group, with its overtones of inferiority, the semi-scientific notions of innate intellectual inferiority, and the relatively unsuccessful school experiences of his predecessors, all combine to create a context in which he will be judged – and into which he will be expected to fit. So there exists a set of expectations about him simply as a result of his group membership, and the evaluations involved affect him in two ways: by shaping both his self-evaluation and others' evaluation of him.

The child's self-evaluation suffers when he compares himself with white children; their advantages, familiarity with the goals of the school, and their ease of learning cause him to select lower, more appropriate targets for himself, and he may not even attempt higher levels of achievement. In this way he circumscribes his own efforts, and then his lack of success is the natural conclusion of a self-fulfilling prophecy. In turn this confirms his lowly evaluation of himself, completing a particularly vicious circle.

In other words, the child provides himself with empirical evidence of his inferiority without realizing how his own attitudes, and before them, white attitudes, make this failure almost inevitable. Irwin Katz, who has done some of the most important research in this area, acknowledges both influences:

The Negro child's feeling of intellectual inferiority is based not only on reality experiences, but reflects an emotional accommodation to the demeaning role in American culture that has been imposed on his group by the dominant white majority.[27]

It seems that these feelings of inferiority become so ingrained that they hold sway over the person even when he does succeed, when they are totally unrealistic. In studies of inter-racial work groups, Negroes who had actually scored as well as their white team-mates on various intellectual tasks nevertheless rated their own performance as inferior. In another study Negroes who were told that their scores were the same as the average white scores (also on intellectual tasks) actually set their goals lower on the next series of tasks, presumably to a more 'appropriate' level.[27]

The second way in which white preconceptions affect the black child in school is through his fellow pupils and teachers. Their evaluations are made real to him in actions specifically directed to him, and in a number of less obvious ways in which their expectations of him are stated or implied. White class-mates may do this through rejection of his friendship, through devaluation of his work or over-evaluation of their own by contrast. Teachers are often equally at fault, sharing the same attitudes, and, through their greater influence, more powerfully affecting the child's view of himself. All these things exert pressure on the child to conform to expectations about him. When the child does fulfil the predictions of these 'significant others' the same circularity occurs, for he only gives further credence to their attitudes.

This very harsh indictment of white attitudes in the school situation is amply borne out by research findings. Katz describes how, in a newly integrated classroom (or in any new inter-racial situation, such as going to school for the first time),

... Negro children would be under some degree of social threat ... Mere indifference on the part of white peers may frustrate their needs for companionship and approval, resulting in lowered self-esteem and the arousal of impulses to escape or aggress. In more extreme instances, verbal harassment and even physical hazing may elicit strong fear responses. These external threats are likely to distract the minority child from the task at hand, to the detriment of his performance.[27]

Katz suggests, with some evidence, that social threat may mar the child's performance by causing him to 'abandon efforts to excel in order not to arouse further resentment and hostility in white competitors'. The desegregation of American schools has illustrated these reactions; Negro children apparently suffer a variety of stress reactions in the inter-racial situation, like loss of appetite, nightmares, lethargy, exhaustion, and so on – in other words the classic symptoms of fear and anxiety. One psychiatrist[28] suggests that this anxiety is more the product of white children's prejudice against the black children than of the latter's worries about schoolwork. Confirmation of this comes from studies of inter-racial summer camps. One study[29] showed that white children actually directed nearly twice as much aggression towards Negro cabin mates as towards white ones. In fact 29 per cent of all actions by white campers towards Negroes were hostile. As a result many Negro children (and whites) showed signs of stress, the more covert variety (enuresis, fears, nightmares, withdrawal, physical symptoms) predominating. From the very earliest research into classroom behaviour, sociometric investigations have shown Negro children withdrawing into their own group in response to white rejection.[30]

Neither are white teachers immune from the prejudices current in the wider society. When *their* behaviour is construed as rejecting or critical of black children, the white children's derogation of them receives tacit support. However, it is not simply a question of overt racial prejudice but rather a complex of perceptions of Negro pupils and expectations about them. Research conducted in the sort of schools which the majority of Negroes attend, that is, schools in deprived areas, shows that the lower the socio-economic status of the pupil enrolment, the smaller the proportion of teachers who enjoyed their work, had personal loyalty to the principal, desired to remain at their present school,

had favourable opinions of the motivation and behaviour of their
pupils, were strongly interested in their pupils, and were themselves competent teachers.[31] Katz interprets these findings as
showing that:

... children from low-income homes, most of whom are Negro, get
more than their fair share of classroom exposure to teachers who are
really unqualified for their role, who basically resent teaching them,
and who therefore behave in ways that foster in the more dependent
students tendencies towards debilitating self-criticism.[32]

Nor are these isolated findings. Other studies paint a similar
picture of teacher-attitudes and show how they are conveyed to
the children. Apparently white teachers more frequently express
dissatisfaction with their job than do Negro teachers, blaming
behaviour-discipline problems and lack of parental interest.
Whereas Negro teachers view pupils as 'fun-loving, happy,
cooperative, energetic and ambitious', white teachers tend to
describe them as 'talkative, lazy, fun-loving, high-strung and
rebellious'.[33] When children are seen as problematic by the
teacher, there is much greater likelihood of friction and unsuccessful relationships between them. And when a whole social class or
racial group is construed in this way *in advance* difficulties arise
from the outset. It has been shown that teachers' contacts with
lower-class children (among whom Negroes predominate) are
more frequent and more negative than their contacts with middle-
class children.[34] It seems that the children who most need acceptance and encouragement from the teacher are actually the ones
who receive it least. Lower-class white and Negro children who
less frequently have the resilient self-esteem of their successful
counterparts, are most vulnerable to further bruising from their
teachers' attitudes. An important investigation[38] of teacher-pupil
relationships showed that those children who had the most
favourable self-images were likely to perceive their teachers as
being more favourable towards them than those who had negative
self-images. The importance of the teacher's preconceptions and
attitudes about class is underlined by the finding that, the higher
the social class of the children, the more they believed teachers to
be favourable towards them, *independently* of their achievements
or lack of them.

All of these teacher-attitudes particularly affect Negro children, for in their case negative *racial* attitudes can be added to negative social class ones. Kenneth Clark,[36] the eminent Negro psychologist and educationist, places much of the blame for ghetto children's educational deprivation with the teachers and school authorities. The attitudes described, he suggests, lead them to view their function as one of 'custodial care and discipline' rather than effective education.

How is it, though, that a teacher's attitudes and expectations of a child can actually affect the child's school-work? Some recent research[24] has produced remarkable evidence about this process at work; it grew out of Rosenthal's[37] finding that in behavioural science research the expectation of an experimenter can affect the responses he obtains from his subjects. In a particular school several classes of children were given a non-verbal intelligence test, which was *said* to be measuring potential for intellectual growth. A proportion of each class were designated as academic 'spurters' and their names were given to their new class teachers at the beginning of the next school year. All the classes were re-tested on the same test twice more at four-month intervals. Overall, the 'spurters' showed considerably greater gains in IQ during this period than did the rest of the children. This might seem unremarkable, were it not for the fact that the 'spurters' had originally been selected from each class not on the basis of their potential for growth, but in a completely random way. In the words of the authors, 'When teachers expected that certain children would show greater intellectual development, those children did show greater intellectual development.' But it was not only in intellectual performance that these children made gains; they were also judged by their teachers to be more likely to succeed, 'as significantly more interesting, curious and happy. There was a tendency, too, for these children to be seen as more appealing, adjusted and affectionate and as lower in the need for social approval.'[38] So those children who were simply *expected* to gain intellectually by their teachers not only did so, but were more favourably regarded by their teachers at the same time.

None of this bodes well for the child who is poor or black or both, and therefore heir to a number of expectations in the mind of the teacher which predict little in the way of success for him. If teachers' expectations do influence performance, the pressure is on him to fail, for he is clearly not expected to succeed. Should he overcome those influences, he is not clear of trouble for it seems that *contradiction of expectations* is not easily accepted. This aspect of the Rosenthal and Jacobson study is perhaps more pessimistic for the minority child's efforts to achieve: they showed that children who were *not* expected to gain intellectually not only showed less gain than those who were, but were regarded less favourably by their teacher when they did gain. 'These may be hazards to unexpected intellectual growth. Classroom teachers may not be prepared to assimilate the unexpected classroom behaviour of the intellectually upwardly mobile child.'[38]

It is clear then, that self-, pupil- and teacher-expectations are stacked against the black child succeeding in school. Nor are his actual school experiences encouraging to him, for many of them involve considerable anxiety. Quite apart from the issue of teacher expectations, the simple fact of a white teacher's race may be perceived as a threat by the child; and

when this source of arousal is added to all others potentially existing in the school of the individual – testing, social rejection, unfamiliar and difficult learning materials, lack of relevant educational training in the family – it becomes apparent that the Negro student may be subjected to many more sources of emotional interference than other disadvantaged groups.[2]

A common factor of all the difficulties we have described is the anxiety they engender in the child. This is certainly an important factor in academic failure, for there has been a great deal of research which has shown that 'anxiety ... [is] more consistently and strongly related to school achievement and intellectual development than other non-intellective characteristics'.[39] Briefly, anxiety and reduced achievement have been shown to go together at all stages in the educational process, from kindergarten to college.

Not surprisingly, Negroes (and other minority-groups) do experience more anxiety in school than do white middle-class children, and their performance on school tests suffers as a result;[40] these children are also very concerned about recognition from peers in school and from authority figures.

Now we know that black children experience conflict about identifying with their own group, that some of them are affected by low self-esteem,[41] and by negative self-evaluations.[42] Clearly these factors play a central part in depressing the child's performance in schools, in the ways described. Regrettably, in the debate about black–white differences in intelligence, the damaging effects of caste on school performance has received much less attention than the effects of 'cultural deprivation'; at best, the emphasis has been on the deprived conditions of the black family and the inadequate preparation for school they are said to provide, rather than the psychological handicaps imposed by an inferior social position. In this chapter the emphasis has been reversed, to afford caste considerations their full importance. For through the child's view of himself and through others' evaluation of him, his performance and in turn his self-image are depressed in a downward spiral.

Remedies

We will pass, for the moment, without comment, to consider the educational policies currently pursued in order to alleviate this situation. The American education system has attempted two remedies for the black child's underachievement in school: *de-segregation* and *compensatory education*. School de-segregation follows from the 1954 Supreme Court ruling that there should be equality of educational opportunity for Negroes and whites alike. Negroes should be allowed to benefit from the superior educational experience provided by white schools. The process is far from complete nearly twenty years after the ruling. It has been deliberately speeded up at one time and slowed down at another by various incumbents of the White House, and pockets of resistance in the South have successfully held out against its implementation there. De-segregation has been achieved by 'bussing' black children into surrounding white neighbourhoods, closing majority-Negro schools and dispersing their populations, and 'pairing' schools and exchanging proportions of each to achieve inter-racial balance.

'Compensatory education' is an umbrella term designating any number of different attempts to improve the quality of education for disadvantaged children. The US Commission on Civil Rights describes it like this:

One approach – remedial instruction – is to give more intensive attention to students in academic difficulty. Remedial techniques usually include reduction of number of students per teacher, provision of extra help to students during and after school, counselling, and use of special teaching materials designed to improve basic skills. Another approach – cultural enrichment – ... attempt[s] to broaden the horizons of poor children by giving them access to activities which ordinarily might be beyond their reach such as field trips and visits to museums, concerts, other schools, and colleges ... A third element ... involves efforts to overcome attitudes which inhibit learning ... to improve self-esteem and to raise confidence by providing successful academic experiences and recognition. A fourth approach ... pre-school education ... seeks to provide disadvantaged children with training in verbal skills and cultural enrichment activities before they enter the primary grades.[43]

Stated in this way the objectives and techniques of compensatory education seem wholly worth while, and certain to improve the lot of the minority child. However, the consensus of opinion seems to be that, with certain notable exceptions, compensatory educational programmes have not delivered the goods. In fact they seem to have had *less* success in boosting achievement than de-segregation programmes. Evaluations of compensatory education projects suggest that the children involved have not reached significantly higher achievement levels than non-participants, and have been surpassed by those who have been integrated into majority-white schools.[2] Both the Coleman Report[44] on 'Equality of Educational Opportunity' and the report of the US Commission on Civil Rights compared the relative performance of black children in racially isolated and de-segregated schools, and provide a lot of evidence of greater gains in achievement for black children in majority-white schools. More recent reviews of compensatory education programmes, while drawing attention to the methodological inadequacies of the studies that have evaluated them, have nevertheless come to essentially the same conclusions (e.g. Passow, 1970,[63] Wilkinson, 1970[64]).

The assertion of the superiority of de-segregation has to be looked at rather carefully because an emotive issue is involved, further complicated by all manner of political considerations. Residential, educational and employment integration have been political articles of faith for liberally minded people for some time. Thus the value-judgement that de-segregation is desirable had been made long before these alternative educational policies were compared for effectiveness, and could conceivably cloud objectivity. There is a little evidence of this in the selection of evidence presented on these issues; some of the *negative, harmful* effects of de-segregation on black children have been rather glossed over. Thus in Weinberg's detailed appraisal of research into the effects of de-segregation he writes: 'De-segregation has most often benefitted the Negro child's self-esteem and virtually never has harmed it.'[45]

Yet Irwin Katz, whose important research in inter-racial settings was mentioned earlier, maintains that

low expectation of success is an important detrimental factor in the performance of minority children attending integrated schools. The evidence is strong that Negro students have feelings of inferiority which arise from an awareness of actual differences in racial achievement, or from irrational acceptance of the white group's stereotype of Negroes.[25]

So bi-racial situations are by no means automatically beneficial; in Katz's[27] experiments, Negroes were found to 'display marked social inhibition and subordination to white partners' in group tasks. In cooperative problem-solving tasks they 'made fewer proposals than did whites and tended to accept the latter's contributions uncritically'. When actually displaying equal ability on tasks, Negroes still rated whites higher. Again, Negroes 'tended to accept passively the suggestions of their white companions' even when these were actually wrong answers to problems. Katz concluded that these dispositions were primarily the result of social threat.

In another experiment, although Negro students performed an

'eye-hand coordination task' better when tested by a white adult than by a Negro adult, when the same task was described as a test of I Q, their performance with the white tester was depressed markedly and elevated slightly with the Negro tester. Eye–hand coordination, says Katz, is not an ability which Negroes are stereotyped as lacking. On intellectual tasks, however, it is possible that 'the Negro subject saw very little chance of meeting the white experimenter's standard of excellence . . . As an additional source of impairment in this situation, low expectancy of success could have aroused fear of incurring the white tester's disapproval (failure threat).'

Katz maintains that there is *not* yet enough evidence to draw firm conclusions about Negro performance in inter-racial situations, pointing to both the positive and negative effects. He catalogues the potentially harmful elements for the black child – social rejection and isolation, accompanied by emotional stress, fear of competition with whites, and unrealistic inferiority feelings – which detract from the benefits of integration. All of these involve stress for the child, and as he emphasizes: 'Research on psychological stress generally supports the assumption that social threat and failure threat are detrimental to complex learning.'

So we have a situation in which de-segregation of schools appears to boost black children's performance more than compensatory education, *in spite of* a number of influences which tend to depress that performance. Katz's experiments might be thought of as looking at the strictly *inter-racial* aspects of the situation, lifting them out of the school context. They demonstrate a number of potentially harmful influences, so that it seems unlikely that *integration per se* – the simple fact of mixing black and white children – is responsible for boosting performance. A review of the evidence for the superiority of de-segregation points in rather the same direction. St John[46] points out that no studies have provided unequivocal evidence that racial mixing alone boosts performance; that *social class* integration and quality of schools may account for quite as much of this superiority as racial integration, for these have not been adequately controlled; and that lack of controls in these studies may have exaggerated the differences between segregated and de-segregated schools, through factors like self-selection (via ambitious parents) of children to be 'bussed', and 'Hawthorne effects' on children studied in this way.

In other words, the superiority of black children's performance in de-segregated schools may have been inflated by biased sampling. Secondly, social class integration may be more important than simple racial integration. That is, at the same time as being racially integrated, black children are also being transported into a higher social class environment in the white schools. On the whole this factor is discussed in terms of the social class background of the black child's white classmates, and the social influences towards achievement exerted on the minority. In situations where whites are in the majority this is said to lead to higher achievement levels for black children. The Coleman Report, for example, found that the 'social class climate' of the school correlated highly with achievement.

Now while the social class background of the pupils may be very important, there are other factors which contribute to the 'social class climate' of the school, and which have been neglected. There is the immediate environment of the school, its fabric and upkeep, the quantity, quality and type of its teachers and teaching materials, its reputation, and so on. We know with absolute certainty that most white schools are better equipped in each of these respects than most black ghetto schools. (For example, we know that there is a strong correlation between the social class of the school and the quality of its teachers, the most proficient teachers being attracted to the most academic schools with the best working conditions.) Yet these crucial factors which largely determine the *quality of the school* have seldom been controlled in comparisons of segregated and de-segregated schools; which leads us to hypothesize an obvious and plausible explanation for the superior performance of 'de-segregated' black children (despite the hazards of inter-racial situations described earlier): namely, that the white schools which black children are integrated with are simply *far superior* schools. Hardly an earth-shattering discovery, but one which, incredibly, appears to have been largely overlooked.

The shortcomings of compensatory education

Or we can approach the problem from the other end. Why is it that, despite enormous expenditure, compensatory education programmes have manifestly failed to improve black children's educational experience to the level enjoyed by white children? First of all, it is difficult to generalize about programmes as they have varied so much from one project to another, so that the term 'compensatory education' covers (it seems) a multitude of sins. Although the overall objectives, listed earlier, are admirable, the content of the programmes themselves could never realize these objectives. Many of the language programmes (e.g. the Peabody Kits) were based on an outdated stimulus-response view of language acquisition, quite apart from the erroneous view of the children's 'language deficits' for which they were designed to compensate. Similarly, the classical music inputs and museum trips of the 'cultural enrichment' programmes could not conceivably attain their objectives, even assuming that the children's culture needed enriching.

Secondly, it emerges rather clearly from evaluations of compensatory education programmes that many have remained almost 'outside' the normal school activities. That is pre-school programmes have tried to improve the child's readiness for school and extra-curricular activities have added 'enrichment' out of school hours, but relatively less attention has been paid to changing and improving the normal daytime educational experience of the child. Thus, O'Reilly writes:[2] 'Typically, compensatory programs are supplementary to the regular school program or may comprise a few short weeks of concentrated effort'. In a similar vein Gordon[47] believes that

it is significant that so much of the current work in the education of the disadvantaged has been directed either at pre-school children or at youngsters who have dropped out of high school. So little attention has been given to investigating the over-all appropriateness of contemporary educational processes. If school people were not such a decent lot, one would think that these two emphases have been so widely accepted simply because they require the least change in the school itself. It often is easier to add extensions than to change the basic structure of institutions.

There are serious criticisms here. Clearly it is ludicrous to expect a vacation-long pre-school programme to compensate for several years' experience of disadvantagement and a group history of oppression and inferior status. Adam (1969)[65] puts this in perspective when he describes 'a Headstart centre [as] not so much a nursery as a crash-course in western infancy which aims to bring the disadvantaged child level with the Spock-raised one between now and next Autumn'. It would be surprising, then, if the evaluation[48] of the Head Start summer programmes had come up with any finding other than that the participants did not achieve lasting gains in cognitive and affective development over non-participants. Significant gains were only achieved in those programmes which lasted for a year before the children started school, but the gains were still not very great, underlining the futility of single summer projects. (Of significance for the de-segregation debate was the finding that programmes based on all-black centres were the most effective.)

It seems that if these deficits are to be made up, programmes should be organized long before children enter school. Gordon[47] makes the point that intervention should begin after birth if we wish to alter this situation; more logically, this should extend to im-proving the environment of the child even before birth. Short of that, it is important that pre-school programmes should begin as early as possible, *but that they should not be a substitute* for improve-ments in school itself. They should also be based on an objective analysis of what the child's 'defects' *are*, an issue we will return to.

Some writers complain that even when school curricula are changed, it is in the direction of intensification, that is, 'more of the same thing', be it teachers, materials or whatever. There seems to have been comparatively little *innovative* change in teaching methods. Nevertheless, this may be adequate for certain areas of learning; an evaluation of one of the few programmes which has produced significant gains in achievement, known as Title I, concluded that 'one effective approach may be nothing more complicated than systematic teaching'.[2] However, in view of the number of unsuccessful projects which have tried just this, two conclusions may be reached: the intensification of existing teaching methods is not great enough to make up the children's deficits, and/or there are other factors connected with achievement which are not being catered to by this method. The US Commission on Civil Rights gives some clue to this in stating the assumptions which lie behind most programmes:

Compensatory education programmes instituted in predominantly Negro schools attended mostly by disadvantaged students rest upon the assumption that the major cause of academic disadvantage is the poverty of the average Negro child and the environment in which he is raised.[43]

No mention here of that complex of factors which retard black achievement deriving from race and caste, independently of poverty. It does seem that more attention has been paid to achievement per se and rather less to boosting self-esteem, group pride and identity; certainly when one reads evaluations of the programmes it is by the yardstick of educational achievement that their success is usually measured. It is also true, of course, that greater achievement is likely to boost self-esteem which would justify this emphasis. However, we have a situation where achievement is not being substantially boosted, so that self-esteem is not growing from that source. In which case we should ask whether it is lack of attention to race and caste factors which is hindering compensatory education, and whether they (operating in the ways described earlier in this chapter) are among the most important factors in under-achievement in the first place. After all, anxiety and self-devaluation, two of the consequences of these factors, have been shown to depress school achievement. Now although 'improving self-esteem and group pride' do figure among the objectives of these programmes, they suffer in translation. They are global and abstract objectives which are difficult to realize in concrete activities. Sometimes the organizers may not understand or be in sympathy with them in the first place:

Such concepts as self-esteem, language development, and academic motivation are frequently little understood by programme directors and teachers alike. The resultant lack of definition leads to a plethora of nonstandardized and varied activities having varying degrees of relationship to the programme objectives, assuming that even the objectives are clear.[2]

Some, however, have met with more success. A programme in San Francisco includes a creative arts centre, while in Philadelphia devices like displays emphasizing the contribution of Negroes to American life and displays of student art work are used to 'raise aspiration levels beyond those held by the child's immediate social environment'. These objectives can be pursued in all-black or majority-black schools. The US Civil Rights Commission heard testimony that this sort of homogeneity assisted curriculum planning and the development of special techniques for overcoming language deficits, for example. To this must be added the finding that Head Start programmes in all-Negro centres were among the most effective, and Stalling's[49] finding that Negro pupils made the greatest gains in achievement *when they remained with Negro teachers and remained in segregated classes* after de-segregation into white schools (that is, a situation of racial homogeneity but vastly improved facilities).

People have raised objections to the idea of all-black schools on the grounds that this is segregation, and that experience has shown the black schools taking part in compensatory education programmes are somehow further stigmatized. The first objection demonstrates the value-judgement to which we drew attention earlier; segregation contravenes the democratic ideal of inter-racial integration. But there is nothing intrinsically wrong with all-black schools, *only with the educational experience that they have, in the past, provided.* Which brings us to the second objection: there need be no stigma attaching to schools involved in compensatory education programmes if these schools are seen to be successful. If the school can become a showpiece, as good as any white school, rather than a patched-up imitation, there will be no question of stigma.

There are a number of lessons here. If we pour resources into all-black or majority-black schools on a massive scale so that they are at least as good as white schools, we create the conditions in which black children's educational deficits can be made up *and* their self-esteem and identity developed. None of the previous attempts at compensatory education appear to have done this even half-successfully, either through an inadequate scale of aid, or a neglect of race and caste factors, or both. Educational achievement and self-esteem go hand in hand, and any attempt to boost either in isolation is doomed to failure. The black child requires both before he can integrate with white people on an equal footing, and to precipitate that integration before both are achieved may bring some successes but also many casualties.

These criticisms and recommendations can be accommodated within the framework of compensatory education as it is currently conceived. However, there is a far more fundamental critique which contests the basic premises of compensatory education; it argues that action programmes cannot help but fail because the analysis of black disadvantagement on which they are based is simply *wrong*.

First of all the authors[50] question the universal assumption of Head Start and similar programmes that black children *do* have linguistic and cognitive deficits. Baratz and Baratz maintain that current linguistic data do not support this assumption; rather that 'Many lower-class Negro children speak a well-ordered, highly structured, but different, dialect from that of Standard English.' While linguistic competence is equated with the latter, linguistic differences are interpreted as deficits. On this argument the black child's speech collides with the Standard English of the school (which is the medium of instruction, expression and complex conceptualization) in much the same way as a West Indian child's *patois* in an English school. Forbes (1971)[66] cites a recent study of language in Pittsburgh which revealed that 'slum children there used 3,200 words, including idioms, not recognized by their teachers or by educational tests'. Add to this the mis-match between his own culture and values, and those of the school and we are some way towards explaining his difficulties and 'under-achievement'. Ginsburg (1972),[26] too, has offered explanations of racial and social class differences in not only language development but also cognitive skills and I Q, which contradict the notion of the 'deprived' and 'inadequate' lower-class child. He concludes that, 'While poverty is not a desirable state and while it may not ennoble those who live in it, it also does not produce serious retardation of their thought-processes.'

These cultural differences are not given due importance because of a more fundamental error on the part of educationists and social policy-makers: an ethnocentric belief that Negroes do not have a separate culture. Cultural differences are recognized, surely, but they are not accorded the respect that anthropologists accord to alien cultures abroad. Rather urban Negro life is seen as a 'deprived', 'disorganized' version of white culture. This has been termed the 'culture of poverty' (or more properly, the 'sub-culture of poverty'). It is based on a long tradition of viewing Negro existence as an unstable, chaotic, amoral disintegration of 'normal' social life, a picture which emerges from the statistics of illegitimacy, father-absence, crime and drug addiction. It centres around the self-perpetuating and self-inflicted inadequate 'life-style of the Negro poor, which disables future generations through its ignorant and ineffective socialization practices.

Valentine[51] has presented a devastating critique of this model which had been the dominant perspective for years. He shows, for example, how theorists have been so concerned with *dis*organization and chaos in Negro life that they resent the opposite when it does appear. He quotes Frazier, the sociologist:

> The behaviour of Negro deserters, who are *likely* to return to their families even after several years of absence, often *taxes the patience* of social workers whose *plans for their families are constantly disrupted*.[52] (Italics added.)

And because of the 'culture of poverty' concept, Valentine argues, poverty is seen as a disabling way of life rather than an involuntary adaptation to an inequitable income distribution. This has the effect of locating the causes of deprivation somehow 'in' the minority and its 'chosen' way of life not in the economic forces which oppress them. Consequently, with the failure of compensatory education programmes in the school it has been necessary to reach further back into the child's life-history to deal with the 'inefficacious' child-rearing practices of mothers and the lack of stimulation in the home. The logical extension of this is the suggestion that specialists should be introduced 'into the home who would not only provide the missing stimulation to the child, but also teach the mother how to raise her children properly'![50]

This model has also been called the 'social pathology' model because it depicts Negro life not as a different culture but as a deficient pathological one. Compensatory education programmes based on this model (as they invariably are) therefore put emphasis on developing the child's competence, thereby improving life-chances; in other words, enabling the poor and black to pull themselves out of poverty by their own bootlaces. Not only is this philosophy ethnocentric and misguided, it actually obstructs progress by distracting attention from the need for structural change, which is the only way the mass of black people can improve their lot. So compensatory education and other programmes speak only to the symptoms of a much deeper malaise, ignoring and even obscuring the causes of these deprivations and 'deficits'. It is rather like ministering to the casualties of a battle, while assuming that they appeared on the battlefield by chance and that their wounds were self-inflicted.

The logic of this analysis leads to the conclusion that there can only be superficial improvements in the educational sphere until the fundamental causes of poverty and racism are dealt with. The wider critique related here conveys the real context in which initiatives like compensatory education are taking place. They are solitary attempts to deal with the outward manifestations of only one aspect of a larger socio-economic condition. To the extent to which governments fail to alter that total picture, so will efforts at compensatory education be circumscribed.

However, this holistic approach and conclusion does not invalidate the previous discussion of smaller issues within compensatory education. While accepting the validity of the analysis, we cannot afford to wait for the revolutionary social change required to implement it. For, realistically, we can see that no government, here or in the US, is going to undertake the radical social action involved in eradicating poverty and racialism, unless compelled to do so. In this regard governments are assisted by social scientists like Daniel Moynihan (one of the foremost proponents of the culture-of-poverty view) who states his belief in the need for active *resistance* to social change quite unequivocally:

Liberals [should] see more clearly their essential interest in the stability of the social order, and that given the present threats to that stability, it is necessary to seek out and make more effective alliances with political conservatives who share that concern.[53]

So there is still a case for lower-order reforms like compensatory education bringing immediate benefits. But these must be undertaken with the eyes open, and not seen as panaceas that will bring justice and equality of opportunity, but simply as a means of equipping some black children to confront their predicament more effectively. But the name 'compensatory education' itself connotes inferiority. Rather we should be pursuing *bi-cultural education*, free of the value-judgements which create 'deficits' from cultural differences. Labelling accepted sub-cultural patterns as pathological or (in the case of children at school) 'wrong' only adds to the devaluation of the minority by the majority. Baratz and Baratz summarize it this way:

Education for culturally different children should not attempt to destroy functionally viable processes of the sub-culture, but rather should use these processes to teach additional cultural forms. The goal of such education should be to produce a bi-cultural child who is capable of functioning both in his subculture and the mainstream.[50]

They give as an example of more appropriate teaching methods the use of Negro dialect in the teaching of reading. These issues will be discussed further in the following chapter. Meanwhile it is important to define the sort of educational milieu in which this philosophy could be enacted, that is, in racially separate or racially integrated schools. Obviously to give this radically different style of education to black children would be easier in all respects in all-black schools; within integrated schools it might tend to reinforce racial division. And we have seen evidence that the former is the case, and evidence of the greater success of all-black centres in the Head Start programme. Against this we have to weigh the higher achievements of 'de-segregated' black children, and against *that*, the caution that these claims may be artificially inflated and more related to the class and quality of the school. In short, if we could improve the quality of black schools to that of white by *positive* discrimination, by massive injections of resources to improve their structures, working conditions, and staff–pupil ratios, we would cater to most of those objections.

One important objection remains: the fact that achievement is only a part of the picture. Equally or more important is the ques-

tion of racial attitudes, and the evidence points in the direction of less polarized attitudes in inter-racial schools. However, a pre-condition of this inter-racial friendship has been shown to be an atmosphere of acceptance between the races in the school. In so many schools this is manifestly not the case, particularly now that 'bussing' has become such a divisive political issue in the US.

It may be that some combination of the alternatives will be the best solution. Black elementary schools could provide a long period of bi-cultural education that would both accustom the child to mainstream cultural patterns and methods of school achievement *and* develop within him self-esteem and a sense of group identity, based in his own cultural heritage. To integrate children on entry to the secondary level would coincide with the normal breaking down and re-forming of friendship groups. The benefits of inter-racial contact would then be built on an equality that does not exist in current efforts at integration. It is precisely this sort of contact – in equal-status situations – which has been shown to break down stereotypes and prejudice. Given that sort of racial atmosphere the negative effects of inter-racial situations on black performance could also be mitigated.

Education and black British children

In the previous pages the research material comes entirely from work with black Americans. Very little of it, however, is specifically 'American' in the sense that it could only have originated there. Through the emphasis on 'caste' influences and deprived material conditions the bulk of the material could be translated into many cultural settings, given certain conditions: namely, the existence of a deprived ethnic or racial minority subject to prejudice and discrimination. And so the findings have an immediate relevance in a number of other inter-racial contexts, not least the situation of 'coloured' immigrants in Britain.

Some of the difficulties encountered by the principal immigrant groups in British schools are essentially cultural, although less a question of cultural *deprivation* than of the mis-match between the culture of the sending societies and that of the host community. To some extent these difficulties are being catered for. They have received recognition from the very beginning, probably because they present themselves in an immediate way through language difficulties, different customs and dress. In response, some special provisions have been made in the education system, for the Asian groups in particular, in the form of orientation and language classes. (Less obvious cultural differences, however, have received scant attention. For a long time West Indian children's *patois* was regarded simply as poor English when in fact it virtually qualifies as a foreign language in its relation to Standard English. Many children who actually needed to learn English almost as a second language only received help to 'improve' their 'bad English' which was not an adequate foundation for complex language skills.) As Townsend[54] has described:

In class [the West Indian child] finds his teacher partly intelligible, he is frequently corrected for speaking bad English although this is the way he and his parents have always spoken their language, and he receives little in the way of special help, although the Asians in his class disappear every day for extra English lessons.

However, the operation of caste distinctions and the ways they enter into the child's educational experience are much less tangible. As yet these influences have received no attention whatsoever in the British education system. Now it is obviously wrong to equate the British and American situations in a simple way and assume that our black children face exactly the same problems; but given the evidence of prejudiced attitudes and their effects on immigrant children, presented earlier, it does seem plausible that some of the processes described may also operate in our schools.

Bhatnagar's[55] recent study of secondary-school children in London showed some of these processes at work. He found immigrant children to be considerably less well-adjusted than English children:

The adjustment level appeared to be strongly related to the status given by the community to the group to which the child belonged. English children were found to be the most adjusted group followed by white immigrants (the Cypriots) with the black immigrants (the West Indians) coming a poor third.

Bhatnagar measured four aspects of adjustment – social acceptability, personal satisfaction, freedom from anxiety and objectivity of social concept – and calculated a mean adjustment score. The West Indian children were found to be the least socially acceptable in the eyes of the other children, the most anxious, and to have the least objective self-concepts. In 'personal satisfaction' the Cypriots and West Indians were not statistically distinguishable, but both scored very much lower than the English group. In the other tests the Cypriots (who qualify as immigrants, and culturally different, but not 'coloured') fell between the English and the West Indians. Nor were levels of adjustment related to the immigrants length of stay in this country, in fact 'a longer stay is just as likely to result in deterioration as in improvement in adjustment.

There also emerged a positive correlation between adjustment and academic achievement: that is, the less well-adjusted immigrant groups did less well on a variety of measures of attainment, I Q, and so on. While the vocational aspirations of the three groups were similar, the expectations of the immigrants were much lower than those of the English children.

Many of the influences described in the last chapter are illustrated in these findings; most important of all is the combination of low social status, low social acceptability, and personal satisfaction, high anxiety, coupled with low school attainment and low expectations, a syndrome with a familiar ring to it. In this country we might have expected cultural factors to be more influential than caste factors, whereas in America they appear to be more evenly balanced. Here we are dealing with the importation of alien culture patterns, rather than the culture of an indigenous minority. Bhatnagar's study, then, should alert attention to the effects of caste-status in British education, appearing in a context thought to be less severely stratified than America.

However, these influences are not entirely separable; they tend to interact and to reinforce one another. Hence in a *caste*-tinted atmosphere, the *culturally* 'different' may be perceived as inferior. This is harmful enough when applied to dress or customs, but has a more serious dimension when it extends to educational assessment. We have seen the effect of teachers' and others' expectations on the child's performance. Caste not only creates expectations of inferiority but colours the interpretation of actual performance. In this context it is easy for the unusual productions of a child from a different culture to be regarded as inferior (or the absence of production through lack of familiarity to be seen as deficiency). This sort of process may well lie behind the problem of West Indian language mentioned earlier. For in a climate of caste, of alien behaviour, discipline problems and learning difficulties, West Indian *patois* was all too easily seen as 'bad English' – that is, as *retarded* language symptomatic of backward children, rather than as normal children's *different* language. This was the result of several factors: (1) the superficial similarities of West Indian dialect and Standard English, (2) the notion of the children as 'culturally deprived' and therefore probably 'linguistically deprived', reinforced by (3) the relative lack of production of language *in the school situation* by West Indian children, particularly the younger ones, who were often withdrawn and silent. It is easy to see how, in the context of the overall picture of West Indian children as members of a lowly and deprived group, these mistakes were made.

But if we acknowledge that the first language of West Indian children is substantially different from Standard English – that it has a different lexis, phonology and syntax – we get a more realistic picture. The situation of a French child coming to an English school illustrates the point: he too would be silent and withdrawn initially, and his difficulties would also continue if he were given no specific instruction which took account of his first language and eased his transfer to the second. There are two points of difference with the West Indian child's situation: one is that the French child in this situation would not be seen as *backward* because of his linguistic difficulties; the second is that in the efforts of the West Indian child to acquire Standard English he suffers from *interference* between the first and second languages because of their surface similarities. In other words, he soon learns that some aspects are 'right' in both languages, and some are not, so that this is an additional source of confusion not suffered by our hypothetical French child, whose two languages are quite dissimilar. (An additional confusion comes from the influence of the local dialects of the child's white peers, which also differ from Standard English.)

It is more difficult to understand why it took us so long to wake up to these facts, when a few minutes' listening to West Indian children talking among themselves out of school makes it clear that they are equally articulate, that their language is very different from Standard English, but is equally complex, rich and descriptive, and communicationally efficient. But the problem is not simply one of teaching children who speak 'West Indian dialect' to use Standard English. Apart from differences between different islands, there are also differences in dialect within islands. For example, there is a continuum of dialects within Jamaica, from the most rural dialects at one extreme to the Jamaican 'Standard English' of the education system at the other (which is still different from 'English Standard English'). Different children will

have learnt different dialects, depending on their parents'
position on that continuum, *their* accommodation to English
speech patterns, the length of their stay here, and so on. And at
this end of the problem we have to recognize that there is a similar
continuum of dialects in Britain which includes Geordie, Scouse,
Brum and Cockney, all of which are far removed from Standard
English. But Standard English is held to be the *correct* form. So
as well as the individual issue with each West Indian child of
where on the (say) Jamaican continuum the child is located, we
have the wider issue of where, on our implicit continuum of
'correct' English, we wish to 'take' the child.

The general answer to the latter issue is that we should attempt
to provide the child with the kinds of spoken, and, particularly,
written language which will enable him to deal with all the situations that will confront him. In other words, as a form of Standard
English is the medium of instruction and assessment in the education system and the passport to higher-paid employment, we
are handicapping the child if we cannot give him this facility.
But the crucial issue is how this can be done without explicitly
or implicitly devaluing his own language. We have to explicate
the language situation: to teach about the *differences* in language,
not that one is 'right' and one is 'wrong', but that all are equally
valid. In other words, we have to depict the learning of different
forms of English *to the child* as a simple instrumental process of
acquiring the tools to do particular jobs, *not* as a process of
acquiring virtue.

With this perspective we can avoid the misunderstandings
(both on our part and the children's) that have surrounded the
issue for so long, and in particular the way connotations of inferiority and 'language difficulties' have reinforced each other.
'Caste influences' and 'language', separately and in interaction,
are the core issues in West Indian children's experience in
school. Both contribute more to attitudes and adjustment, the
expectations surrounding the children, and their achievements
(or lack of them) than any other factors, and yet there has been
very little attention to them. Chapter 7 deals with some specific
strategies that should be tried.

Assessment

The same sort of process operates in the testing of children's abilities. Ferron,[56] in his analysis of the intelligence test performance of 'coloured' children from many different parts of the world, concluded that

... As far as one can make out, poor test performance of coloured children is fundamentally the outcome of emotional and motivational problems involved in the assimilation of Western culture ... Where circumstances are such as to ensure that white and coloured groups share a common way of life and have equal educational opportunities differences are small or non-existent.

However, in this country, white and black groups do not have a common way of life, and while equality of opportunity exists in principle, the kinds of processes described earlier prevent its realization in practice. Not surprisingly, 'under-achievement' in school is a serious problem for immigrant children, West Indians in particular. Here, unspoken assumptions about the intellectual correlates of low caste disguise the role of cultural factors in performance, like the culture-bias of the tests, for example. Thus failure on tests which may be solely due to caste or cultural factors may be interpreted *in a caste climate* as evidence of intellectual inferiority. Culture-bias in tests operates in a variety of ways which are not at all obvious. Apart from the issues of bias in verbal tests because of language difficulty and in non-verbal tests through lack of familiarity with spatial relations, bias extends even to the concrete materials of the test – it has been pointed out that many children are simply unaccustomed to the use of pencils and paper as these seldom appear in their homes. Similar considerations apply to the ordinary week-by-week assessment of schoolwork. Where the society propagates a notion of a group's inferiority it is unreasonable to expect the teacher to be totally immune from it. Unwittingly, judgements are coloured and prophecies fulfilled. And even the social scientists' 'kinder' term, cultural *deprivation*, only adds to connotation of inferiority.

Certainly factors like culture-bias and caste-tinted assessment contribute to the disproportionate representation of West Indian children in schools for the educationally subnormal. For even

apparently 'culture-free' tests can discriminate against the minority child to some extent, but the resulting poor performance is
unremarkable if that is what is expected of a child from an
'inferior' group. Unless it is held that a group is genetically
inferior it is reasonable to say that poor performance of whole
groups and disproportionate ESN classification are simply
measures of inappropriate teaching and assessment.

Fortunately ESN classification only affects a minority of children. Less dramatic labelling occurs through 'streaming',
affecting the majority. Goldman and Taylor, in their survey of
immigrant educational problems,[57] point out that 'although
immigrant children are not being segregated, they are generally
in the 'C' streams or remedial classes because of their *linguistic
disabilities*' (my italics); they add: '. . . this may not be due to low
ability since few authorities have evaluated their ability levels.
Once in these streams, though, it may be difficult to avoid conforming to the achievement level of that stream. Jackson[58]
studied 660 schools in Britain and found that changes of stream
were very rare. Moreover, Douglas[59] found that over a three-
year period the relative attainments of the children in the upper
streams improved, while those of the children in the lower stream
deteriorated. So what may start off as a mis-assessment of ability
may become a self-fulfilling prophecy. This chain of events is
even more disturbing in the light of Goldman and Taylor's
hypothesis that immigrant children may have *above average*
potential in view of their parents' initiative and resourcefulness in
making the emigration.

*

So caste status creates a climate of inferiority around the child
which tends to assimilate other evidence to support it. This
picture structures the interpretation of quite unrelated aspects of
the child's behaviour to 'fit' with the overall evaluation. It goes
without saying that these are largely unconscious processes;
sometimes, however, they are given very explicit support. The
Jensen–Eysenck hypothesis of racial differences in intelligence is a
case in point. This gives quasi-scientific support to the notion
that certain disadvantaged racial minorities are innately intellec-

tually inferior to whites. Of course, this is a theory that the pre-judiced layman has held for years. And so it is naïve in the extreme to maintain, as the authors have done, that this hypothesis is proposed as pure social science with no political intention. This does not absolve them from some responsibility for the inevitable political *effects*, whatever their innocent motivations. A science of race relations does not exist in a social vacuum, and views such as these proposed by respected scientists are seized upon by the mass media and given wide exposure. Obviously they reinforce the idea of 'inferiority' associated with the minorities by giving it a scientific legitimacy; and all the processes we have described – teachers' low expectations, the misinterpretation of cultural differences, and, most of all, the belief in the significance of caste status – are intensified as a result. In this light the propagation of disputed hypotheses as scientific fact becomes far more reprehensible.

British policies

There is no uniform policy for the education of immigrant children in this country, a great deal being left to the discretion of the individual Local Education Authorities. Realization of the need to make special provision for immigrant children has lagged well behind the need itself. The range of LEA provisions, surveyed by Townsend[54] include the following:*

1. Reception centres which provide orientation and cultural adjustment together with basic training. The shock of migration on the child cannot be overestimated; in the space of two or three days many Asian children pass from peasant villages to the crowded classrooms of one of our nineteenth-century inner city schools, receiving any number of cultural and emotional jolts *en route*. It is no exaggeration to say that they move from one reality to an entirely different one. In this context the need for a cushioning phase before total immersion in the new situation seems ab-

*Note: British 'compensatory education' programmes will not be considered here, for they have not yet been adopted on a wide scale as LEA policy, many still being at the 'research and development' stage. Chazan (1973)[67] has recently reviewed their progress so far.

solutely essential, yet only two LEAs in England automatically pass all immigrant children through a reception centre.

2. Full- or part-time language centres, and full- or part-time language classes within normal schools. Because language difficulties have been identified as the immigrants' most pressing educational problem, more resources have been devoted to this aspect than to anything else. There is tremendous variation in the type of instruction given under each type of provision, some concentrating narrowly on linguistic competence, others giving extra tuition in other subjects in which the children are less advanced than native children. One of the main problems seems to be that, even when the focus of the effort is restricted to language teaching, it is difficult to adequately prepare the child for the language demands made on him, particularly at the secondary-school level. Although the child may be able to converse reasonably well, the more specialized subject vocabularies he will require to progress further in school demand the teaching of 'second stage English' as it has been called. It seems that very few authorities have tackled this. Further, the statistics confirm that the overwhelming majority of pupils in the language centres and classes are Asians, for the reasons we have discussed. The West Indians' language needs are not being adequately catered for, so that once again the LEA language provision seem to neglect an important part of their constituency.

3. A third policy is included under the official rubric of 'language provision', although it is arguable whether it should properly be so. This is the policy of *dispersal* of immigrant children from their own neighbourhoods into surrounding areas in order to reduce the proportion of immigrants in 'ghetto' schools. In the original Department of Education and Science circular describing the policy (DES Circular 7/65) it was depicted as partly a response to immigrant language difficulties, and the need to spread the load of extra teacher-attention needed to meet them. However, many people felt that the policy was more a capitulation to the fears and prejudices of white people who were concerned about supposed deterioration of educational standards or who simply opposed the idea of majority-black schools. Such anxieties were fanned during this period by those politicians lobbying for further immigration

control. There were some indications in the circular itself that the policy was directed to this group:

It will be helpful if the parents of non-immigrant children can see that practical measures have been taken to deal with the problem in the schools, and that the progress of their own children is not being restricted by the undue preoccupation of the teaching staff with the linguistic and other difficulties of the immigrant children ... it is to everyone's disadvantage if the problems within the school are allowed to become so great that they cause a decline in the general standard of education provided.

This explains why 'immigrant' children were dispersed, irrespective of whether they were immigrant or not, irrespective of whether they had language difficulties or not, including among them some West Indian children, who, in contrast to what we now know, were then thought *not* to have language difficulties of the same order as the Asians. In other words, the children were dispersed solely on the basis of colour, and despite some educational and social motives (like 'integration') the main purpose of the policy was to assuage white anxieties.

Much of the earlier discussion of de-segregation and 'bussing' in America applies here with equal force. The benefits of inter-racial schooling are mixed benefits, and we need not re-iterate the reasons for this. Even in areas which bus immigrant children this is acknowledged:[60]

When children are taken from their local environment by coach the integration which takes place at school can never be complete. Friendships formed at school cannot be followed up in the children's leisure hours. Children who come by coach are inclined to form groups within a school. If they also have a different language, culture or colour this danger is greatly increased. The immigrant children who are dispersed may experience a deeper sense of isolation from the native community than they would if they had remained in their neighbourhood school – even though that school might be almost all-immigrant.

'Bussing' also militates against the involvement of children in their own community, and formation of neighbourhood friendships, and against involvement of parents in the school. Some research on rural English children[61] showed that children who

travel long distances to school seem more prone to maladjustment; how much greater the damage in the case of black children
when they are made to travel great social and cultural distances
at the same time which necessarily involve a degree of alienation
from the home and the community.

Policies like dispersal institutionalize the recognition of the
disparity between the races. They allow that white people's wish
to remove immigrants from their neighbourhood schools is a
permissible sentiment; by actually implementing this desire they
confirm the immigrants' second-class status and officially endorse
the prejudice.

Of course, multi-racial education is the ideal. But, as we have
argued, this can only be successful on the basis of equality between
the races, which, here as in America, does not exist. Without it
all the pressures of caste and colour, working through prejudice,
rejection, and lowered expectations in the minds of teachers and
pupils, combine to damage the black child's performance, adjustment and fulfilment. Education authorities, schools and teachers
are only slowly realizing that these pressures operate in this
country also. Not surprisingly, then, there has been little official
acknowledgement of the effects of prejudice on the child's performance and adjustment, and even less action.

Bi-cultural education

The education of black children in this country must be *bi-cultural
education*; for so much of what has been written here points to the
protection against prejudice that a positive cultural identity
affords the child. This can best be fostered in schools within his
own community; dispersal dilutes this process and denies the
child the security of his own neighbourhood. Black children have
sufficient educational hurdles in their way without removing
those basic sources of support and security that all other children
enjoy. So neighbourhood schooling is a prerequisite, whatever
concentrations of black children in individual schools might
result. The only obstacle to this is white people's attitudes and
anxieties about large concentrations of black people in one place,
be it schools or residential areas. But there is nothing wrong with

black ghettos – apparently acceptable white ones exist all over the world – only *poor* black ghettos, which is an entirely different issue. So these anxieties should not be allowed to dictate educational policy, to the detriment of black children. For there are some advantages in all-black or majority-black schools, educationally speaking, as we have seen from the American programmes. Further, they would allow the full development of bi-cultural education, which must of necessity entail radically different methods and curricula from the ordinary school.

What would these methods be, indeed what would be the philosophy of bi-cultural education? By defining this we can see, by contrast, how inadequately ordinary schools are geared to the needs of the immigrant child. *Bi-cultural schools* (or indeed multi-cultural schools) *must assume the equality of the two cultural elements, not dilute one and enhance the other*. English and immigrant cultures are not equally valued in ordinary schools, for as institutions of the majority culture they embody that culture. It must no longer be assumed that English language and culture are 'correct' and more valuable; rather they should be regarded simply as a means to successful participation in this society, much as English people regard the learning of a foreign language. Reciprocally, the violence that has geen done to the languages and cultures of the homelands must be repaired. They are not 'deficits' and 'handicaps' to be 'overcome' in the struggle to absorb their English equivalents, but *positive* resources of vitality and creativity. There may be a case for providing instruction in both English *and* immigrant languages, for all pupils. This is one way of increasing communication between pupils and between teachers and pupils, but most importantly it serves to acknowledge the worth of the immigrant languages and cultures. Equal weight should be accorded to immigrant cultures as to English culture in the teaching of history, geography, art, literature, and every other subject. In the primary school the potential for including bi-cultural materials in learning to read and write, number work, art, and drama is enormous. Of course, there will be no tangible benefit from the single instance of a child learning to read about chapattis rather than cats on mats; but cumulatively the endorsement of his own culture by its inclusion in books, teaching

204 Children and Race

materials – indeed in the whole life of the school – must confirm its value in the eyes of the child. This in contrast to the present situation, where the disparity between the culture of the home and the school forces the child to choose between his parents' values and school values, or somehow resolve the two.

After the age of five the school socializes the child for the majority of the day. At present the black child spends the greater part of his waking hours in a place which does nothing to confirm him in an important aspect of his identity. Effectively, he is treated as an English child, albeit a 'coloured' one, and one with certain 'disadvantages'. His own cultural originality is almost entirely ignored, so that he only receives that sense of himself from his parents out of school hours. The bi-cultural school can preserve a continuity, so that the child does not effectively shed his background at the school gate. Many educationists acknowledge the need for such schools but find it difficult to imagine how they could be run in the context of current educational practices and resources. Let us, then, describe the main features and innovations of a bi-cultural community school.

School and community

If the children are to draw strength and support from their own community there must be traffic between the two. It is not sufficient to restrict this to out-of-school hours; there are many ways in which parents and other adults can enrich the normal activities of the school, and in which the school can contribute to community life. First of all, anyone who has worked in largely immigrant schools knows that the children need extra adult attention above all else. Only convention and the insecurities of teachers stand in the way of parents participating in the classroom. Not only will this improve the adult-to-child ratio, but, more importantly, bring persons belonging to the children's own cultural and racial groups into the classroom. Nor need they only assist teachers. Within most communities there is a wealth of talent covering every conceivable ability; let those abilities, interests and crafts be brought into the classroom by parents and other adults and taught to the children during school hours or through clubs and societies afterwards; and let them take the children out into the community to see their workplaces and other activities, so that they understand every facet of their environment. Many adults are shy of speaking publicly to other adults, but most can chat to children at a level they understand about the things they do or their hobbies. Even the most mundane jobs can be fascinating when described by someone who is suddenly cast in the role of an expert or has an enthusiasm for a skill or craft pursued in his spare time. In this way the ordinary members of the community – shopworkers, nurses, busmen, labourers, industrial workers, craftsmen, doctors, railwaymen – will be a familiar part of the school life. And outside their own working hours they can supervise clubs and societies – for other adults as well as the children – around their other interests. The busman who can teach woodwork or guitar or coach sports is contributing to the education of his own and other people's children and at the same time receiving recognition from the community.

In other words, we are leading towards a more general idea of the school as a focus of activities or community centre. For this labels the school as *theirs*, not somehow belonging to teachers from outside, 'The Council' who, as often as not, are associated with establishment attitudes, bureaucracy and obstruction, and the indignities of Social Security, rent debts, and the like. In this way whole families or parts of them can participate in activities together, whether it be craft work, dance, films, talks, sports clubs or simply social meeting, which is the core of any community life. It could also integrate a number of adult concerns like housing, tenants' associations, political groups, legal advice, family-planning services, which would further aid the social education of the children. All in all, parents could become as normal a part of the school landscape as the children themselves, in and out of school time. For this degree of participation to work and continue working the school would have to be the community's school in a very real sense; for the organization of all these activities from the human resources in the community would be beyond the average headmaster's time and energy. In other words, it would require that the school and all its activities were governed and controlled by community representatives and teaching staff working together. Immigrant parents and children would then develop a far more positive orientation towards a school in which they had a voice.

Teaching methods and materials

We have dealt briefly with some of the ways in which schools can be made genuinely bi-cultural. It takes very little imagination to put this into practice once we accept that these will be special schools and will be outside the mainstream of LEA educational policy. Even the fabric of the school can be made more appropriate by sacrificing the 'institutional pastel' paintwork to multi-coloured traditional decorative arts. This can extend to furniture also, dispensing with it completely if desired. Desks often only serve to make a space look 'like a proper classroom' when large painting areas, maths areas, book corners and simple chairs for the children would be less restrictive.

As we have suggested, equal weight should be accorded to both English and immigrant languages and cultures. There is no reason why many teaching materials cannot be produced in parallel, using both languages. Obviously there will be a need for many more teachers fluent in immigrant languages and dialects, but here again parent participation can play an important part. Interpreting the teacher's words and interpreting the children's words to the teacher is one example of this. The teacher and children learn each other's language simultaneously and the shared difficulties will do much to increase empathy and the acceptance of each culture by each other. Needless to say, quite apart from the medium and materials of instruction there are numerous opportunities for culturally relevant content. Every opportunity for developing knowledge about the children's homelands can be utilized, through project work, films, wall-displays and so on. Here again supplementary help from parents and other adults will be invaluable. They can impart first-hand knowledge, teach traditional crafts, cookery, and help to interpret music, dance, drama, literature and art from their own culture.

Some schools already make efforts to draw on the cultural

traditions of their children; but too often this is an occasional thing, produced for special events like Open Days, not a part of the everyday life of the school. Too many schools and teachers retain a slight suspicion of the unfamiliar cultural ways of their pupils, and have neither the knowledge nor the will to use them as a positive educational resource. The teaching of comparative religion and music, even at a very simple level, are examples of the way this sort of approach could enrich the multi-cultural school beyond anything possible in ordinary schools.

One final aspect of the life and atmosphere of the school which is related to teaching methods is the question of discipline. It seems clear from what has already been said that the whole ethos of the multi-cultural school will not be served well by authoritarian teacher–child relationships. For many teachers in immigrant schools the disciplined classroom is the last defence against the tidal wave of energy and disobedience which, they feel, always threatens to engulf them. Some manage to enforce a quiet classroom, but at considerable cost to the spirit of the child. First of all, many of the children come from overcrowded homes where parents must keep them quiet for their own sanity; often children leave school in the afternoon to be confined indoors until their parents return from work, because of the traffic danger in inner-city areas. Others have spent several of their pre-school years in crowded child-minding establishments. Finally, parental discipline may be harsh and erratic, giving rise to frustration and resentment. With this backdrop it is hardly surprising that children confined within small classrooms in schools hemmed in by main roads feel frustrated and often aggressive. To overcome this natural upsurge of energy requires very repressive methods indeed, which by now should be anathema to all teachers. It should be unthinkable to destroy the spirit of any child, but particularly these children. However successful our attempts at multi-cultural education, the society at large will be stacked against the black child for a long time to come; he will need every ounce of resilience and initiative he can muster if he is to secure his rights and fulfil his potential in the face of this opposition. Authoritarian methods will only stamp this out of him. Bi- or multi-cultural schools can make 'free' classrooms work successfully because of the child's greater involvement and identification with the materials and activities than normal. They are in a real sense 'his', and if the battle for quiet and 'obedience' is abandoned both the teacher's and the child's energies can be directed towards the learning experience. Every teacher knows this can happen when the activity in hand *attracts* the child, generating *self*-discipline. This does not solve the problem of the child's accumulated frustrations, although it will draw on some of the energy generated. For this we need to recognize the value of adventure playgrounds and provide them within the school to be used during schooltime. Not only would the children learn construction and measurement and much else besides, but they would be able to live out some of the very real frustrations of the home and the classroom.

Teachers

Clearly the demands made on teachers in such a school will be very great indeed. We need, then, a special kind of teacher to cope with them. Possibly it is unreasonable to expect the present generation of teachers in immigrant schools to have an expert command of the knowledge and techniques required of them. The problems of immigrant schools are a fairly recent development in the careers of older teachers, and there has been little in the way of special training in the colleges for the young teachers. The result is that the teacher knows little more of the cultural backgrounds of her pupils than the average person in the street. But coupled with this is a social ignorance – of the realities of prejudice and discrimination in the society at large or in the classroom itself. It is not necessary to be familiar with the latest research findings, one would have thought, to be able to imagine the effects of prejudice on black children. And yet many teachers are unaware of these things, and persist in using books which portray people like their own pupils in the most derogatory and caricatured way. We will return to this topic in the final chapter.

It is essential that teachers in bi-cultural schools receive special training, so that they can be given all the knowledge they will require. They might also get a glimpse of the immigrant's reality, his view of the world, if they were seconded to live and work in inner city areas during their training. However, instruction will not be sufficient. There are certain qualities of 'natural' teachers which it is very difficult to teach to others; security, warmth, originality, empathy, resilience, self-confidence tempered by humility, authority without authoritarianism, and so on. It is necessary to attract these teachers to bi-cultural schools, for all those talents will be drawn on to the full. To some extent this will happen naturally as people of this type gravitate towards the atmosphere of stimulation and innovation in such schools: the process could be helped by financial inducements, for many 'naturals' have no choice but to apply for higher-paid posts like headships in order to support their own families, and are lost to classroom teaching. Higher pay for bi-cultural school teachers would rectify this and also give status to the school and the jobs.

Above all else we need black teachers; not just for their cultural knowledge and skills but their racial knowledge also – their experience of what it is like to be black in a prejudiced society. Their role and person would embody the contradiction of stereotypes, achieve the respect of white children and combat *their* prejudice, and serve as models with whom black children could unequivocally identify. This does not mean black versions of white teachers, although even this would be an improvement. It means teachers who can really identify with the children, who can understand their experience and validate it from their own lives; who can explain their conflicts and help them to feel positively about themselves and their brothers; and most of all, who can instil the values and sense of identity which will equip the child not to accept this predicament but to confront it. These will inevitably not be white middle-class values, for while these would ease the child's passage into an integrated society, that option is not open to him. So long as discrimination keeps the door closed, to encourage these values in black children involves duplicity. For the very acceptance of these values requires some sacrifice of identity and cultural distinctiveness, a kind of psychological burning of boats behind one. It leaves the child in a no-man's land, having denied his origins and being denied his goal.

The educational obstacles in the way of black people becoming teachers are very great; few will be able to meet the academic qualifications required for teacher-training. But there are many roles within bi-cultural schools which do not require academic skills, given a certain amount of specialist training. Ideally bi-cultural education should begin at the age children are ready for play-groups, these being run within the school premises, continuing through 'nursery' and 'infant' stages in a continuous induction into full bi-cultural education in the primary school. Clearly there is ample scope here for able black people who simply lack paper qualifications. In the longer perspective, adult education (with the help of evening classes in community schools) and reforms within mainstream education (of 'labelling' processes like streaming, misinterpretation of cultural differences, and self-fulfilling expectations) will allow more black people into all types of teaching jobs.

The priority for bi-cultural education is the first ten years of life when the foundations of racial attitudes and self-attitudes are laid down; but it should continue into the secondary school years, also. Ideally community schooling should continue throughout the child's educational career, but comprehensives drawing on large catchment areas preclude this. In any case there are sound arguments for more integrated schooling once the child is secure in his identity and self-esteem and is fulfilling his educational potential. However, there is even more reason for importing the ethos and methods of bi-cultural education into secondary schools, for here they will benefit black and white children alike. This is not a hypothetical or over-idealistic suggestion, for educational experiments of this type are already working successfully in America, notably in Philadelphia.

It goes without saying that bi-cultural education on the scale envisaged here will be expensive. There are two answers to this objection. The first is that the benefit to the whole society of bi-cultural, tolerant, fulfilled individuals cannot conceivably be measured in monetary terms. The second is that if all social policy must be conceived in these terms, let us be clear that this expenditure will not even repay the *interest* on our colonial debt to the immigrant homelands, let alone the debt itself.

7 Education against Prejudice

In the last chapter the primary concern was the education of black children. Now we shall broaden the scope to include the education of white majority-group children, for two reasons: because these children require education in the broadest sense for citizenship within a multi-racial society, and because many of the problems that black children face are imposed by prejudiced white attitudes.

We have argued that parents transmit a particular view of the world in socializing their children, which includes their racial attitudes. When these views are shared by the child's peers and perhaps even his teachers, it means that his entire personal and social environment is tainted in the same way. Where prejudice is intense, racial attitudes are 'in the air' surrounding the child. In this context it is clear that the child has little chance to develop anything but the same attitudes. Given that aggregate of pressures, it seems naïvely optimistic to suggest that school curricula can do very much to counteract this development. Anything other than wholesale changes in adult attitudes (a topic which falls outside the scope of this book) can only scratch the surface of the problem. But there are nevertheless sound arguments for doing everything possible to educate for 'tolerance', even though it seems a long-term strategy, against impossible odds. It is after all only about ten years from beginning primary school to leaving secondary school, so 'education' is not such a long-term solution as is often thought. In the urgency to 'do something', *now* rather than adopt a longer-term approach, we may forget that the children who were starting school when Commonwealth immigration really began are now twenty; had they received some education in 'tolerance' or multi-cultural education, they would be rather more likely to hand on positive attitudes to the generation of children they are now raising.

On the other hand, what is quite wrong is to see education as a panacea; to see it as a substitute for action against discrimination and institutional racism in the wider society. Nor must this action be focused narrowly on overt discrimination. We have to define racial attitudes and behaviour more widely – to include acquiescence in racism, by *acceptance* of inequality, exploitation and devaluation, in which the whole society is implicated.

Race in schools

Certainly one of the biggest obstacles to introducing a more enlightened approach to multi-racial education has been the reluctance of many teachers to admit that 'race' exists as a problem. During the course of the research reported in Chapter Four, I naturally visited many multi-racial schools. While receiving the utmost cooperation, I was told on many occasions that, while I was welcome to conduct my experiments, I was unlikely to find any prejudice as all the children played quite happily together, got on well, even loved one another. Many children undoubtedly do, which is encouraging. But even relatively short periods of observation in the classrooms and playgrounds threw up scores of examples of racial insults and conflicts: 'black bastard', 'Paki-rubbish', and 'jungle-bunny' are common taunts, and when they are introduced into the normal, unimportant playground scuffles between groups of boys, they alter the whole basis of the conflict. Ranks close along racial lines and a trivial incident is escalated into something quite different; it may die down equally quickly, but hostility has been aroused which will taint other contacts, and so on. Invariably children from classrooms that teachers considered happy and 'integrated' evidenced no less hostility on my attitude tests than any others. It seems that many teachers ignore or are simply unaware of 'prejudice' in children. Why should this be?

For a long time it could have been argued that teachers, like many other people, were relatively unaware of the strength of prejudice in the society at large, and were certainly not looking for it in their own classroom; however, for some years now this should not have been the case. In addition their natural goodwill to their children would militate against interpreting their behaviour in this unfavourable way. In other words, they would tend to *not* look at behaviour as being 'prejudiced', if at all possible. Most important, I think, is the factor mentioned earlier, which is related to this: a lingering belief in the 'innocence' of the child. Of course it is unpalatable to impute sentiments like prejudice to young children; and at face value it *would* seem that the child is not intellectually mature enough to assess a complex social issue like 'race' and work out his attitude towards it, prejudiced or otherwise. But as we saw in Chapter 2, this sophisticated process is not necessary. The child need only learn the concepts 'black' and 'white', and concepts like 'bad' and 'good', and marry them to people in the same way as his parents do. So far from the issues being complex, the child only has to grasp some of the simplest concepts that exist, and which are taught to him from infancy. Having picked them up, he may use them without full understanding of their implications, and their likely effect on black children – in other words, without really 'meaning' them. He may use adult racial insults simply to appear adult. But having done so, and set off an angry reaction in a black class-mate, he is called on to defend his action – perhaps physically defend himself. So he now has an emotional investment in those sentiments, because he has to 'stick up' for them. At the same time, the black child's angry response, if not actually confirming the content of the insult, still adds fuel to the white child's feeling of hostility against him. This is just one of the ways in which *knowledge* of adult racial attitudes and stereotypes (without the child actually *feeling* those attitudes) becomes converted into a situation where the child becomes aligned with them *emotionally*. When they are expressed in his behaviour, they tend to be confirmed, both by the act of expressing them 'in public' and by the reactions they elicit from other children. This is a spiral process which may result in all three elements of racial attitudes – the 'cognitive' or information aspects, the 'affective' aspect or feelings, and the behavioural aspects – becoming firmly established, as each element 'tows' the others.

Parents and fellow-pupils are not solely responsible for children picking up prejudiced attitudes. It has to be said that both teachers and teaching materials *can* introduce or reinforce prejudice. This is not an indictment of the entire teaching profession, but of a small minority of teachers who are themselves prejudiced against black people. I may have been unfortunate in my experiences, but I have been too frequently horrified by staff-room conversations to feel that this minority is unimportant. In a non-immigrant school, for example, a small group of teachers expressed some dismay at a news photograph of African statesmen arriving for the Commonwealth Prime Ministers' Conference. The reason was the age-old puerile stereotype of Africans being unable to read or write, having just emerged 'from the trees'. Possibly only a joke in bad taste, but still not the sort of remark that unprejudiced people make; perhaps worse, it was received without censure. It may be unreasonable to expect teachers to be any less prejudiced than the society from which they are drawn; it is none the less distressing to find overt prejudice among people who have such influence over young children, white or black. In immigrant schools their effect may be more harmful. Some totally unsuitable teachers find themselves in this situation through changes in the school population, promotion, and so on. One master, promoted from outside to a position of some influence in a 70 per cent immigrant school referred to his new post as 'teaching down in the jungle', and even in his more humane moments could only see it as 'missionary work'. In planning the school camp, he pressed for regular kit inspections as a precaution against petty theft; when assured that this was not necessary, he suggested that 'that depends on how many Pakis we take'. It may be a coincidence that white children in his class took to wiping paper towels on hair of Asian children to wipe off some of their hair-oil, and threatening other children with them – to 'contaminate' them by touch. That perhaps it was not a coincidence is suggested by the Asian children 'getting back' at him: several of them passed scrawled notes between themselves, each one being duly confiscated. The game was continued just until the teacher in question confiscated an apparently harmless note, only to find his hand wet. The ostentatiously passed note had been covertly but thoroughly chewed beforehand, and was covered in saliva – and

Asian saliva at that. What price racial differences in intelligence ? Hopefully he was an isolated and extreme example; but less obviously derogatory stereotypes have a wider currency among teachers than we like to imagine.

The important point is that rudimentary prejudices flourish and are absorbed even in the classrooms of unprejudiced teachers. One example crystallizes most of what has been said in this book. On the introduction of some new children into a 'liberal' classroom, several children (including the *Indian* girls in the class) were heard to say 'Oh no, not more Indians.'

Were teachers more aware of these things, they might exercise more care in their choice of classroom materials, in their use of language and in examining their own unwitting biases. There is a resistance to each of these. Partly it is habit and lack of imagination – an inability to 'take the role of the other' and imagine the feelings of the black children – but it is also a hangover from an earlier attitude in British race relations – that to acknowledge race was to somehow discriminate oneself. If one was 'colour-blind' and 'tried to treat everyone as equals', by refusing to recognize the problems, they would go away of their own accord. It is now clear that more positive steps have to be taken, that goodwill is not a guarantee against all manner of biases, misperceptions, and expectations of racial groups, and that to ignore the problems is to allow them to continue unchecked. Perhaps the best examples of this are our taken-for-granted, well-tried teaching materials. Many of our best-loved children's books display archaic racial and international attitudes which would never have emerged but for this long overdue pressure towards examination of ourselves and our cultural values.

Children's literature

Perhaps children's literature should not really be separated from the mainstream of English literature, or should be seen in that context. In dealing with black people there remains a significant residue of stereotypes from colonial times, in the tradition described in Chapter 1. In dealing more generally with the colours black and white there is a continuing reflection of cultural colour-

values, in the association of darkness with bad things, evil, wicked-
ness, threat and fear; and whiteness with purity, goodness,
desirability and so on. Marshment's[1] analysis of current adult
fiction bears this out:

> Sometimes [stereotypes] are blatantly vicious, as in Monserrat's
> work, where the African's are presented as savage primitives; some-
> times they are used paternally, like Fleming's definition of James
> Bond's relationship with the Cayman Islander – 'that of a Scots
> laird to his head stalker'; or less explicitly the childlike devotion of the
> 'Negro' to the heroine of *The L-shaped Room*.

In children's literature it's very much the mixture as before,
but often even more out of date: the spirit of Biggles lives on! In
fact, examples are quite hard to find; this well illustrates one of
the major shortcomings of children's books, the virtual omission
of black people. In the case of schoolbooks, Walters has pointed
out that minority racial groups suffer as a consequence: 'The
acceptance of white skin as associated with all that is important
enough to be in books, pictures and "school-learning" tends to
be an unconscious rejection of a child's own colour'.[2] Dorothy
Kuya,[3] writing in a similar vein, talks on the 'humiliation' of the
child whose group is ignored in this way. Not only is the child
deprived of the 'recognition' of his group by the book and by his
classmates, but also of figures with whom he can identify. Although it is only the black child who literally suffers from this
situation, it is also detrimental in a wider sense to white children.
For an unrealistic picture of everyday life is presented which
does not acknowledge the existence of an important minority in
this country; and these children may also latch on to the fact that
black people are not important enough to be included in 'proper
books'. So this must be the first criterion by which we evaluate
children's literature: whether black people are included at all.

The second criterion is whether they are portrayed, explicitly
or implicitly, in a derogatory way. This operates in two ways:
through the disproportionate selection of dark figures for 'bad'
roles, and secondly the attribution of bad characteristics to people
because they are members of a particular racial or national group.
Overlapping with this is a third criterion, which concerns the use
of stereotypes. Stereotypes may be artificially bad, good or

neutral. But they are all bad in the sense that they exaggerate the differences between groups of human beings, and the uniformity within them. While this makes for ease in categorizing people, it distracts attention from the characteristics and experiences which are common to all people, and which *could* be portrayed as a bond between them, and from the huge variation in personality and life-style between individuals within any one of these groups. There is a 'kernel of truth' in many of these stereotypes, or there was once. But they are usually generations out of date, or refer to minorities within the races or nationalities concerned, or practices which are a profoundly *un*important part of their lives. It would be easy indeed to emerge from a childhood spent with some of these books, believing that Africans seldom emerge from the jungle, Chinese men wear pigtails, and that French men (who affect droopy moustaches and dress only in striped jerseys and and black berets) dine exclusively on frogs and snails.

Mary Waddington, who has reached a similar conclusion, describes how many books introduce 'foreign' people through

a romantic and entertaining fantasy of ancient heroes or quaint but abandoned customs. So many books, pictures and films show the unusual and quaint aspects of life in other countries, and children are left with the idea that *all* Dutch children wear clogs, and all Eskimos live in igloos, despite Rotterdam being one of the most modern cities in the world, and Eskimos probably using more helicopters than we in Britain do.[4]

British books, inevitably, view the rest of the world from a British perspective; the quaintness of these images underlines their *differences*. These people deviate from an unspoken norm: the customs, habits and values which constitute the British way of life. Deviation from the 'normal' very often connotes inferiority, as Kozol[5] explains:

It was not that we were told anything was wrong with looking odd or peculiar but simply that we were made to feel, beyond possibilities of redemption, that this 'oddness', this 'differentness', this 'peculiarity' is something from which we can feel ourselves indescribably lucky to have been spared. It is the inexorable quality of differentness which seems so evil here. A bitter little perjury is perpetrated upon

children even before they are old enough to understand exactly why
it is that things that are made to seem so different, strange and peculiar,
are precisely the things which it is easiest to despise.

To summarize these considerations, Gambs[6] has suggested a
number of questions we should ask of the literature we give to
children:

Are minority-group members portrayed as persons to whom the
audience would be sympathetic? Are minority-group members
valued for human qualities? Are undesirable characters (gangsters,
crooks, etc.) portrayed as minority-group members? Are minority
individuals shown in typical roles only (Negroes as porters, servants,
etc.)?

To which we should add the most important question: 'Are they
portrayed as *individuals* (whose group membership is irrelevant)
doing *ordinary*, *unremarkable* things, displaying the normal range
of human characteristics (not special racial or national ones),
who *happen* to be members of a minority-group?'

We will look briefly at a few examples culled from a selection of
books widely available to children. All of them are the work of
authors who, in the estimation of a city librarian, are among the
most popular and frequently read. Although Charles Kingsley's
Water Babies is a well-loved and apparently harmless children's
story, it is a good example of how we accept children's classics
uncritically and pass on some malignant stereotypes in the process. Listen to Kingsley's description of Dennis, an imaginary but
typical Irishman:

You must not trust Dennis, because he is in the habit of giving
pleasant answers: but, instead of being angry with him, you must
remember that he is a poor Paddy, and knows no better; so you must
just burst out laughing; and then he will burst out laughing too, and
slave for you, and trot about after you, and show you good sport if he
can – for he is an affectionate fellow, and as fond of sports as you are
– and if he can't, tell you fibs instead, a hundred an hour; and wonder
all the while why poor ould Ireland does not prosper like England and
Scotland, and some other places, where folk have taken up a ridiculous
fancy that honesty is the best policy.[7]

If that passage at least has a gloss of patronizing warmth, consider
this one where Kingsley describes how 'young ladies walk about

with lockets of Charles the First's hair (or of somebody else's when the Jew's genuine stock is used up)'. Similarly, even C. D. Lewis's apparently benign adventure-stories contain an incident where some boys pawn some toys and describe their meagre payment from the shopkeeper as having been 'Jewed'.[8]

Stereotypes of Frenchmen, whale-eating Eskimos, clog-ridden Dutchmen, and dour penny-pinching Scotsmen abound. Further afield, aliens come in for more exotic treatment; in fact there seems to be a direct relationship between the distance from England of a particular nation, and their potential for bizarre, savage or comic treatment by the author. Arthur Ransome shipwrecks some of his characters off the coast of China. One of their Chinese captors claims to:

> Talkee English velly good. You Melican Missee? Melican boy? ... Chang is a velly gleedy man. Chang wants to get lich quick ... He will make Lord Mayor San Flansisco lite a letter to Amelica.

Naturally all the Chinamen have pigtails and long twisted moustaches, while the women have strapped feet. With the exception of Missee Lee, who was educated in England, they are all shown to be stupid and petty. While the men work, 'Their yellow bodies were naked to the waist ... "like yellow frogs", whispered Roger.'

This brings us on to the treatment of racial as opposed to national groups. First of all let us look at the treatment of 'black' and 'white' as colours which are rich in connotative meaning. They are repeatedly used as descriptive devices to convey atmosphere, mood, threat, human characteristics, morality and to enlist the support of the reader for good over bad. Often characters are 'coloured' in this way to distinguish the goodies and the baddies, Right and Wrong, or most unfortunately, Us and Them. As Kozol[5] remarks:

> Once upon a time there was a woman who had two daughters. One of them was beautiful but the other was ugly ... When you read this ... you know, even before you look, which daughter is going to have yellow hair, and which one will have dark hair.

Like, for example, Marusia, heroine of one fairy-tale of Williams-Ellis's: 'She was a beauty that girl; Marusia the Fair they called her. Her skin was as white as milk ... And what's more, Marusia was as kind and good-natured as she was pretty.'[10] But Charles Kingsley, once again provides the best example of the polarity of black and white. *The Water Babies* is a moral tale of Ellie, 'a clean white, good little darling' of a wealthy family, and Tom, a little chimney sweep. When he enters her room by mistake,

... The room was all dressed in white; white window-curtains, white bed-curtains, white furniture and white walls, with just a few lines of pink here and there ... Under the snow-white coverlet, upon the snow-white pillow, lay the most beautiful little girl that Tom had ever seen. Her cheeks were almost as white as the pillow, and her hair was like threads of gold spread all about the bed ... [Tom] stood staring at her as if she had been an angel out of heaven ... Looking around, he suddenly saw standing close to him, a little ugly, black, ragged figure, with bleared eyes and grinning white teeth. He turned on it angrily. What did such a black ape want in that sweet young lady's room? It was himself reflected in a great mirror.

This symbolic black/white, bad/good theme recurs monotonously throughout the book. Were that not enough, the final associative link is made with black *races* when Tom talks to a family of 'heathens'. They are very stupid and call on a Powwow man to attend their son, who 'rattled, thumped, brandished his thunder-box, yelled, shouted, raved, roared, stamped and danced corry-borry like any black fellow'.

It is too easy to write off these moral tales as archaic and some-how unimportant; to the author's certain knowledge this book is still used in certain multi-racial schools. It takes little imagination to empathize with the immigrant child whose only experience of story-characters who are anything like him, takes this form. Somewhere between the symbolic representation of 'black' and 'white' people and the *actual* portrayal of different races comes the nearly-human 'Golliwogg'. His adventures were originally written in 1900 (by B. and F. Upton); they were inexplicably resurrected in 1967.[11] Golliwogg himself is a ludicrous caricature (see inside the back cover of this book), but the traditional association with black people makes him a more serious influence than he appears. In one of his adventures, the authors manage

to cram *all* the stereotypes of black people into the scenario.
Golliwogg, the laughing crying rubber-lipped nigger minstrel
figure, finds himself in Africa, where he is surrounded by – wait
for it – savage cannibals:

> A fearful tribe of cannibals
> All armed with weapons grim,
> Brandish their spears
> And spite of tears
> Prepare to finish him.

It is said of their kind (and, needless to say, the scalp is not
Golliwogg's):

> This scalp so fair
> He longs to wear –
> Such trophies he holds dear.

Many other stories furnish examples of African savagery,
cannibalism, primitive rites, exotic headgear and clothes, or lack
of them; where stereotypes are not so derogatory, they invariably
stress the simple-minded backwardness and uncultured life
styles of Africans. This shades into the image of the slave-like
'Uncle Tom' figure, happy and lazy, loafing and finger-clicking,
abounding with natural rhythm – the patronizing stereotype of the
American Negro. And, of course, where black Americans do enter
into children's literature this is precisely the treatment they
receive. Two examples stand out: *Nicodemus and His New Shoes*[12]
and the *Little Black Sambo* books[13] (see inside the front cover).
Both depict in words and pictures black people (and perhaps
most damagingly, black children) as laughable doll-like figures,
who speak with music-hall Negro dialects: Nicodemus opines:
'Lawdy lan', if you don't hole dat chile by de han', she is boun'
to git into trouble.' And the children sing a 'characteristic' song:
'I got shoes, you got shoes, All o'God's Chill-un got shoes'.

It may be argued that this is too fine a dissection, and young
children really don't pick up these objectionable overtones. And
some teachers have introduced these series into multi-racial
classrooms for the best reasons, believing that some portrayal of
black figures in books is better than none at all. One can only cite

the experience of a teacher who did this – to find that a child in his class with slightly Afro-styled hair was frequently taunted with the insult 'Little black Sambo'. The story books for slightly older children seem, if anything, worse. They have more scope for travel adventures, more sophisticated ways of describing people's behaviour and so on, which *could* be used to present a more balanced picture than the simpler books for the very young. Instead, stereotyping is just as common, but more elaborate and richer in detail. We are hard put to find examples where books include black people but do not belittle them in one or other of the ways we have discussed.

H. Lofting's Doctor Dolittle* books are among the worst offenders (and among the most popular of children's books). The author feels free to pass on 'adult' racial insults like 'darkies', 'work like niggers', 'coon'; and he puts the following words into the mouth of his character Prince Bumpo (and one can predict, correctly, from his name that he will be dark-skinned and large-lipped):

'White man, I am an unhappy prince. Years ago I went in search of the Sleeping Beauty, whom I had read of in a book . . . I at last found her . . . she awoke. But when she saw my face she cried out "Oh, he's black!" And she ran away and wouldn't marry me . . . If you would turn me white, so that I may go back to the Sleeping Beauty, I will give you half my kingdom and anything else besides.'[14]

The Prince would like blue eyes too; for a time his face is turned 'white as snow, and his eyes, which had been mud-coloured, were a manly grey'. Just to hammer the message home, one of his actions is met with the remark: 'Serve him right, if he does turn black again! I hope it's dark black.'

This sort of material is quite indefensible. It is no exaggeration

---

*It is sometimes argued that the older examples cited here are no longer influential and therefore irrelevant to the debate; children do not read them any more. To take three examples cited so far, Kingsley's *Water Babies* was recently reprinted in a glossy paperback edition, Dr Dolittle's adventures sell upwards of 25,000 copies annually, while *Little Black Sambo* is now in its eighteenth printing (since 1899); the latest (1972) edition is an 'improved' and enlarged version with even a cardboard cut-out model of Black Mumbo and Black Jumbo's favourite son.

to call it racism, albeit in an apparently innocent form. Can there by any doubt that passages like this foster the same feelings in black children who read them – shame over blackness, a desire to be white – sentiments which are echoed in these same children's reactions to the tests described in Chapter 4? And of course they are an open encouragement to prejudice in white children.

Stories which, unlike Dr Dolittle, involve real people, not fantastic figures, should be carefully scrutinized as they come closest to reality. The indefatigable Biggles is only the most famous, or infamous, example of a whole genre. Adventure stories for boys instilling the values of manhood and courage, require dangerous situations with which to confront their heroes. By the same token, their adversaries must be instantly recognizable as brutal and wicked men simply by virtue of their appearance. What better recipe for racial stereotyping? Thus the white men in Foster's *Dragon Island* encounter a tribe of 'the ugliest savages ever created'. On hearing war-drums,

... They [the British] imagined the scenes in the village; the natives, their naked bodies glistening in the firelight; the old man seated by the tom-tom, thumping incessantly; spitting flares, lighting up a ring of cruel faces.[15]

When they are not savage they are merely simple, with child-like pleasures, easily bought by the more intelligent white men:

'I have promised them a stick of tobacco each if they have a meal ready by the time we get there,' explained the hunter with a grin. 'If I know anything about Malays we shall find a feast.'

But Biggles, from his sheer volume of adventure and unrivalled popularity, should have pride of place in any ethnocentric-rogues' gallery. His creator, Captain W. E. Johns, locates him in an atmosphere which is not years out of date but generations. As Barnes has written:

... Captain Johns' socio-political attitudes are those one would associate with a not unduly intelligent Empire builder of the late Victorian 'white man's burden' period.[16]

This is not only evident in isolated incidents but in the whole world-view that emerges from the books – one which is palpably biased and distorted. The reader received the impression

that nearly all the world's surface was jungle and desert, inhabited by bestial savages; that civilization was only to be found in a place called 'Home' or 'England', whence men came by private aeroplane to solve the problems of the dark places of the world; that these problems consisted always of evil men plotting the world's destruction ... that these evil men could easily be recognized – big, black Negroes harsh Prussian officers, fat suave Eurasians.

However, there is a sub-category of coloured people who are invested with some humanity; their qualities however, are usually defined *in relation* to the white man – loyalty to him, trust given to him – and these qualities are credited to the white man's race and culture. For these characters have invariably benefited from the civilizing effect of a British mission school, or have spent time in England. Their virtue often has another significant correlate:

they are usually lighter-skinned. For example, Kadar Bey in *Biggles Flies South.*

was . . . a native, but obviously one of the better class, and his skin was not that much darker than that of a sun-burned white man . . . His clothes were of good quality and might have been made in London; indeed, but for his distinguishing tarboosh, he might have passed for a European.[17]

But even these elevated beings never threaten the white man's superiority. Again, it may be objected that this kind of analysis 'reads too much' racialism into oldfashioned books, where there was no harmful or deliberate intention by the author, and whose influence on the child will be minimal. Perhaps the best rebuttal of this point of view comes from Captain W. E. Johns himself, Biggles's author:

I teach . . . under a camouflage. Juveniles are keen to learn, but the educational aspect must not be too obvious or they become suspicious of its intention. I teach a boy to be a man . . . I teach sportsmanship according to the British idea . . . I teach the spirit of team-work, loyalty to the Crown, Empire, and to rightful authority . . . The adult author has little hope of changing the outlook, politics, or way of life of his reader, whose ideas are fixed. The brain of a boy is flexible, still able to absorb. It can be twisted in any direction . . . upon the actions of his heroes will [a boy's] own character be formed. Upon us, who cater for him at the most impressionable age of his life, rests a responsibility which has been perceived by at least one political party. Biggles, therefore, may have some bearing on the future of the country.[18]

Teachers or parents who want some guidance on worth-while books for children (which include black characters and information about their homelands) would do well to consult two recent bibliographies prepared for this purpose. Of the two, Janet Hill's is the more comprehensive and the more evaluative.[19] However, Judith Elkin's bibliography gives more information about suitability of particular books for particular age-groups.[20] There is a large amount of overlap between them, but both should be compulsory reading-matter for all teachers in multi-racial schools.

The final category of children's books to be covered here is not included in either of these bibliographies. These are the ordinary non-fiction books produced for the majority of children in the country, often before substantial immigration had taken place; in other words: mainstream factual schoolbooks, of two types, children's readers and textbooks for older children.

The books by which children learn to read are obviously the first books with which they have a personal relationship. For the first time the child can read a book alone and absorb its contents first-hand. This novelty value makes those contents very important. They are memorable to the extent that many adults can recall the characters of their first reading books. But most significantly, these readers give access to another world, one of the first alternatives to his here-and-now daily life that the child has encountered. And as the books originate from teachers and parents the child must often equate that world with the 'real' world of adults, which he is about to share. Add to this the mystique surrounding the induction process – learning to read – and the sanctions and rewards offered by adults if he will enthusiastically participate, and it soon becomes clear to the child that there is something very important about this whole thing.

Now we may look at children's readers from a purely structural point of view – the acquisition of vocabulary, grammar, sentence construction, and so on – but the child clearly does not. He cannot help but attend to the contents because in the interests of learning they are repeated with such remorseless regularity. For example:

I like sweets. You like sweets. You and I like sweets. You want toys. I want toys. You and I want toys . . . here are shops. We like shops. We like sweet shops and toy shops.[21]

Recently there has been some long-overdue analysis of this 'world' of school-readers. Childs has looked at the Ladybird reading schemes:

Peter and Jane are privileged people. They live with their family in a comfortable house with a pleasant garden, and they have a friendly dog for company. Father drives a large car. Mother is a good house-wife; she bakes cakes, assiduously waves people good-bye, and purchases execrable hats. They live in a middle-class idyll. As children they are improbable; but in the chintzy world of painted sun-light which they inhabit, they are no doubt firm friends of Dick and Dora (Happy Venture Series), Roy and Carol (Let's learn to read), Ruth and John (Beacon Readers), and everyone's first literary acquaintances, Janet and John.[22]

Even for the middle-class reader there is a marked air of unreality about these books; frozen in the early fifties, a world free of traffic and television, in which children are always obedient, happy, and free to pursue a life of pure hedonism (abetted by adults, unworried by overtime and pay-day – and not a working mother in sight – whose function seems to be to satisfy their children's every whim). Money is unquestioningly available for treats and trips, but above all, for buying things. Our Ladybird hero and heroine are such voracious little consumers that 'keeping up with the Janes' must be an expensive business for their readers. In the course of the first ten short books, they acquire dolls, a rabbit, ball, racing car, fish, boats, a kite, tent, colour camera, balloons, skipping rope, scrapbooks, gun and endless sweets. Peter himself should be given the last word on the subject, as he is seen arranging his toys in a huge new cupboard:

We have a lot of toys. Sometimes I forget about some of them.

Clearly, this semi-detached and sports-jacket world is irrelevant to working-class white children, let alone black children. Stewart[23] looked at the ways the most popular children's reading schemes handled coloured people, and found that American Indians came off worst, stories stressing 'savagery, cruelty, cowardice and ugliness', and that while Negroes were seldom mentioned explicitly, there were any number of stories in which 'the villain or enemy is brown or black with other undesirable characteristics as well'. In the case of Chinese, Japanese, Maoris and Arabs, 'the exotic difference between these people and white people is stressed ... often the foreigner takes on a rather grotesque form and they are to be seen in a subordinate relationship with white people'.

It should be stressed that examples cited here are a small selection from a wealth of similarly angled material. On the whole it is the older books which are the worst culprits, but in many cases their classic status ensures a continuing readership. But even

228 Children and Race

if they were exceptional, or drawn from books which do not have a wide readership, the criticism would still stand. For it should be unthinkable that *any* material which contains any encouragement to prejudice be uncritically available to children in a multi-racial society. And under that rubric we should include material which by omission of black figures presents a distorted picture of the world.

We have gathered together a selection of excerpts from children's literature which, it is felt, are offensive, and contrary to the interests of promoting positive racial attitudes in children. This raises a number of difficult and contentious issues, not least the issue of what, if anything, should be done about them. Some would argue that the 'older' offenders cited here are discounted by their very age; that while the racial values they embody are certainly distasteful, they should be seen in historical context and not pilloried in the 1970s for being inappropriate to an era their authors could never have anticipated. There is some justice in this viewpoint, and there is certainly no intention to censor the authors concerned for retailing the values of their time; their writing must be understood in that context. The only point at issue is whether this material is harmful *now*, when presented to children who know nothing of this context, and when the material reinforces those values we wish to discourage in our society. Clearly, a modern publisher would think very hard before publishing *Little Black Sambo* if he were offered it as a new manuscript today. Here, perhaps, lies the key: few would deny that such books present black people in an unacceptable way, but many people are reluctant to sanction withdrawing children's literature from use, particularly those which enjoy the status of children's classics. Undoubtedly this is largely due to our feelings concerning 'censorship', a principle which is obnoxious to many people. We are not suggesting that book-burning is the solution to this problem, and yet there is a danger that 'discouraging the use' of certain books in schools is coming to be portrayed in that kind of emotive light.

The issue of 'censorship' in this area, is a delicate one, and it is very difficult for concerned liberal people to find themselves arguing for such a thing. Logically, though, we should see it in the context of the amount of censorship we tacitly accept in other areas of our lives, particularly the Press, cinema and television. While the criteria may be misguided, the motive is in theory altruistic; it is for the public good. Many people have a mixture of feelings about this; personally, while I find nearly all political and State censorship thoroughly reprehensible, I am grateful for the constraints placed on right-wing extremists' efforts to incite racial hatred, by the Race Relations Act. Seen in that light, the spectre of censorship, of 'banning free speech', becomes quite a different thing: a voluntary acceptance of limitation on certain kinds of communication in the interests of community relations. Following from this, is it not inconsistent to allow the censorship of racial sentiments for adult ears, while not controlling the influences that children encounter in the same area (who are, additionally, less discriminating and more vulnerable)? Rightly or wrongly, we already accept this kind of 'censorship' in other areas of children's literature. How many children's books deal with sexuality, or political issues? And nearer to our topic, it is significant that there are relatively few books which contain anti-Semitic sentiments, despite the presence of a substantial Jewish minority in Britain for generations, and periods of anti-Semitism in our history. This reflects both self-censorship and a current climate of public opinion which is, if not pro-Jewish, at least anti-anti-Semitism in principle.

The most cogent criticism of the idea of withdrawing racially objectionable books has come from Mike Phillips, who argues that they should be retained to demonstrate to children that there *is* prejudice in English life and literature – 'a knowledge which most black children had better be used to by the time they learn to read'.[45] My own feeling is that this is correct, with certain reservations. Firstly, the question of age is crucial. While this kind of awareness should be fostered, it is simply not possible for children to evaluate books in that context at the age-levels for which these books are intended. While the simple 'black–bad, white–good' message can be absorbed by even a five-year-old, the concepts necessary to discuss and combat these sentiments in anything other than those simplistic terms are far too advanced. Secondly, it requires teachers of considerable awareness and sensitivity to handle these issues, and not every teacher is thus endowed. Finally, although teachers and children in majority-black schools may have a consciousness of the issues that would foster this kind of discussion, this will be less true in non-black areas, where the books' message may be absorbed without critical comment. Certainly, though, older children could benefit from reading these books and the discussion they would stimulate.

On balance, I would argue for discouraging the use of this kind of material with young children; we have to weigh the sacrifice of literary merit against possible harmful effects, and my own feeling is that English children's literature is rich enough to survive this slight incursion. And there is a more positive aspect, too: the production of positively beneficial books to replace them. It is unfortunately true that the books which deal with black people in an accepting and acceptable way are the exception; but they do exist (and in increasing numbers), and should be introduced into all schools to replace the dangerous and outdated material described here. A select list of some of the better examples is given in Appendix 2.

If any other evidence were needed it is provided by children themselves. Just as the white children in a class described earlier latched on to the insulting aspects of the Little Black Sambo books, so do black children respond to books which feature 'people like them' in a warm and exciting way. A measure of this is the rate at which different types of book are read, borrowed and even taken home by the children. Ezra Jack Keats's books (for example, *Peter's Chair*[24]), which are attractively written and illustrated adventures of a young black boy, are far and away the most popular books in a multi-racial classroom that I visited frequently. Within a few months copies have been replaced as their predecessors were literally worn out. Similarly, Leila Berg's 'Nippers'[25] stories, which describe the lives of inner-city children (who are more familiar with gas-meters than with Peter and Jane's lawns and rhododendrons), are firm favourites with white working-class children.[25] They, too, are dog-eared with use, while Dick and Dora languish on the shelves practically unread. Both 'Nippers' and the 'Breakthrough to Literacy'[33] series include some black figures, but not nearly enough. Probably the best single scheme in this respect is the 'Sparks' multi-racial Infant Reading Scheme.[34]

Overall, though, there are very few books which are *all* good. So many otherwise acceptable books are marred by particular passages or even individual sentences, which detract from the remainder of the beneficial material in the book. For example, it seems particularly careless that in a multi-racial book, expressions like 'things look black' for so-and-so should be used. Similarly Eric Allen's book, *The Latchkey Children*,[26] is an acceptable book until we get to the passage where a black character, Duke Ellington Binns, is described like this: 'Duke was watching him, his eyes shining like new florins in his boot-polish face.' Now, no black child is going to be unaffected by that sort of description. It would be foolish at the present time to reject out of hand all books which contain any reference of this kind. However, they might be restricted to use for reading aloud to the class, so that the teacher can censor offending passages.

Less susceptible to censorship are illustrations; this is unfortunate, for not only are they the most accessible part of books to all children, irrespective of reading ability, but they also contain some of the worst offences. White artists do seem to have a stereotyped notion of black facial features, or a limited ability to represent them. Also the illustration is by its very nature a description encapsulated in a few lines, requiring key features to be accentuated beyond realism; and if the text it describes is itself stereotyped, the result is often much worse. Again, humour is often and important aspect of the book and exaggeration is an accepted way of achieving this; but so often this amounts to caricature which can be very harmful. There is a difference between *a* funny white man, and black men who are funny *because* of their features.

The effect of 'cartoon' type illustrations depends on their context. They are far less harmful, if at all, against a background which is bizarre or abstract. Ezra Jack Keats's books exemplify in the best possible way how 'unrealistic' illustrations of both blacks and whites can be perfectly acceptable. His illustrations clearly represent a world which is larger than life, and the vibrant colours and forms in the background make that fact unambiguous.

Both the story-line and the illustrations convey a warm and appealing atmosphere which is wholly acceptable, a fact which is underlined by their popularity amongst black and white children alike.

Where story books go for an artistic impression of realism accentuation of colour and facial features is also common, for the reasons mentioned. Two alternatives suggest themselves. 'Lenny lives in the West Indies' manages to combine real photographs of people with a narrative story (see inside the front cover of this book), which is in many ways the best solution.[27] But line drawings are cheaper and realistic ones are possible. The illustrations to Mary Cockett's 'Another home, another country' (see inside the back cover) are by far the most successful that the author has encountered.[28] They could probably best be imitated by preparing drawings from photographs, not from the too-exotic imagination of most of the artists encountered.

Textbooks

Although the books fall outside the clientele we have dealt with in this book, namely primary school children, we should briefly mention textbooks for older children. As early as 1962, Stephen Hatch[29] pointed out some of the rabid stereotyping of races and nationalities that passes for fact in history and geography textbooks – and these taken from comprehensive schools which might have been expected to adopt a more enlightened approach. Glendinning[30] has more recently analysed history textbooks and apparently found little change over the intervening nine years, the same mixture of jingoism, ethnocentric versions of events and historical developments, or at best patronage of underdeveloped peoples, predominating. Cameron[31] points out that much of the reason for this is a passing of the buck between teachers and publishers, neither taking the initiative to secure changes in archaic textbooks, which are therefore reprinted in their original form. She cites the example of a book published by Blackie, whose title gives some clue to its imperial perspective: *Our Neighbours and Their Work for Us.* First published in 1935 and most recently reprinted in 1965, it contains the following, concerning the West Indies: 'The heat of the sun makes the work of growing sugar too hard for white people. Even the natives on the plantations work in very light loose clothes'. Or *Work in Other Lands* published in 1935 tells us that in Ceylon ' each of the plantations where the tea is grown and picked and packed is looked after by a white man ... He sees that all the people who work on his plantation work well and honestly.'

As Cameron comments, 'presumably he has to keep his eyes peeled'. That passage appears in the *revised* 1956 edition; one cannot help wondering what it was like before.

Many teachers have realized the potential harm that material such as this can do to both black and white children; but they are handicapped through inadequate book allowances, so that they cannot simply root out all the old books, as they would have very few left. Here a lead might be given by the LEAs, for example, by taking a decision that a large capital sum be immediately allocated to replacing biased literature in schools. This would also have the effect of bringing the issue to the attention of those people who are not yet aware of it; and we can be sure that such a move would be warmly supported by the publishers. This begs the question of whether the LEAs are aware of the issue, and here the evidence is not encouraging. An all-party group of MPs wrote to 200 LEAs to ask what they were doing in this direction.[32] Only 29 authorities could be described as actually giving a lead, and although half the total gave sympathetic and helpful replies, there was a disturbing tardiness of response from some of the main conurbations with large immigrant populations. Rather too many responses (which were, after all, from chief education officers) showed a tendency to bureaucratic buck-passing, blind faith in teachers and their books, or a simple inability to understand the issues at all. One chief education officer 'would be surprised if our teachers chose books which increased colour prejudice', while one myopic reply at least grasped half the point:

The points which are made will be borne in mind and I would however, like to inform you:
(1) There are very few schools in Sunderland with any immigrant children.
(2) There is no school in Sunderland with as many as 10 immigrant children on the roll.

But all children require education for citizenship in a multi-racial society, not just those in immigrant areas.

What is to be done?

(1) AWARENESS There is no longer any reason why schools and even parents should remain unaware of these issues. It is time for an educational campaign, in the very widest sense, to simply disseminate the facts that (a) rudimentary racial attitudes of a 'prejudiced' kind are already developing in children by the age of five, and (b) prejudice, whether directly from other people or implicit in books and comics, hurts and damages black children. A concerted initiative by LEAs, teachers' unions, parent–teacher associations, black community groups and organizations like the National Association for Multi-Racial Education, and, most importantly, colleges of education, could ensure that parents, teachers and future teachers are acquainted with the facts. This is obviously a prerequisite for any further action (and may in itself begin a process of change towards accepting attitudes); yet at present only a minority of primary teachers seem to be aware of these basic facts.

(2) UNDERSTANDING This does *not* mean a missionary sympathy with black children. *Empathy* is perhaps a better word, for it involves being able to take the part of the child and understand his experience from *his* perspective, not just an adult one. Needless to say this must include 'taking the part' of both white and black children. It is necessary for the teacher to understand the social pressures on the child: from parents who may make disparaging remarks about 'blacks' or prevent the child from bringing home black friends; from friends who may ostracize him for associating with 'smelly' Asian children. Why *should* the child develop accepting attitudes when the society around him palpably rejects these people, and all the pressures are to ac-quiescence?

The teacher's projection of himself into the role of the black child is more difficult; but he can start by reading some of the accounts of people who have turned their skin black to do this,[44] and 'add in' the feelings of vulnerability of a young child, in an

alien culture. On a more organized basis, the potential of drama
and group role-playing for achieving this is only just starting to be
explored. The organizations mentioned could pursue this, and at
the very least, the books should be required reading.

(3) TRAINING   The preparation given by colleges and depart-
ments of education for teaching in 'immigrant' schools is, with a
few notable exceptions, inadequate. Typically, two or three lectures may be devoted to this (as one of a number of 'problem areas'
for teachers) or there may be a whole course offered as a special
option among several others. Educational institutions as much as
everyone else have got to wake up to the fact that we live in a multi-
racial society, and cater to that fact. Not only do potential teachers
of black children need all kinds of special knowledge and training,
but all teachers should appreciate the basic facts of racial and
cultural diversity, and be able to educate their children towards
positive racial attitudes and behaviour. This requires that
education for teachers in training includes these issues as a central
part of the curriculum, not a peripheral, special field. This would
include information about the cultural backgrounds of the immigrants, their experiences and social situation in this country,
language difficulties, the facts of racism and its intrusion into the
life of the child, his experience in school and the outside world.
And at the practical level, the implications of these issues for
educational practice must be thoroughly drawn out in the way
attempted in this chapter. This is the very minimum we can do,
though obviously more comprehensive strategies would be pre-
ferable. Only in this way can we begin to cope with the wells of
ignorance about black people and their lives that trainee teachers
share with the public at large.

A wider and more difficult problem concerns practising teachers, many of whom have a similar need for information. Compulsory in-service training is one solution and experience of
teachers' discussion groups centring on these issues* suggests
that these can be enormously influential in breaking down stereotypes and providing information. Another avenue which should

*Note: See, for example, the National Foundation for Educational Re-
search 'Education for a Multi-Racial Society' Project. Details, forthcoming,
from NFER, Upton Park, Slough, Berks.

be exploited further is the exchange arrangements with teachers in the immigrants' homelands. Perhaps with these innovations we might avoid in the future a situation which recently confronted me, and though an isolated and extreme example, demarcates the limits of ignorance that can exist: after some conversation at cross-purposes, it emerged that a teacher in a 50 per cent black school with whom I was talking was under the impression that West Indian children came from Western India; not surprisingly she was rather puzzled by their dissimilarity with the 'other' Indian children. The anecdote is related not to satirize the teacher, but to pose the question of what other misconceptions, perhaps more harmful, survive in teachers' minds through the inadequate preparation they have received for multi-racial education.

(4) IN THE CLASSROOM   Given some awareness and understanding, the teacher will already have begun to examine her own racial attitudes. It is too much to expect any person to divest themselves of these attitudes overnight, but *recognition* of them is the first step. This must involve honesty and often quite painful admissions. Did she not feel slightly repulsed by her first contact with oiled Asian hair? Is West Indian English *really* as good as Standard English? Are they not a bit slower, too? Or can *immigrant* children, of whatever colour, really be *expected* to do as well as English children, with all those 'problems'? It is so easy to fall into, or never emerge from, any of these traps, whereby expectations which are lowered even for 'good', 'sympathetic' reasons set off that pernicious cycle of lowered achievements.

So the teacher first of all has to examine minutely her own attitudes and bring them into the open to herself. In this way she has a better chance of evaluating them rationally than if they remain suppressed, but implicit in her behaviour. From this basis she can begin to build a teaching environment in her classroom that will offer some resistance to the racial attitudes current in the wider society. There are a number of specific ways in which this can be attempted:

(a) Language of the teacher: Even radical teachers may unwittingly behave in ways which harm black children and fuel white evaluations of them. I refer to the fact that nearly all our teachers have been brought up within this culture and use its language in conventional ways. I recently overheard one such teacher say to a West Indian girl, in a very affectionate voice, 'Shirley, you are a little blackmailer', realizing the error instantly, but too late to prevent the child being upset. As we have seen, evaluations based on colour, particularly black and white, have permeated our language since Biblical times, and probably before. The very antiquity of the 'pure' and 'good' connotations of white and the 'evil' connotation of black, somehow adds to their credibility, as though they are part of the natural order of things, and in some way real. In a few seconds one can think of any number of examples in current usage: blackleg, blackguard, black sheep, black spot, black mark, to black-ball, blacklist and so on. All denote bad things. The words themselves are only symptomatic of cultural colour associations of long standing; no doubt they assisted the justification of our earlier 'race relations' exploits in Africa and elsewhere. But now we must suppress these usages, even reverse them. We could start by bringing Black Beauty out of the realms of the animal kingdom; and why not even a black Beauty and a white Beast ? Only in that sort of way can we begin to make *nonsense* of the colour values implicit in our language and literature. *Obviously* these things are only of marginal importance; but we should regard the task as one of destroying the context into which prejudices about *people's* colour can so easily be fitted.

(b) West Indian language: In the last chapter it was argued that West Indian language difficulties and their interpretation added to the devaluation of the child in school. We have to design strategies to deal with this as it acts as a brake on the child's achievement, which in turn reinforces the process. The perspective we should adopt is that of teaching language skills that the child will need while not deprecating his own language. Clearly the priority is reading for so much of the child's subsequent education depends on this skill; of the other aspects, written and spoken language: the former is the more important and 'talk reform' more questionable. If any confirmation of these priorities were needed we only have to look at the relative emphasis given to these skills by West Indians themselves in their supplementary schools.

The inclusion of black figures and culturally relevant themes in books and materials will assist this process by the greater involvement of the child. But it has been suggested that we might go further and produce reading materials *in* West Indian dialect (much in the same way as Joan Baratz is doing in the States with Negro Non-Standard English). The theory is that learning to read in the child's own language will provide a greater basis of confidence than the present system where the child has to learn the language *and* learn to read simultaneously. There is a lot to be said for this, particularly as it would tangibly recognize the worth of the child's own language, but there are also obvious difficulties. The child would at some point have to transfer to Standard English, as in the case of Initial Teaching Alphabet. However, this is an empirical question, and should be an urgent area for research. Certainly recent work, like the Concept 7–9 Dialect Kit,[43] which is a large step in the right direction, needs to be developed further. The kit aims at developing language and reasoning skills, taking account of common West Indian language difficulties, but there is a need for a more individually directed system which allows for the different locations of children on the 'dialect continuum' mentioned in the last chapter.

(c) Books: We have dealt with this issue at some length, but let us simply draw out the main priorities. Teachers can collectively press for changes in this area, or act individually, as a few enterprising teachers have done, to produce their own materials.

i *Inclusion* of black figures in children's books, that is, in picture books, story books, readers and reading schemes, and information books. The guiding principle for their portrayal is that they should be *ordinary* figures, with the same range of characteristics and abilities as white figures, but who *happen* to be black.

ii *Revision* of many standard English children's books to remove derogatory references to blackness and black people, both in text and illustrations.

iii *Production* of new books, more specifically directed to black children. These should cover both the cultural backgrounds and the children's present situation in urban Britain. Of the former category, those already available tend to over-emphasize poverty, underdevelopment, and simple rural life-styles; while reality should not be distorted, more emphasis should be laid on modernization and technological development in the immigrant homelands. There are very few books which deal with immigrant children in Britain. Although there are a number of American books showing black characters in an urban landscape, these obviously omit Asian-type figures. They can be used to good effect in the short term, but there is a pressing need for British equivalents to be produced.

(d) Audio-visual aids and cultural materials: There is an enormous potential for really exciting work with posters, photographs, wall-charts, tapes, records, cross-cultural music, cookery, dressmaking and craftwork. There is no need to reiterate these points beyond saying that most of the proposals (in the previous chapter) for work in bi-cultural schools are equally applicable and equally important to schools with not a single immigrant pupil. For white children, too, will learn to respect those things which are 'important enough' to be enshrined in educational materials.

There are, then, individual and group strategies that teachers can pursue to improve materials. Many individual teachers with good ideas in this direction have been prevented from translating them into practice by the constraints of time, money and materials, and technical expertise. But recent experience in Bristol has shown that there are abundant resources of each of these in Colleges of Art and Polytechnics. Thus is has been possible to create a variety of innovative educational materials of high quality, with the help of local art students as a part of their final year projects. This has been stimulating for both the students and the teachers involved, quite apart from the tangible benefits of the materials themselves. Produced in any other way, these materials would have eaten up a large chunk of the average school's annual capitation allowance; instead, an array of work cards, books, reading-games and any amount of other visual aids, educational toys, music, film and video-tapes, are in production at a tiny fraction of their normal cost to the schools (the majority being provided free).* Not least, it has given the teachers an insight into the widely different financial philosophies of primary and higher education!

Of course, this has been achieved on a group basis, but our experience suggests that any teacher who asks for help of this kind is likely to get a cooperative reception. Other *group* activities should include representations to educational publishers, so that teachers can save themselves even this trouble. There are indications that the publishers are becoming increasingly sensitive to the inadequacies of their books and materials for multi-racial schools. They *want* ideas and feedback for their efforts, and teachers' groups and organizations must step in and take this initiative. In this way, perhaps, we can prevent some of the more obvious mistakes that are being made in the attempt to 'up-date' children's books. In 1970 Geoffrey Chapman published 'The Chapman Readers' written by Bakewell and Woods, a reading-scheme specifically directed at multi-racial schools. Unfortunately the authors chose as the central character a bizarre golliwog figure (tousle-haired and grass-skirted) called Pronto. In mitigation it should be said that he is dark green rather than black, but apart from that he makes Little Black Sambo look like Eldridge Cleaver (see inside the back cover of this book). When we consider the capital cost of producing a new reading-scheme, it is clear that teachers have a responsibility to ensure that the money is spent in more useful ways. It is worth noting that 'The Chapman Readers' are no longer in print.

(5) TEACHING 'RACE' Since 'race' has hardly been acknowledged as an issue in British primary schools, it is not surprising that there has been little effort to *positively* teach tolerant attitudes. In any case, because very young children's race 'attitudes' seem

* Note: for individual teachers working alone, illustrative material depicting black figures can be a problem. The most accessible sources of these are occasional issues of the Colour Supplements in the *Observer*, *Sunday Times* and *Daily Telegraph*. The new black magazine *Focus* provides another source, while the Inner London Education Authority magazine *Contact* contains many pictures of West Indians, Asians and English children in the school situation. Some more general sources of books and information are given in Appendix I.

to consist mainly of simple evaluations of the races, without a lot of information to back them up, teaching *facts* about race may be attacking the wrong part of the problem.

However, an early study of this age-group in America, having established that 'prejudiced' racial and religious attitudes did exist in their subjects, set about trying to change both the children's attitudes and behaviour through a programme of 'intercultural education'.[35] The reader is advised to refer to the original text for details of the experiment; but, in outline, the purpose was to influence this attitude development through two types of teacher philosophy, methods and teaching materials. 'One experimental condition was designed to support democratic intercultural values, the second to maintain or foster group prejudices common in our culture.' (The second condition was not quite so unethical as it appears: it amounted to a programme based on a status quo philosophy, which assumed that the development of prejudice was the norm. So it was less a deliberate intervention to increase prejudice than the continuation of methods in widespread use, which, in contrast to the other condition, did little to try and prevent prejudice developing.) Exposure of these different programmes was achieved by forming 'clubs' of children within particular classes, who were withdrawn from the body of the class for certain curriculum areas:

The neighbourhood was chosen as the curriculum area for the experimental material of both clubs. (It is frequently the context if not the theme of first or second grade social studies.) The neighbourhood was particularly suitable for the purposes of this experiment since it was within the firsthand experience of the children and offered a good possibility of interpretation from either ... point of view. How people live, the work they do, the way they celebrate holidays, worship, get along with neighbours, etc., were learned through real and make-believe trips, stories, recordings, dramatizations, parties, painting pictures, meeting people, of their own or other neighbourhoods.

Here is a *small* selection of the specific experimental objectives of a number of the sessions, and the precise ways in which they were pursued. The objectives and methods listed are only those of the 'tolerance teaching programme':

Objectives	Methods
To help the children perceive the neighbourhood as multi-cultured, to accept the people who live in it . . . (regardless of differences). To challenge the Jewish stereotype.	Construction of map, location of shops and personalities on it, exchange of information about people and places. Story-telling about 'Mr Cohen' and other minority figures.
To help the children know that people do different kinds of work . . . that all work and all workers are important.	Role-playing in different jobs. Discussion of how each one helps neighbourhood – illustrated by describing what happens when any one stops. Visits to work places. Conversations with workers, etc.
To challenge the children's stereotype of Negro people. To prepare children for a successful social experience in which racial differences will not be a source of hostility and conflict. To provide [that] experience on the occasion of Thanksgiving. To demonstrate acceptance and friendliness of Negro and white adults (teachers and parents) in a social situation.	Story-telling with incidental Negro characters. Preparation for inter-racial party with black guest of honour. Black and white adults at party behave non-stereotypically and with friendliness. Post-party group discussions.
To provide a situation in which (a) conflicts over colour differences are acknowledged (b) good human relations in spite of colour differences are also acknowledged.	Symbolic story-telling in terms of brown and white animals. Link made with humans. Further discussion of children's feelings about party, and plans for another.
To challenge the children's stereotype of 'Catholic', to give them an opportunity to express fears, misconceptions, and 'anti'	Party at which Sister is introduced to parents, and acts as games-leader. Children tell what they know of neighbourhood and

Objectives	Methods

feelings as well as an opportunity to develop positive feelings towards a Catholic Sister. To provide a second social experience in which Negro and white adults as well as children participate.

ask questions. Sister explains about her habit, the church, etc., counteracts children's fears of nuns.

To have the children perceive 'America' as the sum of many neighbourhoods and 'Americans' as all the people in the neighbourhoods.

Teacher plays record of popular song about America. Begins a discussion leading to a map/picture of interlocking people and neighbourhoods which go to make up the country. Includes occupations, celebration days.

To challenge the children's stereotype of Jews through a social situation in which a Jewish cultural observance is seen as part of American life and Jewish people are seen at home in the familiar roles of family members.

Discussion on walk to house. Introduction to family. Play traditional games, given information about Jewish customs and holidays. Discussion of how to include it on map.

To summarize their experience through the painting so that the children perceive and accept the diversity which characterizes American life: so that America is perceived as including all the different people in it, and is seen as an extension of the neighbourhood.

Children review all their work and discuss it, finally representing it on the mural.

Even this abbreviated version makes it clear that here was an attempt to deal with the issues of race, religion, culture, and nationality head-on, through the study of the neighbourhood where they all coalesce. But did this approach work?

The short answer is yes. On before–after tests of the children's attitudes, the proportion of the 'experimental' group who responded towards Negroes in hostile terms decreased from 46 per cent to 23 per cent. Similar trends were recorded for attitudes towards Jews. This compared with trends in the reverse direction for the 'prejudiced', 'status quo' comparison group, and small random changes in control groups. The programme did not result in a large number of children totally accepting Negroes; rather the main trend was from hostility to ambivalence. However, it was a short programme occupying relatively little of the school day, so that dramatic changes would be unlikely, if not suspect.

A more recent but less ambitious study has come up with equally optimistic findings. The authors, Litcher and Johnson,[36] tested the effects on white children's attitudes of using 'multi-ethnic' reading-books, compared with control groups who were given traditional readers. The children's racial attitudes were tested before and after a four-month period of exposure to these books, using doll and picture tests of the type described in Chapter 3. This is how the authors sum up their findings:

> The results of this study dramatically indicate that the use of multi-ethnic readers in an elementary school will result in more favourable attitudes towards Negroes. The data ... indicate that the reader decreased the preference for one's own racial group over the other ... The multi-ethnic reader resulted in a reduction of the amount of social distance placed between the white and Negro racial groups ... the children in the experimental groups were less likely to exclude a child on the basis of race than were the controls ... [and] ... were less likely to attribute negative traits to Negroes and positive traits to whites.

In the words of the authors of the earlier study, their experimental programme started from the premise that 'group membership of persons' should not be 'a topic which is taboo and avoided'. The second study used a more oblique approach, but one which clearly recognized and presented the fact of racial diversity. Both approaches contrast with the attitude of many teachers who seldom deal with the issue at all, believing that even to recognize racial or cultural differences is somehow discriminatory. The notion of taboo is very appropriate; for when children sense that adults veto certain subjects, like sex, for example, their interest tends to become more aroused than if the topic had been dealt with as a matter of course. Probably this happens because the taboo issue gives the child a glimpse into the world of adults. He is naturally intrigued and wants to know more. More dangerously, it may simply make him anxious to reproduce adult attitudes, as a way of *being* grown-up. Discoveries from the adult world are related very quickly to friends, as they are prestigious items of information. In this way we may heighten the importance of race as an issue to children simply by virtue of a disapproving or secretive attitude towards it being raised in their presence.

There is some further evidence, this time from Britain and involving older children, which points in the same direction as the American studies. Part of the Schools Council-Nuffield Humanities Curriculum Project was devoted to a study of the effects of classroom discussions of race on the race attitudes and friendship choices of adolescents. The discussions took place over a period of 6–8 weeks involving some twenty to thirty hours of participation by the students. These did not take place in a vacuum, but in response to a specially prepared teaching programme which included journalism, politicians' speeches (like Powell), official publications, political propaganda, news photographs, documentary film, features films, records, novels and non-fiction, poetry and drama. The discussions were chaired by a teacher who strove to remain neutral as far as possible.* The situation is not comparable with younger children, for here there can be intellectual discussion of abstract ideas based on complex concepts and information; there is the possibility of influencing the cognitive or information aspects of attitudes by confronting them with authoritative alternative facts. Rationality has the opportunity of overcoming the simple emotional aspect of attitudes. Nevertheless, the principle of dealing with 'race' head-on is the same, and had similar results to the experimental programme with young children:

*Note: It should be said that this approach engendered considerable controversy, particularly with respect to the viability (or indeed the ethics) of a neutral 'chairman' conducting discussions of materials, some of which were palpably racist in content.

The effects of the experiment, although not generally significant, tended to suggest a shift in the direction of inter-ethnic tolerance.[37]

'Significant' of course, refers to statistical significance, which is not at all the same thing as 'real' significance. It might be argued that for a programme covering a few weeks in the lives of adolescents to exert any influence over their racial attitudes is a highly significant result indeed. These slight increases in inter-ethnic tolerance were not restricted to their expressed attitudes, but extended to their choices of friends on a sociometric test as well.

Of course, the purpose of bringing black figures into children's literature and bringing black culture into the classroom is not simply to promote more positive attitudes among white children; all the evidence that has been gathered together in this book points to the need to foster more positive attitudes towards black people among black children themselves. Again, there is evidence that this can be effective. David Johnson studied the effects of teaching black history to a group of black American children via a 'Freedom School' in Harlem.[38] The children participated in the school for two hours each Saturday morning over a period of four months, learning about both African history and the history of the American Negro. They ranged from 8 to 13 years old; they were interviewed before and after the programme and given various child personality and attitude tests. Johnson reports that

... The Freedom School ... seemed to have some effect on the boys in the areas of self-attitudes, equality of Negroes and whites, attitudes towards Negroes, and attitudes towards civil rights. That is, they became more confident in themselves, more convinced that Negroes and whites are equal, more positive towards Negroes, and more militant towards civil rights.

The same changes were found among the girls, though less strongly. The parents of these children were all involved in the civil-rights movement, so it could be argued the children would be more disposed than other children towards accepting these beliefs. Equally, though, it is likely that the parents would have encouraged such attitudes long before the Freedom School was organized, so that the *change* in attitudes it produced is the more remarkable.

Other studies have produced similar changes in self-concept and attitudes towards blackness with much younger black children both in elementary schools[39] and in the pre-school years.[40] One study, though a small-scale one, is particularly important because it not only demonstrates that these effects can be achieved in racially mixed situations (as opposed to exclusively black projects) but also that the effects can carry through to the children's *behaviour*. Belle Likover[41] worked with a group of girls on an inter-racial summer camp which they attended on a daily basis. By concentrating on a small group – twenty-six girls in all – it was possible to study the effects of her programme on the children's interaction with each other. Only half of them participated in the experimental programme, the other half serving as a basis for comparison. In the first week of the camp, the programme was the same for both groups; both worked on the theme of Jewish holidays.

Black history was introduced to the girls in the experimental group at the beginning of the second week through many program forms, including stories, dance, song, art and discussion. The counselor, with help from the camp director, translated the historical material to a level appropriate for 6–7 year old girls. Using the camp's general theme for the second week – independence and freedom – the experimental group concentrated its attention on the struggles of blacks for freedom . . . During the third week . . . the girls explored the contributions that blacks have made to American society under the program theme, great Americans. Biographical material about Negro heroes (like Martin Luther King and John Henry) was presented.

During the same period the control group dealt with the issues of freedom of speech and American heroes in a more general way without the emphasis on black people. However, the race issue was not avoided: 'Discussions of the girls' feelings about race were stimulated by the introduction of two picture books, *In Henry's Backyard* and *Your Skin and Mine*. Both books present classical anthropological concepts about race in a form that elementary-school children can understand'. Three measures were used to evaluate the effectiveness of the programme: a measure of the extent to which each child behaved positively towards members of the other race, as rated by counsellors and a non-participant observer at the end of the first and fourth weeks of the camp; daily records of each child's behaviour towards the children of the opposite race, and interviews with the girls' mothers to find out what racial attitudes the children relayed at home as a result of their daily experiences. Each of the interaction measures showed a significant increase in cross-racial contact and friendship in the experimental group, compared to a minimal change in the control group. These changes were corroborated by the mothers' accounts of their children's comments and reactions to the experience. The black mothers showed appreciation of the increased self-confidence and self-respect their children had developed. None of them knew about the experiment until the end of the interview.

It should be said that not all race teaching programmes have been as conspicuously successful as those described here. It is fair to say, though, that those which have failed have often been very limited in scope and would have required near-miraculous conversions to have registered significant changes in attitude. A case in point is Miller's[46] optimistic attempt to influence adolescents' prejudices on the basis of a three-hour teaching programme, or Greenberg and his associates, who attempted a similar objective with college students by means of a single lecture.

In Britain, work in this area is only just beginning in the primary school, although this is the age-range at which we must start if we wish to try and circumvent or affect the early development of prejudice. The author is currently conducting an action research project with 5–9-year-old children in a number of London and Bristol primary schools which deals directly with these issues. We are looking at the effects of (a) black teachers and (b) multi-racial, multi-cultural literature and curricula on children's racial attitudes, both black and white. This involves the introduction of a vast amount of teaching material (multi-racial books, reading-games, work-cards, visual aids, etc.) into the classrooms of a number of West Indian, Asian and English teachers, and assessing the effects on the children's attitudes after a year's exposure to these influences. The philosophy behind the project should be apparent from all that has been said here. We hope that, for the white children, the formation of a close relationship with a black person in a position of respect and affection will affect the formation of their attitudes towards black people in general, and that the black teachers will help to foster a secure sense of identity in their black children. Similarly, the teaching materials are designed to present black people and their cultural backgrounds in a positive and accepting way, and as an unremarkable part of the child's school experience. At the time of writing the analysis of the data from this project is at an early stage. It is not possible to draw firm conclusions, but there are already clear indications of a beneficial effect on the children's attitudes, of both black teachers and multi-racial materials, particularly in the case of the black children in the study. Detailed results of the study should be published soon after the appearance of this book. A list of the books selected for the experiment appears in Appendix 2.

Most of the work with young children described here, particularly the prolonged programmes, has had a remarkably high success rate with both black and white children. The only reservation we need have about educational attempts to eradicate prejudice and its effects concerns the pressures exerted by society in the opposite direction. As such, we are catering to the symptoms rather than the causes of the problem. Though the title of this last section, 'What is to be done?', is culled from Lenin, there is nothing revolutionary about the proposals either in conception or in effect. It has not been my purpose in this chapter to present a packaged 'solution' to the 'problems' of multi-racial education, or the wider issues of racism and racial attitude development. Education is merely one of many inputs into the child's attitudes; the combination of the other, often contrary, forces is probably more important. In other words, the innovations suggested here *must* be made, at the very least, but not as a cure-all, rather with our eyes open. The school is simply one area of influence on the child which may be amenable to reform, among many others which are less so.

In conclusion

This book has described some of the more subtle consequences of racism and suggested some limited, though proven, remedies for some of its aspects. People in this society do not become 'prejudiced' on attaining adulthood; they learn attitudes towards black people from infancy by their socialization within a culture in which these attitudes are widely held. Racism is deeply rooted in British culture but has only been recognized as such since the immigration of black people brought the issue home. If, with Martin Buber, we believe that a society may be termed human in the measure to which its members confirm one another, then our society is found lacking, in its treatment of black people. The lack of that confirmation has been seen to damage black children from an early age by undermining their acceptance of themselves and their group. Hopefully, in the technicalities of 'out-group identification' and other shorthands we have not lost sight of the referents of these terms: the black minorities and their economic, social and psychological oppression by the dominant white majority. In this book as in others the reader should heed Sivanandan's caution that

... We need also to examine the stupefying phrases that sociologists and educationalists in particular have come to use when they speak, for instance, of disadvantaged children, unrealistic aspirations, of our children and your children. Who disadvantaged the children? Why are their aspirations unrealistic? ... Children are the continuing measure of our humanity and we stand or fall by what we do to them.[42]

Appendices and References

Appendix I
Sources of books, material and information concerning the lives and backgrounds of black people in Britain

Institute of Race Relations Library
247–9 Pentonville Road, London, N1   01–837 0041

Race Today
Monthly publication of Towards Racial Justice, 74, Shakespeare Road, London, SE24   01–737 2268

Community Relations Commission
15–16 Bedford Street, London, W1   01–836 3545

Commonwealth Institute Library
Kensington High Street, London, W8   01–602 3252

Voluntary Committee on Overseas Aid and Development
69 Victoria Street, London, SW1   01–799 3863

School of Oriental and African Studies
Malet Street, London, WC1

Africa Centre
38 King Street, London, WC2   01–836 1973

Oxfam
274 Banbury Road, Oxford   0865 56777

New Beacon Books
76 Stroud Green Road, London, N4   01–272 4889

Bogle-L'Ouverture Publications
141 Coldershaw Road, London, W13   01–579 4920

Books from India
32 Coptic Street, London, WC1   01–580 1228

The Independent Publishing Company
38 Kennington Lane, London, SE11 (Books from India)
01–735 2101

Pam's Sikh Bookshop
17 Abbotshall Road, London, SE6   01–698 5010

National Association for Multi-Racial Education
c/o Otto Polling, The Northbrook Centre, Penn Road, Slough,
SL2 1PH

American Council on Inter-racial Books for Children, Inc.
29 West 15th Street, New York, NY 10011, USA

Drum & Spear Press, Inc.
1371 Fairmont Street, Washington, DC, USA

Appendix 2

A select list of multi-racial books for the primary school

AUTHOR	TITLE	PUBLISHER
(a) West Indian background		
Stoppelman, J. W. F.	*Jamaica*	Benn
Caldwell, J. C.	*Let's Visit the West Indies*	Burke
Cockett, M.	*Another Home, Another Country*	Chatto, Boyd & Oliver
Ness, E.	*Josefina February*	Chatto, Boyd & Oliver
Prescod, S.	*We live in Jamaica* (Books 1–3)	Collins
Palmer, C. E.	*The Cloud with the Silver Lining*	Deutsch
Cousins, P. M.	*Queen of the Mountain*	Ginn
Richardson, B.	*Sugar in Guyana*	Ginn
Williams, W.	*We Live in Guyana*	Ginn
Bentley, J. D.	*Toussaint L'Ouverture of the West Indies*	Hulton
Sherlock, P. M.	*West Indian Story*	Longmans
Sherlock, P. M.	*Anansi the Spider Man*	Macmillan
Bolt, A.	*Lenny Lives in the West Indies*	Methuen
Borely, C.	*Nelson's New West Indian Readers*, Introductory Books 1 & 2	Nelson
Sherlock, P. M.	*West Indian Folk Tales*	Oxford
Craig, K.	*Emmanuel and his Parrot*	Oxford
Craig, K.	*Emmanuel Goes to Market*	Oxford
Abrahams, R. D.	*Humphrey's Ride*	Routledge & Kegan Paul
Abrahams, R. D.	*The Bonus of Redonda*	Routledge & Kegan Paul
Hughes, L.	*The First Book of the Caribbean*	Ward
(b) Asian background		
Mehta, R.	*Ramu: A Story of India*	Angus & Robertson

AUTHOR	TITLE	PUBLISHER
Arora, S. L.	*What Then Raman*	Blackie
Funai, M.	*The Tiger, the Brahman and the Jackal*	Bodley Head
Darbois, D.	*Gopal: His Life in India*	Chatto, Boyd & Oliver
Sucksdorff, A. B.	*Chendru: the Boy and the Tiger*	Collins
Fawcett, R.	*How Did They Live: India*	Gawthorn
Lang, A.	*The Olive Fairy Book*	Longmans
Bryant, S.	*The Greedy Cat and the Parrot*	Methuen
Forsberg, V.	*Salima Lives in Kashmir*	Methuen
Silverstone, M. & Miller, L.	*Bala, Child of India*	Methuen
Watson, J. W.	*India: Old Land, New Nation*	Muller
Gray, J. E. B.	*Indian Tales and Legends*	Oxford
Papas, W.	*Taresh the Tea-Planter*	Oxford
Thoger, M.	*Shanta*	Puffin
Hughes, J.	*Ditta's Tree*	Puffin
Norris, M.	*Young India*	Wheaton
Various Authors	Children's Books from India	Children's Book Trust of New Delhi (available from Oxfam, see Appendix I.)
Khandpur, S.	*Junior's Animal World Series*	Ratnabharati (available from Books from India, see Appendix I)
Teta, J.	*Pakistan in Pictures*	Sterling Press

(c) Miscellaneous books with multi-racial themes or backgrounds

Showers, P.	*Your Skin and Mine*	Black
Showers, P.	*Look at Your Eyes*	Black
Milburn, C.	*My Five Senses* series	Blackie
Fisher, *et al.*	*Sparks* multi-racial Infants' Reading Scheme	Blackie
Kornitzer, M.	*The Holywell Family*	Bodley Head
Shoesmith, K. A.	*Do You Know About Hair?*	Burke
Baker, E.	*I Want to be a Secretary*	Chambers
Huston, A. & Yolen, J.	*Trust a City Kid*	Dent
Gittings, J. G.	*Let My People Go*	Hulton
van Stockum, H.	*Mogo's Flute*	Longmans

AUTHOR	TITLE	PUBLISHER
Ballard, M.	*Benjie's Portion*	Longmans
Chijioke, F. A.	*Beginning History: Ancient Africa*	Longmans
Joseph, J.	*Tim and Terry*	Longmans
Joseph, J.	*Judy and Jasmin*	Longmans
Steptoe, J.	*Stevie*	Longmans
Pope, R.	*Is It Always Like This?*	Macdonald
Usborne, P.	*In the Park*	Macdonald
Mwangi, Z.	*Africa: From Early Times to 1900*	Macmillan
Various authors	selected titles from the *Nippers* series: *Saturday Morning, Thigh's Team, In the Park, Eight Days to Christmas, The Wedding Tea, Julie's Story, Paul's Story, The Lost Money, The Pretenders, Tip's Lot, Ginger, The Boy in the Park.*	Macmillan
Keeping, C.	*Charley, Charlotte and the Golden Canary*	Oxford
Barrett, J.	*Old Macdonald Had Some Flats*	Piccolo
Bawden, N.	*On the Run*	Puffin
Bawden, N.	*The Runaway Summer*	Puffin
Brown, R.	*A Saturday in Pudney*	Puffin
Fox, P.	*How Many Miles to Babylon*	Puffin
van der Loeff, A. R.	*Everybody's Land*	Univ. of London Press
Monjo, F.	*The Drinking Gourd*	World's Work
Bonsall, C.	*The Case of the Hungry Stranger* (and series)	World's Work
Lexau, J.	*The Rooftop Mystery*	World's Work
Greenfield, E.	*Bubbles*	Drum & Spear Press (see Appendix I)
Klimowicz, B.	*When Shoes Eat Socks*	Abingdon Press, N.Y. (available from New Beacon Books, see Appendix I)
Clifton, L.	*Some of the Days of Everett Anderson*	Holt, Rinehart & Winston
Bond	*Brown is a Beautiful Colour*	Franklin-Watts Inc.

AUTHOR	TITLE	PUBLISHER
Brothers & Holsclow	*Just One Me*	Follett Publishing Co.
Bonham, F.	*Mystery of the Fat Cat*	Dell (available from Bogle L'Ouverture Ltd, see Appendix I)
Keats, E. J.	*Goggles*	Puffin and Bodley Head
	Hi Cat, A Letter to Amy Peter's Chair, The Snowy Day, Whistle for Willie, Pet Show	

References

Introduction

1. Sivanandan, A., and Kelly, C. (1972): *Register of Research on 'Commonwealth Immigrants' in Britain, 1972*, London, Institute of Race Relations.
2. Milner. D. (1973): 'The Future of Race Relations Research in Britain: A Social Psychologist's View', *Race*, **15**, (i), pp. 91-9.

Chapter 1

1. Lippmann, W. (1927): *Public Opinion*, London, Allen & Unwin.
2. Aristotle: *Politics*, Book xxx, I, London, Heinemann, 1958.
3. Cassian, J. (1958): translated by O. Chadwick in *Western Asceticism*, London, S.C.M. Press.
4. Jordan, W. D. (1969): *White over Black*, Baltimore, Penguin Books Inc.
5. De Gomara, Francisco Lopez (1555): cited in W. D. Jordan, op. cit.
6. Gergen, K. J. (1967): 'The Significance of Skin-Colour in Human Relations', *Daedalus*, Journal of the American Academy of Arts and Sciences, Spring 1967, pp. 390-406.
7. Bastide, R. (1967): 'Color, Racism and Christianity', *Daedalus*, Spring 1967, pp. 312-27.
8. Baker, R. (1589): 'The First Voyage of Robert Baker to Guinie . . . 1562'. in Richard Hakluyt, *The Principall Navigations, Voiages and Discoveries of the English Nation*, London, 1589.
9. Curtin, P. D. (1964): *The Image of Africa: British Ideas and Action 1780-1850*, Madison, University of Wisconsin Press.
10. Segal, R. (1966): *The Race War*, London, Cape.
11. Boulainvilliers, Count Henri de, cited in J. Barzun: '*Race: A Study in Superstition*, New York, Harper & Row, 1965.
12. Linnaeus, K. (1735): '*Systema Naturae*', cited in P. D. Curtin, op. cit.

13. Barzun, J. (1965): *Race: A Study in Superstition*, New York, Harper & Row.

14. Gossett, T. F. (1965): *Race: The History of an Idea in America*, New York, Schocken Books.

15. Stanton, W. (1960): '*The Leopard's Spots; Scientific Attitudes towards Race in America 1815–59*, Chicago, University of Chicago Press.

16. Long, E. (1774): *History of Jamaica*, vol. II, London.

17. Banton, M. (1967): *Race Relations*, London, Tavistock.

18. Knox, R. (1850): *The Races of Men: A Fragment*, London, Renshaw.

19. Gibbes, R. W. (1851): 'Death of Samuel George Morton, MD', *Charleston Medical Journal*, 6, pp. 594–8.

20. Galton, F. (1869): *Hereditary Genius: An Inquiry into Its Laws and Consequences*, London, Macmillan.

21. Thomas, W. I. (1904): 'The Psychology of Race Prejudice', *Amer. J. Sociol.*, 9, (v), pp. 593–611.

22. Ross, E. A. (1908): *Social Psychology*, New York, Macmillan.

23. Macdougall, W. (1908): *Social Psychology*, London, Methuen.

24. Allport, F. H. (1924): *Social Psychology*, Cambridge, Mass., Houghton Mifflin.

25. Baker, R. S. (1964): *Following the Color Line*, first published in 1908, reprinted New York, Harper, 1964.

26. Washington, B. T. (1945): *Up from Slavery*, London, O.U.P.

27. Fishel, L. H. & Quarles, B. (1970): *The Black American: A Documentary History*, New York, Morrow.

28. Bogardus, E. S. (1925a): 'Social Distance and Its Origins', *J. App. Sociol.*, 9, pp. 216–26.

29. Bogardus, E. S. (1925b): 'Measuring Social Distance', *J. App. Sociol.*, 9, pp. 299–308.

30. Thurstone, L. L. (1931): 'The Measurement of Social Attitudes', *J. Abnorm. & Soc. Psychol.*, 36, pp. 249–69.

31. Lasker, B. (1929): *Race Attitudes in Children*, New York, Holt.

32. Bettelheim, B., and Janowitz, M. (1950): *The Dynamics of Prejudice*, New York, Harper & Bros.

33. Adorno, T. W. *et al.* (1950): *The Authoritarian Personality*, New York, Harper.

34. Myrdal, G. (1944): *An American Dilemma: The Negro Problem and Modern Democracy*, New York, Harper.

35. Pettigrew, T. F. (1958): 'Personality and Socio-cultural Factors in Inter-Group Attitudes: A Cross-national Comparison', *J. Confl. Resol.*, 2, pp. 29–42.

36. Du Bois, W. E. B. (1964): *Souls of Black Folks*, Greenwich, Conn., Fawcett.
37. Baldwin, J. (1964): *Nobody Knows My Name*, London, Michael Joseph.
38. Baldwin, J. (1963): *The Fire Next Time*, London, Michael Joseph.
39. Kardiner, A., and Ovesey, L. (1951): *The Mark of Oppression*, New York, Norton.

Chapter 2

1. Ashley Montagu, M. F. (1968): *Man and Aggression*, New York, O.U.P.
2. Berger, P. L., and Luckmann, T. (1966): *The Social Construction of Reality*, New York, Doubleday.
3. Sullivan, H. S. (1955): *Conceptions of Modern Psychiatry*, London, Tavistock.
4. Jones, E. E., and Gerard, H. B. (1967): *Foundations of Social Psychology*, New York, Wiley.
5. Horowitz, E. L., and Horowitz, R. E. (1936): 'Development of Social Attitudes in Children', *Sociometry*, 1, pp. 307–38.
6. Johnson, N. B. (1971): 'Some Aspects of the Formation of National Concepts in Children'. Unpubl. Ph. D. dissertation, University of London, 1971.
7. Laing, R. D. (1969): *The Politics of the Family*, Toronto, Canadian Broadcasting Corporation.
8. Sears, R. R. (1957): 'Identification as a Form of Behavioural Development', in D. B. Harris (ed.): *The Concept of Development*, Univ. of Minnesota, pp. 149–61.
9. Sanford, N. (1955): 'The Dynamics of Identification', *Psychological Review*, 62, pp. 106–18.
10. Mussen, P. (1967): 'Early Socialization: Learning and Identification', in *New Directions in Psychology*, vol. 3, New York, Holt, Rinehart & Winston.
11. Freud, S. (1924): *Collected Papers*, vol. 4, London, Hogarth Press.
12. Freud, S. (1949): *Group Psychology and the Analysis of the Ego*, London, Hogarth Press
13. Freud, S. (1949): *An Outline of Psycho-analysis*, New York, Norton.
14. Mowrer, O. H. (1950): *Learning Theory and Personality Development*, New York, Ronald Press.
15. Bronfenbrenner, U. (1960): 'Freudian Theories of Identification and Their Derivatives,' *Child Development*, 31, pp. 15–40.

16. Freud, A. (1946): '*The Ego and the Mechanisms of Defence*, New York, Int. Univ. Press.
17. Whiting, J. W. M. (1960): 'Resource Mediation and Learning by Identification', in I. Iscoe and H. W. Stevenson (eds.): *Personality Development in Children*, Austin, Univ. of Texas Press.
18. Freud, S. (1933): *New Introductory Lectures on Psycho-analysis*, New York, Norton.
19. Sears, R. R., Rau, L., and Alpert, R. (1965): *Identification and Child-Rearing*, Stanford Univ. Press.
20. Bandura, A., and Huston, A. C. (1961): 'Identification as a Process of Incidental Learning', *Journal of Abnormal and Social Psychology*, **63**, pp. 311–18.
21. Bandura, A., and Walters, R. H. (1963a): 'Aggression', in *Child Psychology*, part 1, Chicago, Nat. Soc. for the Study of Education, pp. 364–415.
22. Walters, R. H. (1966): 'Implications of Laboratory Studies on Aggression for the Control and Regulation of Violence', *Ann. Amer. Acad. Polit. & Soc. Sci.* **364**, pp. 60–72.
23. Kuh, D. Z., Madsen, C. H., and Becker, W. C. (1967): 'Effects of Exposure to an Aggressive Model and Frustration on Children's Aggressive Behaviour', *Child Development*, **38**, pp. 739–46.
24. Bandura, A., Ross, D., and Ross, S. A. (1961): 'Transmission of Aggression through Imitation of Aggressive Models', *J. Ab. & Soc. Psych.*, **63**, pp. 575–82.
25. Pushkin, I. (1967): Private communication.
26. Mosher, D. L., and Scodel, A. (1960): 'Relationships between Ethnocentrism in Children and the Ethnocentrism and Authoritarian Rearing Practices in Their Mothers', *Child Development*, **31**, pp. 369–76.
27. Laing, R. D. (1961): *The Self and Others*, London, Tavistock.
28. Secord, P. F., and Backman, C. W. (1964): *Social Psychology*, New York, McGraw-Hill.
29. Morland, J. K. (1966): 'A comparison of Race Awareness in Northern and Southern Children', *American Journal of Orthopsychiatry*, **36**, pp. 22–31.
30. Tajfel, H., Bundy, R. P., Billig, M., and Flament, C. (1971): 'Social Categorization and Intergroup Behaviour', *European J. Soc. Psych.*, **1**, pp. 149–78.
31. Tajfel, H. (1970): 'Aspects of National and Ethnic Loyalty', *Social Science Information*, **9**, pp. 119–44.
32. Piaget, J. (1928): *Judgment and Reasoning in the Child*, London, Routledge.

33. Piaget, J., and Weil, A. (1951): 'The Development in Children of the Idea of the Homeland and of Relations with Other Countries.' *Inter. Soc. Sci. Bull.*, 3, pp. 561-78.

34. Jahoda, G. (1962): 'Development of Scottish Children's Ideas and Attitudes about Other Countries', *J. Social Psychol.*, 58, pp. 91-108.

35. Tajfel, H., and Jahoda, G. (1966): 'Development in Children of Concepts and Attitudes about Their Own and Other Nations: A Cross-national Study', *Proc. XVIIIth Internat. Congress Psychol.*, Moscow, 1966, Symp. 36, pp. 17-33.

36. Johnson, N. B., Middleton, M. R., and Tajfel, H. (1970): 'The Relationship between Children's Preference for and Knowledge about Other Nations', *Brit. J. Soc. & Clin. Psychol.*, 9, pp. 232-40.

37. Johnson, N. B. (1966): 'What Do Children Learn from War Comics?', *New Society*, 7 July 1966.

38. Horowitz, E. L. (1940): 'Some Aspects of the Development of Patriotism in Children', *Sociometry*, 3, pp. 329-41.

39. Middleton, M. R., Tajfel, H., and Johnson, N. B. (1970): 'Cognitive and Affective Aspects of Children's National Attitudes', *Brit. J. Soc. & Clin. Psych.*, 9, pp. 122-34.

40. Tajfel, H., Nemeth, C., Jahoda, G., Campbell, J. D., and Johnson, N. B. (1970): 'The Development of Children's Preference for Their Own Country: A Cross-national Study', *Internat. J. Psychol.*, 5, pp. 245-53.

41. Tajfel, H., Jahoda, G., Nemeth, C., Rim, Y., and Johnson, N. B. (1972): 'The Devaluation of Children of Their Own National and Ethnic Group: Two Case Studies', *Brit. J. Soc. & Clin. Psychol.*, 11, pp. 88-96.

42. Tajfel, H. (1970): private communication.

Chapter 3

1. Porter, J. D. R. (1971): *Black Child, White Child*, Cambridge, Mass., Harvard Univ. Press.

2. Williams, J. E. (1964): 'Connotations of Color-Names among Negroes and Caucasians', *Perceptual and Motor Skills*, 19, pp. 721-31.

3. Williams, J. E., Morland, J. K., and Underwood, W. L. (1970): 'Connotations of Colour Names in the US, Europe and Asia', *Journal of Social Psychology*, 82, pp. 3-14.

4. Williams, J. E. (1970): 'Connotations of Racial Concepts and Colour Names', in M. L. Goldschmid (ed.), *Black Americans and*

White Racism, New York, Holt, Rinehart & Winston, 1970, pp. 38–48.

5. Harbin, S. P., and Williams, J. E. (1966): 'Conditioning of Color Connotations', *Perceptual and Motor Skills*, **22**, pp. 217–18.

6. Renninger, C. A., and Williams, J. E. (1966): 'Black-white Color-connotations and Race Awareness in Preschool Children', *Perceptual and Motor Skills*, **22**, pp. 771–85.

7. Mosher, D. L., and Scodell, A. (1960): 'Relationship between Ethnocentrism in Children and the Ethnocentrism and Authoritarian Rearing Practices in Their Mothers', *Child Development*, **31**, pp. 369–76.

8. McCandless, B. R., and Hoyt, J. M. (1961): 'Sex, Ethnicity and Play Preference of Pre-School Children', *Journal of Abnormal and Social Psychology*, **62**, pp. 683–5.

9. Allport, G., and Kramer, B. M. (1946): 'Some Roots of Prejudice', *Journal of Psychology*, **22**, pp. 9–39.

10. Orwell, G. (1939): 'Boy's Weeklies' in his *Collected Essays*, London, Secker & Warburg, 1961.

11. Johnson, N. B. (1966): 'What Do Children Learn from War Comics', *New Society*, 7 July 1966.

12. Laishley, J. (1972): 'Can Comics Join the Multi-racial Society?', *Times Education Supplement*, 24 November 1972, p. 4.

13. Himmelweit, H., Oppenheim, A. N., and Vince, P. (1958): *Television and the Child*, London, Oxford University Press.

14. Dominick, J. R., and Greenberg, B. S. (1969): 'Communication among the Urban Poor: Blacks on TV: Their Presence and Roles', Report no. 8, Project CUP, Department of Communication, Michigan State University.

15. Greenberg, B. S., and Dominick, J. R. (1969): 'Television Behaviour among Disadvantaged Children', Report no. 9, Project CUP, Department of Communication, Michigan State University.

16. Greenberg, B. S. (1971): 'Children's Reactions to TV Blacks', Report no. 14, Project CUP, Department of Communication, Michigan State University.

17. Husband, C. (1972): 'The Media', *Race Today*, **4**, no. 9, p. 307.

18. Husband, C. (1972): 'The Media', *Race Today*, **4**, no. 10, p. 338.

19. Jones, K., and Smith, A. D. (1970): *The Economic Impact of Commonwealth Immigration*, Cambridge University Press.

20. Goodman, M. E. (1964): *Race Awareness in Young Children*, New York, Collier Books.

21. Stevenson, H. W. and Stewart, E. C. (1958): 'A Developmental

Study of Racial Awareness in Young Children', *Child Development*, **29**, pp. 399–409.

22. Horowitz, E. L. (1936): 'Development of Attitude towards Negroes', *Archives of Psychology*, no. 194.

23. Radke, M., Trager, H. G., and Davis, H. (1949): 'Social Perceptions and Attitudes of Children', *Genetic Psychology Monographs*, **40**, pp. 327–447.

24. Ammons, R. B. (1950): 'Reactions in a Projective Doll-Play Interview of White Males Two to Six Years of Age to Differences in Skin-Colour and Facial Features', *Journal of Genetic Psychology*, **76**, pp. 323–41.

25. Morland, J. K. (1958): 'Racial Recognition by Nursery School Children in Lynchburg, Virginia', *Social Forces*, **37**, pp. 132–7.

26. Morland, J. K. (1963): 'Racial Self-Identification: A Study of Nursery School Children', *Amer. Cath. Sociol. Rev.*, **24**, pp. 231–42.

27. Radke, M. J., and Trager, H. G. (1950): 'Children's Perceptions of the Social Roles of Negroes and Whites', *Journal of Psychology*, **29**, pp. 93–103.

28. Vaughan, G. M. (1963): 'Concept Formation and the Development of Ethnic Awareness', *J. Genet. Psychol.*, **103**, pp. 93–103.

29. Vaughan, G. M. (1964a): 'Ethnic Awareness in Relation to Minority-Group Membership', *J. Genet. Psychol.*, **103**, 119–30.

30. Morland, J. K. (1969): 'Race Awareness among American and Hong Kong Chinese Children', *Amer. J. Sociol.*, **75**, (3), pp. 360–74.

31. Morland, J. K. (1962): 'Racial Acceptance and Preference of Nursery School Children in a Southern City'. *Merrill-Palmer Quart.*, **8**, 271–80.

32. Lambert, H. C., and Taguchi, Y. (1961): 'Ethnic Cleavage among Young Children', *Jour. Abnorm. & Social Psychol.*, **62**, pp. 380–82.

33. Criswell, J. H. (1937): 'Racial Cleavage in Negro–White Groups', *Sociometry*, **1**, pp. 87–9.

34. Criswell, J. H. (1939): 'A Sociometric Study of Race Cleavage in the Classroom', *Arch. Psychol.*, no. 235.

35. Clark, K. (1955): *Prejudice and Your Child*, Boston, Beacon Press.

36. Harding, J., Proshansky, H., Kutner, B. and Chein, I. (1967): 'Prejudice and Ethnic Relations', in G. Lindzey and E. Aronson (eds.): *Handbook of Social Psychology*, vol. 5, Cambridge, Mass., Addison-Wesley.

37. Trager, H. G., and Radke-Yarrow, M. (1952): *They Learn What They Live*, New York, Harper.

38. Radke, M., and Trager, H. G. (1950): 'Children's Perceptions of the Social Roles of Negroes and Whites', *J. Psychol.*, **29**, pp. 3–33.

39. Minard, R. D. (1931): 'Race Attitudes of Iowa Children', *Univ. Iowa Stud. Char.*, **4**, (2).

40. Muhyi, I. A. (1952): 'Certain Content of Prejudices against Negroes among White Children of Different Ages', unpubl. Ph.D. dissert., Columbia Univ., 1952.

41. Blake, R., and Dennis, W. (1943): 'The Development of Stereotypes Concerning the Negro', *Jour. Abnorm. & Social Psych.*, **38**, pp. 525–31.

42. Radke, M., Sutherland, J., and Rosenberg, P. (1950): 'Racial Attitudes of Children', *Sociometry*, **13**, pp. 154–71.

43. Lipset, S. M. (1959): 'Democracy and Working Class Authoritarianism', *Amer. Sociol. Rev.*, **24**, pp. 482–501.

44. Bird., C., Monachesi, E. D., and Burdick, H. (1952): 'The Effect of Parental Discouragement of Play Activities upon the Attitudes of White Children towards Negroes', *Child Development*, **23**, pp. 13–53.

45. Landreth, C., and Johnson, B. C. (1953): 'Young Children's Responses to a Picture and Inset Task Designed to Reveal Reactions to Persons of Different Skin-colour', *Child Development*, **24**, pp. 63–80.

46. Chein, I., and Hurwitz, J. I. (1950): 'The Reactions of Jewish Boys to Various Aspects of Being Jewish', New York, Jewish Centre Division, National Jewish Welfare Board.

47. Chyatte, C., Schaefer, D. F., and Spiaggia, M., (1951): 'Prejudice Verbalisation among Children', *J. Educ. Psych.*, **42**, pp. 421–31.

48. Singer, D. (1967): 'Reading, Writing and Race Relations', *Trans-action*, June 1967, pp. 27–31.

49. Mussen, P. H. (1950): 'Some Personality and Social Factors Related to Changes in Children's attitudes towards Negroes', *Jour. Abnorm. & Soc. Psych.*, **45**, pp. 423–41.

50. Deutsch, M., and Collins, M. (1951): *Inter-racial Housing – a Psychological Evaluation of a Social Experiment*, Minneapolis, Univ. of Minnesota Press.

51. Mackenzie, B. K. (1948): 'The Importance of Contact in Determining Attitudes towards Negroes', *Jour. Abnorm. & Soc. Psych.*, **43**, pp. 417–41.

52. Koch, H. L. (1946): 'The Social Distance between Certain Racial, Nationality and Skin-Pigmentation Groups in Selected Populations of American Schoolchildren', *J. Genet. Psych.*, **68**, pp. 63–95.

53. Springer, D. V. (1950): 'Awareness of Racial Difference by Pre-Schoolchildren in Hawaii', *Gen. Psych. Mon.*, **41**, pp. 215–70.

54. Vaughan, G. M. (1964b): 'The Development of Ethnic Attitudes in New Zealand Schoolchildren', *Gen. Psych. Mon.*, **70**, pp. 135-75.

55. Radke-Yarrow, M., Trager, H. G., and Miller, J. (1952): 'The Role of the Parents in the Development of Children's Ethnic Attitudes', *Child Development*, **23**, pp. 13-53.

56. Gough, H. G., Harris, D. B., Martin, W. E., and Edwards, M. (1950): 'Children's Ethnic Attitudes: 1: Relationship to Certain Personality Factors', *Child Development*, **21**, pp. 83-91.

57. Allport, G. W., and Kramer, B. M. (1946): 'Some Roots of Prejudice', *J. Psych.*, **22**, pp. 9-39.

58. Horowitz, E. L., and Horowitz, R. E. (1938): 'Development of Social Attitudes in Children', *Sociometry*, **1**, pp. 307-38.

59. Adorno, T. W., Frenkel-Brunswik, E., Levinson, D. J., and Sanford, E. N. (1950): *The Authoritarian Personality*, New York, Harper.

60. Harding, J., Proshansky, H., Kutner, B., and Chein, I. (1969): 'Prejudice and Ethnic Relations', in G. Lindzey and E. Aronson (eds.): *Handbook of Social Psychology*, vol. 5, Reading, Mass., Addison-Wesley.

61. Christie, R., and Jahoda, M. (1954): *Studies in the Scope and Method of the Authoritarian Personality*, Glencoe, Illinois, Free Press.

62. Titus, H. E., and Hollander, E. P. (1957): 'The California F-Scale in Psychological Research, 1950-55, *Psych. Bull.*, **54**, pp. 47-64.

63. Gough, H. G., Harris, D. B., and Martin, W. E. (1950): 'Children's Ethnic Attitudes: 2: Relationship to Parental Beliefs Concerning Child Training', *Child Development*, **21**, pp. 169-81.

64. Horowitz, R. E. (1939): 'Racial Aspects of Self-Identification in Nursery-School Children', *J. Psych.*, **7**, pp. 91-9.

65. Clark, K. B., and Clark, M. P. (1939): 'The Development of Consciousness of Self and the Emergence of Racial Identification in Negro Pre-School Children', *J. Soc. Psych.*, *SSPSI Bulletin*, **10**, pp. 591-9.

66. Clark, K. B., and Clark, M. P. (1947): 'Racial Identification and Preference in Negro Children', in T. M. Newcomb and E. L. Hartley (eds.): *Readings in Social Psychology*, New York, Holt, 1947, pp. 169-78.

67. Goodman, M. E. (1946): 'Evidence Concerning the Genesis of Inter-racial Attitudes', *American Anthropologist*, **48**, pp. 624-30.

68. Porter, J. D. (1963): 'Racial Concept Formation in Pre-School Age Children', unpubl. Master's thesis, Cornell Univ., 1963.

69. Hartley, E. L., Schwarz, S., and Rosenbaum, M. (1948a): 'Child-

ren's Use of Ethnic Frames of Reference: An Exploratory Study of Children's Conceptions of Multiple Ethnic Group Membership', *J. Psych.*, **26**, pp. 367–86.

70. Hartley, E. L., Rosenbaum, M. and Schwartz, S. (1948b): 'Children's Perceptions of Ethnic Group Membership', *J. Psych.*, **26**, pp. 387–98.

71. Goodman, M. E. (1952): *Race Awareness in Young Children*, Cambridge, Mass., Addison-Wesley.

72. Deutsch, M. (1960): *Minority-Group and Class Status as Related to Social and Personality Factors in Scholastic Achievement*, Monograph 2, Society for Applied Anthropology, Cornell University, New York.

73. Butts, H. (1963): 'Skin-Colour Perception and Self-Esteem', *J. Negro Educ.*, **32**, pp. 122–8.

74. Palermo, D. S. (1959): 'Racial Comparisons and Additional Normative Data on the Children's Manifest Anxiety Scale', *Child Development*, **30**, pp. 53–7.

75. Mussen, P. H. (1953): 'Differences between the T.A.T. Responses of Negro and White Boys', *J. Consulting Psych.*, **17**, pp. 373–6.

76. Ritchie, J. E. (1963): *The Making of a Maori*, Publications in Psychology, no. 15, Victoria, University of Wellington.

77. Thompson, R. H. T. (1953): 'Maori Affairs and the New Zealand Press', *Journ. Polynesian Soc.*, **62**, pp. 363–83.

78. Werner, N. E., and Evans, I. M. (1968): 'Perception of Prejudice in Mexican–American Preschool Children', *Perceptual and Motor Skills*, **27**, pp. 1039–46.

79. Bruner, J. S., and Goodman, C. C. (1947): 'Value and Need as Organising Factors in Perception', *J. Abnorm. & Soc. Psych.*, **42**, pp. 33–44.

80. Johnson, G. B. (1950): 'The Origin of the Spanish Attitude towards the Anglo and the Anglo Attitude towards the Spanish', *J. Educ. Psych.*, **41**, pp. 428–39.

81. Fishman, J. A. (1955): 'Negative Stereotypes Concerning Americans among American-born Children Receiving Various Types of Minority-Group Education', *Gen. Psych. Mon.*, **51**, pp. 107–182.

82. Harris, A., and Watson, G. (1946): 'Are Jewish or Gentile Children More Clannish?', *J. Soc. Psych.*, **24**, pp. 71–6.

83. Meltzer, H. (1939): 'Group Differences in Nationality and Race Preferences of Children', *Sociometry*, **2**, pp. 86–105.

84. Zeligs, R., and Hendrickson, G. (1933): 'Racial Attitudes of Two Hundred Sixth Grade Children', *Sociol. Soc. Res.*, **18**, pp. 26–36.

85. Gregor, A. J., and McPherson, D. A. (1966): 'Racial Preference and Ego-Identity among White and Bantu Children in the Republic of South Africa', *Gen. Psych. Mon.*, **73**, pp. 217-53.

86. Clark, K. (1965): *Dark Ghetto*, New York.

87. Kirscht, J. P., and Dillehay, R. C. (1967): *Dimensions of Authoritarianism: A Review of Research and Theory*, Lexington, University of Kentucky Press.

88. LaPiere, R. (1934): 'Attitudes vs Actions', *Social Forces*, **13**, pp. 230-37.

89. Milner, D. (1973): 'The Future of Race Relations Research in Britain: A Social Psychologist's View', *Race*, **15**, (i), pp. 91-9.

90. Vernon, P. E. (1938): *The Assessment of Psychological Qualities by Verbal Methods*, Medical Research Council, Industrial Health Research Board, Report no. 83, London, H. M. Stationery.

91. Deutscher, I. (1966): 'Words and Deeds: Social Science and Social Policy', *Social Problems*, **13**, (iii), pp. 235-54.

92. Minard, R. D. (1952): 'Race Relationships in the Pocahontas Coal Field', *J. Soc. Issues*, **8**, (i), pp. 29-44.

93. Wicker, A. W. (1969): 'Attitudes versus Actions: The Relationship of Verbal and Overt Behavioral Responses to Attitude Objects', *J. Soc. Issues*, **25**, (iv), pp. 41-78.

Chapter 4

1. Rose, E. J. B., *et al.* (1969): *Colour and Citizenship: a Report on British Race Relations*, London, O.U.P. for I.R.R.

2. Lawrence, D. (1969): 'How Prejudiced Are We?', *Race Today*, **1**, no. 6, pp. 174-6.

3. Deakin, N., *et al.* (1970): *Colour, Citizenship and British Society*, London, Panther Books.

4. Political and Economic Planning (1967): *Report on Racial Discrimination*, London, Political and Economic Planning.

5. Daniel, W. W. (1968): *Racial Discrimination in England*, Harmondsworth, Penguin Books.

6. Smith, M. G. (1965): *The Plural Society in the British West Indies*, Berkeley, University of California Press.

7. Lowenthal, D. (1970): 'Black Power in the Caribbean', letter in *Race Today*, **2**, no. 3, pp. 94-5.

8. Lowenthal, D. (1972), *West Indian Societies*, London, O.U.P. for I.R.R.

9. Fitzherbert, K. (1967): *West Indian Children in London*, Occasional papers on social admin., no. 19, London, Bell.

10. Bowker, G. (1968): *The Education of Coloured Immigrants*, London, Longmans.
11. Hiro, D. (1967): *The Indian Family in Britain*, London, N.C.C.I.
12. Goodall, J. (1968): 'The Pakistani Background', in R. Oakley (ed.): *New Backgrounds*, London, O.U.P. for I.R.R.
13. Narain, D. (1964): 'Growing Up in India', *Family Process*, 3, (i), pp. 127–54.
14. Bell, R. (1968): 'The Indian Background', in R. Oakley (ed.), op. cit.
15. Pushkin, I. (1967): 'A Study of Ethnic Choice in the Play of Young Children in Three London Districts', unpubl. Ph. D. dissertation, University of London.
16. Clark, K. B., and Clark, M. P. (1947): 'Racial Identification and Preference in Negro Children', in T. M. Newcomb and E. L. Hartley (eds.): *Readings in Social Psychology*, New York, Holt, pp. 169–78.
17. Trent, R. D. (1954): 'The Colour of the Investigator as a Variable in Experimental Research with Negro Subjects', *J. Soc. Psych.*, 40, pp. 281–7.
18. Kraus, S. (1962): 'Modifying Prejudice: Attitude Change as a Function of the Race of the Communicator', *Audio-visual Communication Review*, 10, pp. 14–22.
19. Freedman, P. I. (1967): 'Race as a Factor in Persuasion', *J. of Exper. Educ.*, 35, pp. 48–52.
20. Summers, G. F. and Hammonds, A. D. (1966): 'Effects of Racial Characteristics of Investigator on Self-enumerated Responses to a Negro Prejudice Scale', *Social Forces*, 44, pp. 515–18.
21. Jahoda, G., Thomson, S. S., and Bhatt, S. (1972): 'Ethnic Identity and Preferences among Asian Immigrant Children in Glasgow: A Replicated Study', *Europ. J. Soc. Psych.*, 2, (1), pp. 19–32.
22. Greenwald, H. J., and Oppenheim, D. B. (1968): 'Reported Magnitude of Self-misidentification among Negro Children: Artifact?' *J. Pers. & Soc. Psych.*, 8, pp. 49–52.
23. Morland, J. K. (1962): 'Racial Acceptance and Preference of Nursery School Children in a Southern City', *Merrill-Palmer Quarterly*, 8, pp. 271–80.
24. Morland, J. K. (1963): 'Racial Self-Identification: A Study of Nursery-School Children', *Amer. Catholic Sociol. Rev.*, 24, pp. 231–42.
25. Morland, J. K. (1966): 'A Comparison of Race Awareness in Northern and Southern Children', *Amer. J. Orthopsychiatry*, 36, pp. 22–31.

26. Hraba, J., and Grant, G. (1970): 'Black is Beautiful: A Re-Examination of Racial Identification and Preference', *J. Pers. & Soc. Psych.* **16**, pp. 398–402.

27. Goodman, M. E. (1964): *Race Awareness in Young Children*, New York, Collier Books.

28. Klineberg, O., and Zavalloni, M. (1969): *Nationalism and Tribalism among African Students*, Paris, Mouton.

29. Sattler, J. M. (1973): 'Racial Experimenter Effects', in K. S. Miller and R. S. Dreger (eds.): *Comparative Studies of Blacks and Whites in the United States*, New York, Seminar Press.

30. Kawwa, T. (1965): 'A Study of the Interaction between Native and Immigrant Children in an English School with Special Reference to Ethnic Prejudice', unpubl. Ph.D. dissertation, Inst. of Educ., University of London.

31. Laishley, J. (1971): 'Skin-Colour Awareness and Preference in London Nursery School Children', *Race*, **13**, (i), pp. 47–64.

32. Brown, G. and Johnson, S. P. (1971): 'The Attribution of Behavioural Connotations to Shaded and White Figures by Caucasian Children', *Brit. J. Soc. & Clin. Psych.*, **10**, pp. 306–12.

33. Richardson, S. A., and Green, A. (1971): 'When is Black Beautiful? Coloured and White Children's Reactions to Skin-Colour', *Brit. J. Educ. Psych.*, **41**, pp. 62–9.

34. I.R.R. Library Staff (1973): 'Books, Libraries and Racism', *Race Today*, **5**, no. 10, pp. 301–8.

35. Clarke, E. (1966): *My Mother Who Fathered Me*, London, Allen & Unwin.

36. Sivanandan, A. (1969): *Coloured Immigrants in Britain: A Select Bibliography*, London, Inst. Race Relations, Special Series.

37. Dummett, A. (1973): *A Portrait of English Racism*, Harmondsworth, Penguin.

38. Humphry, D. (1972): *Police Power and Black People*, London, Panther Books.

39. Humphry, D., and John, A. (1970): *Because They're Black*, Harmondsworth, Penguin.

40. Holroyde, P., *et al.* (1970): *East Comes West: A Background to some Asian Faiths*, London, Community Relations Commission.

41. Searle, C. (1973): *The Forsaken Lover: White Words and Black People*, Harmondsworth, Penguin.

42. Rex, J., and Moore, R. (1967): *Race Community and Conflict: A Study of Sparkbrook*, London, Oxford University Press for I.R.R.

43. Allen, S. (1972): *New Minorities, Old Conflicts: Asian and West Indian Migrants in Britain*, New York, Random House.

44. Ramchand, K. (1965): 'The Colour Problem at University: a West Indian's Changing Attitudes', in H. Tajfel and J. Dawson (eds.): *Disappointed Guests*, O.U.P. for I.R.R.

45. Patterson, S. (1963): *Dark Strangers*, London, Tavistock.

46. Rowley, K. G. (1968): 'Sociometric Study of Friendship Choices among English and Immigrant Children', *Educational Research*, 10, (ii), pp. 145–8.

47. Kawwa, T. (1963): 'Ethnic Prejudice and Choice of Friends amongst English and Non-English Adolescents', unpubl. M.A. dissert., University of London.

48. Saint, C. K. (1963): 'Scholastic and Sociological Adjustment Problems of the Punjabi-speaking Children in Smethwick', unpubl. M. Ed. dissert., Univ. of Birmingham.

49. Durojaiye, M. O. A. (1970): 'Patterns of Friendship Choices in an Ethnically-mixed Junior School', *Race*, 12, (ii), pp. 189–200.

Chapter 5

1. Seward, G. H., (1956): *Psychotherapy and Culture Conflict*, New York, Ronald Press.

2. Mussen, P. H., (1953): 'Differences between the T.A.T. Responses of Negro and White Boys', *Journal of Consulting Psychology*, 17, pp. 373–6.

3. Palermo, D. S., (1959): 'Racial Comparisons and Additional Normative Data on the Children's Manifest Anxiety Scale', *Child Development*, 30, pp. 53–7.

4. Deutsch, M., (1960): *Minority Group and Class Status as Related to Social and Personality Factors in Scholastic Achievement*, Monograph 2, Society for Applied Anthropology.

5. Hammer, E. F., (1953): 'Negro and White Children's Personality Adjustment as Revealed by a Comparison of Their Drawings (H-T-P)', *Journal of Clinical Psychology*, 9, pp. 7–10.

6. Kleiner, R. J., Tuckman, J., and Lavell, M., (1960): 'Mental Disorder and Status Based on Race', *Psychiatry*, 23, pp. 271–4.

7. Jaco, E. G., (1960): *The Social Epidemiology of Mental Disorders*, New York, Russell Sage Foundation.

8. Dreger, R. M., and Miller, K. S., (1968): 'Comparative Psychological Studies of Negroes and Whites in the U.S., 1959–65', *Psychological Bulletin*, Monograph Supplement 70 (iii) part 2.

9. Dreger, R. M., and Miller, K. S., (1960): 'Comparative Psychological Studies of Negroes and Whites in the U.S.', *Psychological Bulletin*, 57, pp. 361–402.

10. Milner, E., (1953): 'Some Hypotheses Concerning the Influence

of Segregation on Negro Personality Development', *Psychiatry*, **16**, pp. 291–7.

11. Bateson, G., Jackson, D. D., Haley, J., and Weakland, J. (1956): 'Towards a Theory of Schizophrenia', *Behavioural Science*, **1**, pp. 251–64.

12. Laing, R. D. (1963): *The Divided Self*, London, Tavistock.

13. Kardiner, A., and Ovesey, L., (1951): *The Mark of Oppression*, New York, Norton.

14. Brown, C., (1966): *Manchild in the Promised Land*, London, Cape.

15. U.S. Commission on Civil Rights (1967): *Racial Isolation in the Public Schools*, Washington, U.S. Govt. Printing Office.

16. Pettigrew, T. F., (1964): *A Profile of the Negro American*, Princeton, Van Nostrand.

17. Brody, E. B. (1963): 'Colour and Identity Conflict in Young Boys: Observations of Negro Mothers and Sons in Urban Baltimore', *Psychiatry*, **26**, pp. 188–207.

18. Stone, I. F. (1966): *New York Review of Books*, 18 August 1966.

19. Fanon, F. (1968): *Black Skin, White Masks*, London, MacGibbon & Kee.

20. Jahoda, G. (1961): *White Man*, London, O.U.P. for Inst. of Race Relations.

21. Ritchie, J. E. (1963): *The Making of a Maori*, Victoria, Univ. of Wellington Publications in Psychology, no. 15.

22. Dai, B. (1953): 'Some Problems of Personality Development among Negro Children' in Kluckhohn, C., and Murray, H. (eds.) *Personality in Nature, Society and Culture*, New York, Knopf.

23. X, Malcolm (1968): *The Autobiography of Malcolm X*, Harmondsworth, Penguin Books.

24. Baldwin, J. (1964): *Nobody Knows My Name*, London, Joseph.

25. Kleiner, S., and Parker, R. (1966): *Mental Illness in the Urban Negro Community*, New York, The Free Press.

26. Allport, G. (1954): *The Nature of Prejudice*, Cambridge, Addison-Wesley.

27. Sartre, J-P. (1948): *Anti-Semite and Jew*, New York, Schocken Books.

28. Baughman, E. E. (1971): *Black Americans*, New York, Academic Press.

29. McDonald, R. L., and Gynther, M. D. (1965): 'Relationship of Self and Ideal-Self Descriptions with Sex, Race and Class in Southern Adolescents', *Journal of Personality and Social Psychology*, **1**, pp. 85–8.

30. Wendland, M. M. (1967): 'Self-Concept in Southern Negro and

White Adolescents as Related to Rural-Urban Residence', unpubl. Ph.D. dissert., Univ. of N. Carolina at Chapel Hill.

31. Rosenberg, M., and Simmons, R. G. (1972): *Black and White Self-Esteem: The Urban School-Child*, The Arnold and Caroline Rose Monograph Series in Sociology, American Sociological Association.

32. Friedman, N. (1969): 'Africa and the Afro-American: The Changing Negro Identity', *Psychiatry*, **32**, (2), pp. 127–36.

33. Isaacs, H. R. (1964): *The New World of Negro Americans*, Viking Press, Compass Edition.

34. Hraba, J., and Grant, G. (1970): 'Black is Beautiful: A Re-Examination of Racial Preference and Identification', *J. Pers. & Soc. Psychol.*, **16**, pp. 398–402.

35. Harris, S., and Braun, J. R. (1971): 'Self-Esteem and Racial Preference in Black Children', Proceedings of the 79th Annual Convention, APA, 1971.

36. Morland, J. K. (1972): 'Racial Attitudes in Schoolchildren', Final Report, U.S. Dept. of Health, Education and Welfare, Project no. 2–0–009.

37. Bagley, C. (1969): 'The Social Aetiology of Schizophrenia in Immigrant Groups', *Race Today*, **1**, no. 6, pp. 170–4.

38. Hensi, L. K. (1968): 'Psychiatric Troubles of Immigrants', *New Society*, 1 February 1968, pp. 162–3.

39. Deakin, N. (1970): *Colour, Citizenship and British Society*, London, Panther.

40. P.E.P. (1967): *Report on Racial Discrimination*, London, Political and Economic Planning.

41. Griffin, J. H. (1962): *Black Like Me*, London, Collins.

42. Humphry, D., and John, A. (1971): *Because They're Black*, Harmondsworth, Penguin Books.

43. Paige, J. M. (1970): 'Changing Patterns of Anti-White Attitudes among Blacks', *Journal of Social Issues*, **26**, pp. 67–86.

44. Brigham, J. C. (1971): 'Views of White and Black Schoolchildren Concerning Racial Differences', Revision of a paper read at the meeting of the Mid-Western Psychological Association, Detroit, May, 1971.

45. Carpenter, T. R., and Busse, T. V. (1969): 'Development of Self-Concept in Negro and White Welfare Children', *Child Development*, **40**, pp. 935–9.

46. Zirkel, P. A., and Moses, E. G. (1971), 'Self-concept and Ethnic Group Membership among Public School Students', *American Educational Research Journal*, **8**, pp. 253–65.

47. Floyd, J. (1973): 'Self-Concept Development in Black Children', mimeograph, Univ. of Rochester.
48. Howe, D. (1973): 'Fighting Back: West Indian Youth and the Police in Notting Hill', *Race Today*, 5, (11), pp. 333-7.

Chapter 6

1. Pasamanick, B., and Knobloch, H. (1961): 'Epidemiological Studies on the Complications of Pregnancy and the Birth Process', in G. Caplan (ed.): *Prevention of Mental Disorders in Children*, N.Y., Basic Books.
2. O'Reilly, R. P. (1970): *Racial and Social Class Isolation in the Schools*, N.Y., Praeger.
3. Deutsch, C. P. (1968): 'Environment and Perception', in M. Deutsch, I. Katz, and A. R. Jensen (eds.): *Social Class, Race and Psychological Development*, N.Y., Holt, Rinehart & Winston.
4. Deutsch, C. P. (1964): 'Auditory Discrimination and Learning: Social Factors', *Merrill-Palmer Quart.*, 10, (iii), pp. 277-96.
5. Jensen, A. R. (1968): 'Social Class and Verbal Learning', in Deutsch, Katz and Jensen, op. cit.
6. Bernstein, B. (1962): 'Linguistic Codes, Hesitation Phenomena and Intelligence', *Language and Speech*, 5, (i), pp. 31-46.
7. MacDonald, M., McGuire, C., and Havighurst, R. (1949): 'Leisure Activities and the Socio-economic Status of Children', *Amer. J. Sociol.*, 54, pp. 505-19.
8. Deutsch, M. P. (1963): 'The Disadvantaged Child and the Learning Process', in A. H. Passow (ed.): *Education in Depressed Areas*, N.Y., Columbia University Press.
9. Milner, E. (1951) :'A Study of the Relationship between Reading Readiness in Grade One Schoolchildren and Patterns of Parent-Child Interactions', *Child Dev.*, 22, pp. 95-122.
10. Stendler, C. B. (1961): 'Social Class Differences in Parental Attitude Towards School at Grade One Level', *Child Dev.*, 22, pp. 37-46.
11. Rosen, B. C. (1946): 'The Achievement Syndrome: A Psycho-cultural Dimension of Social Stratification', *Amer. Sociol. Rev.*, 21, pp. 203-11.
12. Terrel, G., Durkin, K., and Wiesley, M. (1959): 'Social Class and the Nature of the Incentive in Discrimination Learning', *J. Abnorm. & Soc. Psych.*, 59, pp. 270-72.
13. Dreger, R. M., and Miller, K. S. (1969): 'Comparative Psychological Studies of Negroes and Whites in the U.S., 1959-1965', *Psych. Bull.*, Monograph Suppl. 70, (iii), pp. 1-58.

14. Montague, D. O. (1964): 'Arithmetic Concepts of Kindergarten Children in Contrasting Socio-economic Areas', *Elementary Schools Journal*, **64**, pp. 393–7.

15. Coleman, H. A. (1940), 'The Relationship of Socio-economic Status to the Performance of Junior High School Students', *J. Exper. Educ.*, **9**, pp. 61–3.

16. Siller, J. (1957): 'Socio-economic status and conceptual thinking', *J. Abnorm. & Soc. Psych.*, **55**, pp. 365–71.

17. Eels, K., Davis, A., Havighurst, R. J., Vergil, E., and Tyler, R. (1951): *Intelligence and Cultural Differences*, Chicago, University of Chicago Press.

18. Abrahamson, S. (1952): 'Our Status System and Scholastic Rewards', *J. Educ. Sociol.*, **25**, pp. 441–50.

19. Hill, E. H., and Giammatteo, M. C. (1963): 'Socio-economic Status and Its Relationship to School Achievement in the Elementary School', *Elementary English*, **40**, pp. 265–70.

20. Wylie, R. C. (1963): 'Children's Estimates of Their Schoolwork Ability, as a Function of Sex, Race and Socio-economic Status', *J. Pers.*, **31**, pp. 203–24.

21. McKee, J. P., and Leader, F. B. (1955): 'The Relationship of Socio-economic Status and Aggression to the Competitive Behaviour of Pre-School Children', *Child Dev.*, **26**, pp. 135–41.

22. Bledsoe, J. C. (1959): 'An Investigation of Six Correlates of Student Withdrawal from High School', *J. Educ. Res.*, **53**, pp. 3–6.

23. Rist, R. C. (1970): 'Student Social Class and Teacher Expectations: The Self-fulfilling prophecy of Ghetto Education', *Harvard Ed. Rev.*, **40**, pp. 411–51.

24. Rosenthal, R., and Jacobson, L. (1968): *Pygmalion in the Classroom*, N.Y., Holt.

25. Silberman, C. E. (1970): *Crisis in the Classroom*, N.Y., Random House.

26. Ginsburg, H. (1972): *The Myth of the Deprived Child*, Englewood Cliffs N.J., Prentice-Hall.

27. Katz, I. (1968): 'Factors Influencing Negro Performance in the De-segregated School', in Deutsch, Katz and Jensen, op. cit.

28. Coles, R. (1963): *The De-Segregation of Southern Schools: A Psychiatric Study*, N.Y., Anti-Defamation League.

29. Yarrow, M. R. (1958): 'Inter-personal Dynamics in a De-segregation Process', *J. of Social Issues*, **14**, (i).

30. Criswell, J. H. (1939): 'Social Structure Revealed in a Sociometric Re-Test', *Sociometry*, **2**, pp. 69–75.

31. Herriott, R. E., and St. John, N. H. (1966): *Social Class and the Urban School*, N.Y., Wiley.

32. Katz, I. (1967): 'The Socialization of Academic Motivation in Minority-Group Children', in D. Levine (ed.): *Nebraska Symposium on Motivation*, 1967, Lincoln, University of Nebraska Press, pp. 131–91.

33. Gottlieb, D. (1964): 'Teaching and Students: The Views of Negro and White Teachers', *Sociol. Educ.*, **37**, pp. 345–53.

34. Hoehn, A. J. (1954): 'The Study of Social Status Differentiation in the Classroom Behaviour of 19 Third Grade Teachers', *J. Soc. Psych.*, **39**, pp. 269–92.

35. Davidson, H. H., and Lang, G. (1960): 'Children's Perceptions of Their Teachers' Feeling towards Them Related to Self-perception, School Achievement and Behaviour', *J. Exper. Educ.*, **29**, pp. 107–18.

36. Clark, K. B. (1965): *Dark Ghetto*, N.Y., Harper & Row.

37. Rosenthal, R. (1966): *Experimenter Effects in Behavioural Research*, N.Y., Appleton Century Crofts.

38. Rosenthal, R., and Jacobson, L. (1968): 'Self-fulfilling Prophecies in the Classroom', in Deutsch, Katz and Jensen, op. cit.

39. O'Reilly, R. P. (1969): 'The Relationship of Anxiety, Creativity, Intelligence and Prior Knowledge of Program Content to Children's Performance with Programmed Instructional Materials', unpubl. doctoral disserts., Cornell Univ.

40. Philips, B. N., and McNeil, K. (1968): 'Differences between Anglo and Non-Anglo Children on Factorial Dimensions of School Anxiety and Coping Style', paper presented to Amer. Educ. Res. Assoc., Chicago, 1968.

41. Deutsch, M. (1960): 'Minority Group and Class Status as Related to Social and Personality Factors in Scholastic Achievement', *Monograph, no. 2, Society for Applied Anthropology*, pp. 1–32.

42. Keller, S. (1963): 'The Social World of the Urban Slum Child: Some Early Findings', *Amer. J. Orthopsych.*, **33**, pp. 823–31.

43. U.S. Commission on Civil Rights (1967): *Racial Isolation in the Public Schools*, Washington, U.S. Govt Printing Office.

44. Coleman, J. S. (1966): *Equality of Educational Opportunity*, Office of Education, U.S. Department of Health, Education and Welfare, U.S. Govt Printing Office.

45. Weinberg, M. (1968): *Desegregation Research: An Appraisal*, Bloomington, Phi Delta Kappa.

46. St John, N. (1970): 'Desegration and Minority-Group Performance', *Review of Educ. Res.*, **40**, (i), pp. 111–33.

47. Gordon, E. W. (1968): 'Programs of Compensatory Education', in Deutsch, Katz and Jensen, op. cit.

48. Westinghouse Learning Corporation and Ohio University (1969): *The Impact of Head Start*, Bladensburg, Maryland.

49. Stallings, F. H. (1959): 'A Study of the Immediate Effects of Integration on Scholastic Achievement in the Louisville Public Schools', *J. Negro Educ.*, **28**, pp. 439–44.

50. Baratz, S. S., and Baratz, J. C. (1970): 'Early Childhood Intervention: The Social Science Base of Institutional Racism', *Harvard Ed. Rev.*, **40**, pp. 29–50.

51. Valentine, C. A. (1968): *Culture and Poverty*, Chicago, Univ. of Chicago Press.

52. Frazier, E. F. (1966): *The Negro Family in the U.S.*, Chicago, Univ. of Chicago Press.

53. Moynihan, D. P. (1967): 'The Politics of Stability', speech to National Board, Americans for Democratic Action, 23 September 1967.

54. Townsend, H. E. R. (1971): *Immigrant Pupils in England*, Slough, National Foundation for Educational Research.

55. Bhatnagar, J. (1970): *Immigrants at School*, London, Cornmarket.

56. Ferron, O. (1965): 'The Test Performance of "Coloured" Children', *Educ. Res.*, **8**, (i), pp. 42-57.

57. Goldman, R. J., and Taylor, F. M. (1966): 'Coloured Immigrant Children: A Survey of Research Studies and Literature on Their Educational Problems and Potential', *Educ. Res.*, **8**, (iii), pp. 163–83.

58. Jackson, B. (1964): *Streaming: An Educational System in Miniature*, London, Routledge & Kegan Paul.

59. Douglas, J. W. B. (1964): *The Home and School*, London, MacGibbon & Kee.

60. Education Committee, Ealing International Friendship Council (1968): *The Education of the Immigrant Child in the London Borough of Ealing*.

61. Lee, T. (1957): 'On the Relation between the School Journey and Social and Emotional Adjustment in Rural Infant Children', *Brit. J. Ed. Psych.*, **27**, (ii), pp. 107-14.

62. Pidgeon, D. A. (1970): *Expectation and Pupil Performance*, London, N.F.E.R.

63. Passow, A. H. (ed.): *Reaching the Disadvantaged Learner*, New York, Teachers College Press, Columbia University.

64. Wilkerson, D. A. (1970): 'Compensatory Education Programmes across the Nation', in A. H. Passow (ed.): *Reaching the Disadvantaged Learner*, op. cit., pp. 1–17.

65. Adam, R. (1969): 'Project Headstart: LBJ's One Success', *New Society* 14, no. 370, pp. 681–3.
66. Forbes, J. D. (1971): 'The Mandate for an Innovative Educational Response to Cultural Diversity', in J. C. Stone and D. P. DeNevi (eds.): *Teaching Multi-Cultural Populations*, N.Y., Van Nostrand.
67. Chazan, M. (1973): *Compensatory Education*, London, Butterworth.

Chapter 7

1. Marshment, M. (1971): 'The Black Man in Fiction', *Race Today*, 3, (vi), pp. 206.
2. Walters, E. (1966): 'Some Factors in the Background and Experience of West Indian Children which May Affect Their Progress and Behaviour in English Schools', unpubl. paper, cited in E. J. B. Rose *et al.*: *Colour and Citizenship*, London, O.U.P. for I.R.R., 1967.
3. Kuya, D. (1971): in 'School-Books Attacked for Warped Outlook on Race', *Guardian*, 17 April 1971.
4. Waddington, M. (1967): 'Education for One World: The Teacher's Field of Action', *New Era*, 48, pp. 55–62.
5. Kozol, J. (1967): *Death at an Early Age*, Harmondsworth, Penguin Books.
6. Grambs, J. D. (1967): *Human Relations and Audio-Visual Materials*, an Intergroup Educational Pamphlet, National Conference of Christians and Jews, cited in M. Waddington, op. cit.
7. Kingsley, C. (1973): *The Water Babies*, London, Pan Books.
8. Lewis, C. D. (1966): *The Otterbury Incident*, London, Bodley Head.
9. Ransome, A., (1941): *Missee Lee*, London, Cape.
10. William-Ellis, A. (1963): *Round the World Fairy Tales*, Glasgow, Blackie.
11. Upton, B. and F. (1967): *The Golliwogg's Bicycle Club*, London, Longmans.
12. Hogan, I. (1956): *Nicodemus and His New Shoes*, London, Dent.
13. Bannerman, H. (1971): *Little Black Sambo*, London, Chatto & Windus.
14. Lofting, H. (1972): *The Story of Doctor Doolittle*, Harmondsworth, Penguin.
15. Foster, K. (1951): *Dragon Island*, London, University of London Press.
16. Barnes, T. R. (1960): 'Captain Johns and the Adult World', in B. Ford: *Young Writers, Young Readers*, London, Hutchinson.

17. Johns, W. E. (1969): *Biggles Flies South*, London, Collins.
18. Dixon, R. (1972):'Racialism in Children's Literature', *Teachers Against Racism Bulletin*, no. 2, June 1972.
19. Hill, J. (1971): *Books for Children: the Homelands of Immigrants in Britain*, London, I.R.R.
20. Elkin, J. C. (1971): *Books for the Multi-racial Classroom*, Birmingham Library Association, Youth Libraries Group.
21. Murray, W. (1965): *Ladybird Key Words Reading Scheme, Reader 2b*.
22. Childs, C. (1971): 'Doing What Comes Naturally', *Guardian*, 14 April 1972.
23. Stewart, I. (1970): 'Readers as a Source of Prejudice', *Race Today*, 2, (i), pp. 27–8.
24. Keats, E. J. (1973): *Peter's Chair*, Harmondsworth, Penguin.
25. Berg, L. (1972): *Little Nippers*, Basingstoke, Macmillan.
26. Allen, E. (1968): *The Latchkey Children*, London, O.U.P.
27. Bolt, Anne (1970): *Lenny Lives in the West Indies*, London, Methuen.
28. Cockett, Mary (1969): *Another Home, Another Country*, London, Chatto, Oliver & Boyd.
29. Hatch, S. (1962): 'Coloured People in School Text-Books', *Race*, 4, (i), pp. 63–72.
30. Glendinning, F. (1971): 'Racial Stereotypes in History Textbooks', *Race Today*, 3, (ii), pp. 52–4.
31. Cameron, S. (1971): 'Prejudice in the Printed Page', *The Teacher*, 19 November 1971.
32. Price, C. (1971): 'Whiter Than White Textbooks', *New Statesman*, 29 October 1971.
33. Mackay, D., *et al.* (1970): *Breakthrough to Literacy*, London, Longmans.
34. Fisher, R. M., *et al.* (1972): *Sparks: An Infant Reading Scheme for Children in an Urban Environment*, Glasgow, Blackie.
35. Trager, H. G., and Yarrow, M. R. (1952): *They Learn what They Live: Prejudice in Young Children*, New York, Harper.
36. Litcher, J. H., and Johnson, D. W. (1969): 'Changes in Attitudes towards Negroes of White Elementary School Students after Use of Multi-ethnic Readers', *J. Educ. Psych.*, 60, (ii), pp. 148–52.
37. Verma, G. K., and McDonald, B. (1971): 'Teaching Race in Schools', *Race*, 13, pp. 187–202.
38. Johnson, D. W. (1966): 'Freedom School Effectiveness: Changes in Attitudes of Negro Children', *J. of Applied Behav. Science*, 2, (iii), pp. 325–30.

39. Bunton, P. L., and Weissbach, T. A. (1971): 'Attitudes towards Blackness of Black Pre-School Children Attending Community-controlled or Public Schools', mimeograph, Pomona College.

40. Golin, S. (1971): 'Project Self-Esteem: Some Effects of an Elementary School Black Studies Programme', *Proceedings, 79th Annual A.P.A. Convention*.

41. Likover, B. (1970): 'The Effect of Black History on an Inter-racial Group of Children', *Children*, **17**, (v), pp. 177–182.

42. Sivanandan, A. (1969): 'Race: The Revolutionary Experience', *Race Today*, **1**, (iv), pp. 108–9.

43. Wight, J., *et al.* (1972): *Concept* 7–9, Leeds, E. J. Arnold; for Schools Council.

44. Griffin, J. H. (1962): *Black Like Me*, London, Collins.

45. Phillips, M. (1973): 'The Acceptable Face of Racism', *Race Today*, **5**, (10), pp. 306–7.

46. Miller, H. J. (1969): 'The Effectiveness of Teaching Techniques for Reducing Colour-Prejudice', *Liberal Education*, **16**, pp. 25–31.

Penguin Education

Library of Education

Academic Freedom   *Arblaster*
Arnold on Education   *Ed. Sutherland*
Celebration of Awareness   *Illich*
Centuries of Childhood   *Ariès*
Children in Distress   *Clegg/Megson*
Children Solve Problems   *de Bono*
Child's Discovery of Space   *Jean and Simone Sauvy*
Compulsory Miseducation   *Goodman*
County Hall   *Kogan with Van der Eyken in
  conversation with Cook/Pratt/Taylor*
Cultural Action for Freedom   *Freire*
Culture Against Man   *Henry*
Deschooling Society   *Illich*
Dog-Exercising Machine   *de Bono*
Education and Jobs   *Berg*
Education for a Change   *Colin/Mog Ball*
Education for Democracy   *Ed. Rubinstein/Stoneman*
Education: Structure and Society   *Ed. Cosin*
Education, the Child and Society   *Ed. van der Eyken*
Essays on Education   *Henry*
Fantasy and Feeling in Education   *Jones*
Forsaken Lover   *Searle*
Free Way to Learning   *Ed. Head*
General Education   *Ed. Yudkin*
Half Way There   *Benn/Simon*

Penguin Education

Library of Education

Juniors   *Razzell*
Language of Primary School Children   *Connie/Harold Rosen*
Language, the Learner and the School   *Barnes/Britton/
Rosen/LATE*
Last Resort ?   *Ed. Newell*
Lawrence on Education   *Ed. Joy/Raymond Williams*
Learner Teacher   *Otty*
Letter to a Teacher   *School of Barbiana*
Look at Kids   *Berg*
Lost for Words   *Creber*
Multi-Racial School   *Ed. McNeal/Rogers*
New Polytechnics   *Robinson*
Paint House   *McGuire*
Pedagogy of the Oppressed   *Freire*
Politics of Education   *Kogan/Crosland/Boyle*
Pre-School Years   *Van der Eyken*
Reading, How to   *Kohl*
Relevance of Education   *Bruner*
Resources for Learning   *Taylor*
School is Dead   *Reimer*

Penguin Education

Library of Education

School That I'd Like   *Ed. Blishen*
Simulation in the Classroom   *Taylor/Walford*
Spare the Child   *Wills*
Special Child   *Furneaux*
Speech and the Development of Mental Processes in the
    Child   *Luria/Yudovich*
State School   *Mackenzie*
Teaching as a Subversive Activity   *Postman/Weingartner*
Television and the People   *Groombridge*
36 Children   *Kohl*
Time for School   *Mitchell*
Tinker, Tailor   *Ed. Keddie*
Two Worlds of Childhood   *Bronfenbrenner*
Understanding Children Writing   *Burgess and Others*
What's the Use of Lectures   *Bligh*

Penguin Education

Sociology Readings

Cognitive Sociology   *Circourel*

Decisions, Organizations and Society   *Ed. Castles/ Murray/Potter*

Ethnomethodology   *Ed. Turner*

Industrial Man   *Ed. Burns*

Introducing Sociology   *Worsley and members of the Social Anthropology and Sociology Department, Manchester University*

Language and Social Context   *Ed. Giglioli*

Logic of Sociological Explanation   *Boudon*

Modern Sociology: Introductory Readings   *Ed. Worsley and members of the Social Anthropology and Sociology Department, Manchester University*

Mythology   *Ed. Maranda*

Poverty   *Ed. Jack/Janet Roach*

Problems of Modern Society   *Ed. Worsley and members of the Social Anthropology and Sociology Department, Manchester University*

Race and Social Difference   *Ed. Baxter Sansom*

Rules and Meanings   *Ed. Douglas*

Social Administration   *Ed. Birrell/Hillyard/Murie/Roche*

Social Anarchism   *Baldelli*

Social Inequality   *Ed. Beteille*

Sociological Perspective   *Ed. Thompson/Tunstall*

Sociological Portrait   *Ed. Barker*

Sociology of Law   *Ed. Aubert*

Sociology of Religion   *Ed. Robertson*

Sociology of Science   *Ed. Barnes*

Sociology of the Family   *Ed. Anderson*